THE
MAMMOTH
AND THE
MOUSE

THE
MAMMOTH
AND THE
MOUSE

*Microhistory and
Morphology*

Florike Egmond
and
Peter Mason

The Johns Hopkins University Press
Baltimore and London

The Johns Hopkins University Press
2715 North Charles Street
Baltimore, Maryland 21218-4319
The Johns Hopkins Press Ltd., London

Library of Congress Cataloging-in-Publication Data
will be found at the end of this book.
A catalog record for this book is available from the British Library.

ISBN 0-8018-5477-6
ISBN 0-8018-5478-4 (pbk.)

The floor of time is always giving way beneath us and our feet go through into the cellars below, while we imagine ourselves to be in the top storey of the present.

Robert Musil, *The Man without Qualities*

CONTENTS

ILLUSTRATIONS

PREFACE

IS MICROHISTORY INEVITABLY CONFINED TO THE LOCAL, THE specific, even the marginal? Are the morphological correspondences that can be detected over long periods of time and vast geographical expanses too enormous for the historian to handle?

This book represents an attempt to bridge two fields of cultural research, microhistory and morphology: to raise the specific above the level of the trivial without reducing comparison to the level of the nondescript. We argue that a morphological method drawing on the insights of the Bologna school, associated with the historian Carlo Ginzburg, is particularly fruitful within certain domains of the study of culture, especially with regard to the distinction between popular and learned culture. At the same time, we engage in a critical dialogue with recent microhistorical studies, sometimes questioning the more speculative aspects of these writings.

Impinging on the disciplines of cultural studies, anthropology, history, and art history but belonging to none of them, the main lines of the argument are propounded in seven chapters, arranged in three parts. The material under discussion ranges in time from antiquity to the nineteenth century, though the focal center lies in the early modern period. Each part is preceded by a brief introduction outlining the main theoretical points at issue and offering wider contexts in which the detailed discussions of the individual chapters might be set. Thus, the introduction to part I discusses the development of a morphological method in the hands of such scholars as Goethe, Galton, Wittgenstein, and Ginzburg. In particular, it discusses the relation between the significant and the trivial, as well as the need to rethink the concept of historical context. The introduction to part II discusses the problem of comparison and commensurability in both history and anthropology, and the introduction to part III deals with the relation between chronological succession or periodization and the temporality characteristic of *longue durée*.

The urge to work together on this book originated in the spring of 1989, when Carlo Ginzburg was in the Netherlands for a few days to present his latest book-length publication, *Storia notturna*. With very few exceptions, the Dutch reception to both Ginzburg and his work was decidedly hostile. Most of his critics who committed themselves to print hardly displayed a very thorough knowledge of his writings; one even erred on the other side in displaying knowledge of a work that Ginzburg had never written.

Even though, or perhaps precisely because, we came from different backgrounds (one of us is trained as a historian; the other holds degrees in classics and anthropology), we realized that this was evidently a work that would repay serious reading and rereading. Our instinctive response was a sense of the need to join in the fray to ensure that these exciting ideas were at least given a fair hearing. On second thought, however, it seemed wiser to abstain from such local battles; it was obvious that Ginzburg was quite capable of running rings round his detractors on his own. Instead, we set ourselves the task of carrying out a number of case studies that, though in themselves tangential to the content of *Storia notturna*, would, we hoped, demonstrate the potential of Ginzburg's morphological method in a variety of settings. The proof of the pudding would be in the eating. If our readings are close, it is because we see little point in any other kind of reading; if the inquiry is critical—and it will be obvious that our engagement with the works of Ginzburg and others retains its own distance—this is because we regard *critical inquiry* as a pleonasm.

Although each chapter tends to reflect the particular expertise of one of us, we see them all as the products of joint reflection and discussion. At the same time, we have not attempted to come up with a unison on every issue; in a work that highlights the plurality of possible contexts, it would seem strange to want to iron out every trace of difference between one authorial voice and another. Moreover, other voices besides our own are present in the form of citations or other borrowings. At times these quotations have involved us in the use of terminology that we ourselves would refrain from using. We have not eliminated such words from our text, for they form part of the various discourses we analyze. In most cases, however, they should be taken to appear *sous rature*.

While we have made every effort not to perplex the reader unduly, any inquiry that leaps across time and space with seven-league boots, as ours does at times, is bound to have a vertiginous effect. The fault, we would plead, is not entirely ours; and we gladly leave the last word on this score, as on many others, to Laurence Sterne (*The Life and Opinions of Tristram Shandy* 1.14):

Could a historiographer drive on his history, as a muleteer dri-
ves on his mule,—straight forward;—for instance, from Rome
all the way to Loretto, without ever once turning his head aside
either to the right hand or to the left,—he might venture to fore-
tell you to an hour when he should get to his journey's end;—
but the thing is, morally speaking, impossible: For, if he is a man
of the least spirit he will have fifty deviations from a straight line
to make with this or that party as he goes along, which he can
no ways avoid.

ACKNOWLEDGMENTS

FIRST AND FOREMOST, WE ARE GRATEFUL TO CARLO GINZBURG FOR discussion of a number of points, for the idea for the architecture of the present work, and for demonstrating the meaning of *rigore elastico*. In addition, the authors would like to express their special thanks to those who have commented on parts of the present manuscript: Esther Cohen (Jerusalem), Maarten Jansen (Leiden), Adam Jones (Leipzig), Mayke de Jong (Utrecht), Michel Perrin (Paris), Guido Ruggiero (Miami), and Allan Lund (Munich). Every page has improved from Joanne Allen's meticulous editing. And thanks to John Blake for rescuing the title.

Although none of the chapters in the present volume have previously been published in their present form, elaborations of some of this material have appeared in *History Workshop* 41 (1996), *Thamyris* 1, no. 1 (1994), *The Classical Tradition and the Americas,* edited by W. Haase and M. Reinhold, 1, pt. 2 (1996), the *International Journal of the Classical Tradition* 2, no. 2 (1995), and *Dutch Jewish History III: Proceedings of the 5th Symposium on the History of the Jews in the Netherlands,* edited by Jozeph Michman (Assen, 1993). We are grateful to the editors of these publications for agreeing to the use of this material in the present work.

PART I

INTO THE
ARCHIPELAGO

There is much to be gained by neither believing
nor yet disbelieving everything.

Philostratus, *Life of Apollonius of Tyana*

THE MAMMOTH ROOM OF CHARLES WILLSON PEALE'S MUSEUM IN
Philadelphia contained not only the skeleton of a mammoth that Peale
had recently excavated but also the skeleton of a mouse, intended as an object of contrast with the mammoth. The juxtaposition of the gigantic and the
minute—in the eyes of some, of the sublime and the ridiculous—implies a
relation of both inclusion and opposition. As representatives of natural
kinds, the mammoth and the mouse were included within the Great Chain
of Being, linking various levels of animal taxonomy with one another. At a
more symbolic level, however, the mammoth conjured matters of national
political importance, for it could be used to set the new American institutions within a historical framework going back millennia. The mouse, on
the other hand, as a symbol of an insignificant but persistent rodent, is a
threat to history: as a symbol of *tempus edax rerum,* it nibbles away at the
foundations of history and undermines its vast edifices.

The reduction of scale of historical research is one of the main characteristics of the historians who have been developing what has come to be
called *microhistory.* There is no need for us to repeat the excellent analysis
of the emergence of microhistory by Edward Muir (1991). As has been pointed
out by Grendi (1994), Revel (1994), and others, there is no school of microhistory; no microhistorical program has ever been produced; and despite
the importance of the work of Carlo Ginzburg and the journal *Quaderni*

storici, microhistory is not confined to Bologna. Taking as its cue Aby Warburg's dictum "God is in the detail," this finely focused ethnographic history represented a move away from the abstractions of a sociologically or institutionally inspired historiography towards individual persons and individual cases. To quote Muir: "Their [microhistorians'] work responds to the once-dominant preoccupation among historians with quantitative social science, the *longue durée,* and immobile history, and it returns to interpreting utterances and beliefs, to describing brief dramatic events, and to envisioning a past characterized more by abrupt changes than by deep structural continuities" (1991, vii).

As Carlo Ginzburg and Carlo Poni stressed in their programmatic "The Name and the Game," first published in 1979, it was not the business of microhistory to limit itself to verifying, on its own scale, the macrohistorical (or macroanthropological) rules that have been elaborated elsewhere (Ginzburg and Poni 1991, 9). Recovering the lost peoples of Europe could not mean simply allowing their microhistories to be swallowed up by a larger, totalizing, and immobile grand history. The focus on the micro level was not an addition to history, much less a subtraction from it. As Revel stressed, what the microhistorical perspective offers is not an attenuated, partial, or mutilated version of macrosocial reality but a *different* version (1994, 561).

Yet, as Edward Muir formulates the question, "How can historians concerned with trifles avoid producing trivial history?" (1991, xiv). Are "marginal phenomena" necessarily of marginal importance? (Egmond 1986, 8). How is one to particularize without falling into the trap of anecdotal history? (Egmond 1993b, 14). It is with respect to these central questions that the work of Carlo Ginzburg in particular assumes crucial importance. In his seminal work *The Cheese and the Worms* (1980) he conducted an intensive study of the records of the interrogations of a sixteenth-century miller, Menocchio, in order to reconstruct the private worldview of this obscure individual. However, on the basis of clues contained in Menocchio's testimony, Ginzburg managed to reconstruct the contours of an "obscure, almost unfathomable, layer of remote peasant traditions" (xxiii). Continuing the archaeological metaphor, he states: "In Menocchio's talk we see emerging, as if out of a crevice in the earth, a deep-rooted cultural stratum so unusual as to appear almost incomprehensible" (58). Menocchio's cosmogony proved to fit into a millenarian cosmological tradition.

The case of Menocchio clearly spoke—or was made to speak—to larger issues. But regarding *how* obscure, marginal, or unusual cases can be used to address crucial historical issues, microhistorians differ, at least in their personal modi operandi. Whereas Ginzburg stresses the relevance of the well-documented exceptional case precisely because it is exceptional, Muir looks for equally richly documented "regular" cases that can be used to throw light on more general sociocultural issues. Ruggiero does both, employing fragmented evidence as well as more extensively documented archival cases to recover and recount the poetics of everyday life. As Ginzburg has shown in "Clues: Roots of an Evidential Paradigm," this question has implications which go far beyond the mere matter of typicality (Ginzburg [1986] 1990b, 96–125; cf. Revel 1994, 567–68, and Burke 1992, 41). Microhistorical research also raises the equally intriguing questions whether comparison can play any part in it and whether there is any way to connect microhistory and the study of the *longue durée*. Again opinions and approaches differ. Ginzburg refers to Kracauer's remarks about Marc Bloch's *Feudal Society* as "a constant back and forth between micro- and macrohistory, between close-ups and extreme long-shots, so as to continually thrust back into discussion the comprehensive vision of the historical process through apparent exceptions and cases of brief duration" (1993, 27). A similar use of the photographic metaphor—from close up to Antonioni's *Blow-Up*—is made by Revel (1994, 554–55, 572). Other microhistorians share this emphasis on discontinuities and the heterogeneity of history, as well as a profound distrust of models and theories that cover up and smooth over such gaps and ruptures and an interest in narrative forms that enable historians to do justice to such crevices without completely destroying the coherence of their own "tales." There is an intrinsic relation between the form of exposition and the production of a certain type of intelligibility (570), and it is precisely at this point where narrative form and analytical approach meet (and should not clash) that morphology plays a crucial part. It is an interest in these themes that has made us venture into the complex domains of historical context, continuity, comparison, and representation. This book consists of a series of attempts to explore the scope and limits of microhistory. Morphology is both our main means of transport through time as well as space and the perspective that guides our explorations.

Morphology links us, again, to the work of Carlo Ginzburg. His researches into the diffusion of cults with shamanistic undercurrents, which culminated in his monograph on the witches' sabbath ([1989] 1990a), have been on a scale closer to that of the mammoth than to that of the mouse, spanning thousands of miles and thousands of years in an attempt to ground historically the resemblance between beliefs encountered in sixteenth-century Friuli and the myths and rites of Siberian shamans. All the same, in the collecting and sifting of evidence, the methodology remains strictly and stringently philological; it is the use to which that evidence is put that is unconventional (Muir 1991, xviii).

In making huge geographical and chronological leaps, Ginzburg was pursuing a method that was much more morphological than historical (Ginzburg [1986] 1990b, xii). Although the roots of microhistory do not seem to go back beyond the 1960s (Ginzburg 1994), morphological concerns were very much in the air during the first two decades of the century. During that period morphological interests were reflected in a variety of disciplines, as evidenced by such diverse studies as Vladimir Propp's *Morphologie du Conte,* A. Jolles' *Einfache Formen,* and the early art historical writings of Roberto Longhi (Ginzburg 1982, 9; cf. Ginzburg [1989] 1990a, 27 n. 58). An important figure in this development was the British scientist and explorer Francis Galton (1822–1911). He had served on committees of the British Association for the Advancement of Science for the investigation and publication of the national or local types of race prevailing in different parts of the United Kingdom and demonstrated a possible method for determining a type in 1877. Photographs of as many as eight different criminals were aligned in register to produce a composite portrait of a type. The method was used to establish criminal types, mental-disease types, and racial types; Galton's composite of "the Jewish type" was published in 1885 (Green 1985; Poignant 1992, 60–61). The defect of the composite, of course, was that its success in representing the type was inevitably at the expense of the individual, one of the considerations that led the psychiatrist Adolf Meyer to develop the life chart as a way of representing individuality as a type of one (Leys 1991).

Fingerprinting might be seen as the reverse procedure, in that it made it possible to distinguish members of an indistinct mass by a specific, individual biological mark. It is interesting to note that the introduction of fingerprinting in Europe was spearheaded by the same Galton, who took his lead from a report of its use by the British administration in Bengal (Ginzburg [1986] 1990b, 122–23).

Both Freud, in *The Interpretation of Dreams* ([1900] 1976, 218ff.), and Wittgenstein, in a lecture on ethics given to the Heretics Society in Cambridge in 1929 (see Wittgenstein 1993, 38), expressed an interest in Galton's method, and both referred explicitly to Galton's work. Implicitly, the starting point of their reflections could be traced further back, to the morphological reflections of Goethe, encapsulated in their most literary form in his novel with the unlikely title *Die Wahlverwandtschaften*, generally rendered in English as *Elective Affinities* (Goethe [1809] 1971). Wittgenstein's reflections on morphology are concentrated in two works: "Remarks on Frazer's *Golden Bough*," a collection of notebook jottings spanning the period from 1931 to the late 1940s (Wittgenstein 1993, 119–55), and *Philosophical Investigations*, dating from the late 1940s (Wittgenstein 1958). In these texts Wittgenstein introduced the notion of "family resemblances"—"a complicated network of similarities overlapping and criss-crossing: sometimes overall similarities, sometimes similarities of detail" (1958, §66)—to suggest a way of dealing with phenomena that are related to one another in many different ways but do not share any one thing in common.

Ginzburg acknowledges his indebtedness to Wittgenstein's remarks on Frazer ([1986] 1990b, xii). However, whereas Wittgenstein considered morphological analysis as an alternative to historical research, Ginzburg has sought to demonstrate that although the morphological method may be useful as a heuristic device, it only becomes convincing when external evidence can be used to confirm the formal resemblances. This strategy can be seen most clearly in Ginzburg's study of Piero della Francesca (1985), where stylistic considerations are overdetermined by historically documented material. Ginzburg follows the same procedure in his reflections on a watercolor study of peonies by Martin Schongauer: an early dating of this nature study to ca. 1472 on stylistic grounds requires, and finds, substantiation in "hard" dating on the basis of the watermark (Ginzburg 1995; cf. Levenson 1991, cat. no. 202). Similar considerations guide his treatment of the witches' sabbath. Thus at the end of *Ecstasies* ([1989] 1990a) Ginzburg shifts from morphological points of resemblance to the establishment of a historical sequence. The integration of history and morphology he attempts is not a mixture in equal proportions, for the lengthy work of classification in terms of morphology has a preliminary, provisional status. Ultimately it is subsumed to historical ends.

In the studies in morphology and microhistory that follow we have tried to pay attention to the specific nature of each case. All the same, as discrete points within historical discourse, they are linked to one or more of the others, like islands in an archipelago rather than nations within a single landmass. Each case study is part of a morphological chain linked by family resemblances. The result is not devoid of context, for without a context there can be no meaning. On the contrary, we are faced with a continuous process of *recontextualization,* of the "reconstruction of the plurality of necessary contexts" (Revel 1994, 561), leading to unexpected linkages between chains of morphological resemblance. Of course, not just any recontextualization will do—Revel refers to "necessary" contexts—but there certainly is a wide range of possibilities, and like Wittgenstein, we see no grounds for giving primacy to any specific context on the assumption that it is in some way "authentic" or "primary."

1

EXCURSIONS

IN THE THORAX OF THE MAMMOTH

IN OUR PURSUIT OF FAMILY RESEMBLANCES, WE START WITH THE activities of a portrait painter in Philadelphia in the late eighteenth century. Our trajectory leads via London in the mid-nineteenth century to Ostend in the early nineteenth and The Hague in the sixteenth and includes, among others, the colorful figures of a beachcomber (Adriaen Coenen), a reconstructor of prehistoric animals (Charles Willson Peale), and a military adventurer (Herman Kessels). In the process, we raise some questions bearing on the relation between "popular culture" and "learned culture" and on the relation between disinterested academic activity and the entertainment of the show. Interest in popular entertainment and recreation—the realm of so-called popular culture—has often been contrasted with the loftier themes of political and intellectual history. The present chapter questions the validity of such a distinction. On the one hand, the representatives of "learned culture" could get up to some very amusing antics. On the other, people whom we would probably tend to associate with "popular culture" could come up with startling contributions to knowledge. And if our discussion itself seems to be a kind of hybrid, equally in place in the academy and in the fair, the reader is asked to consider how it could be otherwise.

In 1800 the author of a paper on the Giant Sloth (Megalonyx) of Virginia,[1] president of the American Philosophical Society, and third president of the United States of America, Thomas Jefferson, made attempts to extract a mammoth from Shawangunk, Ulster County, near West Point. At the time his efforts were unsuccessful, but when the saddler, repairer of bells and watches, sculptor, painter, engraver, soldier, propagandist, civic official, museum curator, zoologist, botanist, and inventor Charles Willson Peale heard of the discovery of gigantic bones in the area, he set off with his son Rembrandt for Shawangunk, with funds from Jefferson and the American Philosophical Society in his pocket, to study and sketch the bones. Later in the same year, Peale designed and built a chain-and-bucket pump to prevent the site from flooding, hired a number of locals to assist with the digging, and proceeded to supervise the excavation of the bones of what was later to be reassembled as a mastodon.[2]

Interest in enormous bones was nothing new. The discovery of large bones had been connected with the existence of giants at least from the time of the early church fathers, who derived biblical support for the existence of giants before the time of Noah from Genesis 6:4 ("There were giants in the earth in those days"). As late as the seventeenth century the French humanist Nicolas Fabri de Peiresc wrote to his Italian counterpart Cassiano dal Pozzo on 2 August 1635: "Although I would in no way wish to deny the truth of the tradition of giants in general, nonetheless, I would readily doubt that all the bones that are found in various places are giants' bones."[3] Twenty-five years later a Dutch minister and physician, J. Picardt, was arguing that the presence of megalithic remains in certain parts of the Netherlands was evidence that they had been inhabited in primeval times by fierce "terrible barbarian and cruel giants" (Picardt 1660, 27). In fact, it was not until the nineteenth century that giants were relegated to the realm of folklore (Schnapper 1986; Bolens-Duvernay 1988).

In North America, fossils had been found at Big Bone Lick in the Ohio Territory since the 1740s, and Peale had already been commissioned to make drawings of bones from the area in the 1780s (Peale 1983, 568 n. 33). Ten years later he was busy collecting whale bones on a trip to Delaware (Peale 1988, 56). Indeed, it was mammoth bones, along with a dried paddlefish and his collection of portraits, that prompted Peale to set up a museum in the 1780s. As Peale himself said in a broadside issued in 1792, "We have seen bones of an enormous size, which have been found in divers parts of America, and [about] which no tolerable idea at present can be formed of what kind of beasts they were. But if such a number of those bones were collected together, and made into a complete skeleton, it would lead to an illustration of the animal by analogy: a work that I believe may yet be executed" (15–16).

The concatenation of circumstances in 1801, when Peale was making his mammoth haul, in Shawangunk must have seemed to provide him with the opportunity to make his dream come true. He realized it in three ways. First, the mastodon itself was recreated within the walls of Peale's museum in Philadelphia, one of the first of its kind in the United States of America. Second, his son Rembrandt wrote a ninety-two-page *Historical Disquisition on the Mammoth, or Great American Incognitum, an Extinct, Immense, Car-*

Fig. 1. *The Exhumation of the Mastodon,* by Charles Willson Peale, 1806–8. Oil on canvas, 58.7 cm × 127 cm. Courtesy of the Peale Museum, Baltimore City Life Museums.

nivorous Animal, Whose Fossil Remains Have Been Found in America.[4] Third, Peale himself completed a large oil painting (58.7 cm × 127 cm) entitled *The Exhumation of the Mastodon* in 1808 (fig. 1). All three exhibits—the presentation of the skeleton, its textual representation in the *Disquisition,* and the visual representation of its excavation—were on permanent display in the Mammoth Room of Peale's museum.

Peale's mammoth, however, is not just an episode in the history of the life sciences or the history of collections; it clearly has a place in the history of representations. But we have chosen it as an instance of a high specific gravity (though a gravity combined with hilarity, as we shall see), in which presentations and representations condense a range of experiences that are both symptomatic and constitutive of a specific moment in cultural history.

In discussing some of the several strands that come together in an event of microhistory, we move around this epicenter in ever-widening circles in an attempt to present certain characteristics of a longer timespan without sacrificing the attention to detail for the sake of the *longue durée*.

To begin *ab ovo*, Charles Willson Peale (1741–1827) was the oldest son of Charles Peale (1709–50), an official in the London General Post Office who was sentenced to death as a young man for forgery and had his sentence commuted to transportation to the American colonies. Four years after his father's death, the twelve-year-old Charles Willson Peale was apprenticed to a saddler. When his artistic talents were discovered, he was sent to London to study the art of painting, and he returned to Maryland to set up as a portrait painter at the end of 1769. After the disruption of the Revolutionary War, he continued as a highly successful portraitist in Philadelphia. A list of the portraits in his collection of celebrated personages in 1784 includes a large number of high-ranking military figures, government ministers, a count, a marquis, and two barons (Peale 1983, 634–35). It was in Philadelphia that Peale expanded his portrait gallery to form part of a museum in 1786.

There was little of the academic about these beginnings. Peale's father spent the last years of his life as master of Kent County School, sustaining a belief that his family possessed landed estates which proved after his death to lack any foundation. Charles Willson Peale's apparent ability to move relatively freely in the circles of the conservative gentry of Maryland was largely due to his program of self-education; in turn, through a feedback process, his education was promoted through the contacts he made. His work as a portrait painter for those with the status or wealth to commission a portrait also helped him to further his aspirations, and his practical activities in the museum inevitably brought him into contact with the world of learning,[5] as he corresponded with well-known international figures such as the French zoologist Étienne Geoffroy Saint-Hilaire (1772–1844) and the British naturalist and president of the Royal Society Joseph Banks (1743–1820).[6] When Peale decided to give a lecture course on natural history, he was treading on dangerous ground, as Philadelphia had a well-trained professional in the field in the person of Dr. Benjamin Smith Barton (1766–1815), a member of the first generation of professional naturalists in the United States, who had been appointed as the first professor of natural history at the University of Pennsylvania in 1789. There was certainly an element of professional jealousy in the relations between the two men,[7] but it was clear from the start that Peale saw himself as a popularizer of science. That he lectured in his museum, not in the university, and that his were the first scientific lectures in America to which women were invited indicates this (Peale 1988, 258 n. 5).

This appeal to a broad public, which also had pecuniary motives, entailed having recourse to methods of presentation that were themselves popular in kind. Throughout his life, Charles Willson Peale was a consummate showman. An early example of this talent dates from 1785, the year before he opened his museum, when he converted one end of his portrait gallery into a small theater and presented a series called "Perspective Views with Changeable Effects."[8] Using transparencies and lamps, he attempted to reproduce natural phenomena such as a thunderstorm, a sunrise, or the various hues of fire to vocal and musical accompaniment. Despite Peale's attempt to cut costs by using a barrel organ to replace the live musicians, the venture failed to yield the profit he had hoped for.

In the following year he began collecting specimens for a museum of natural history, which also bear witness to his sense of the dramatic in using art to imitate nature. An early visitor to the museum was astonished to behold two men who looked exactly alike until he perceived that one of them was a waxwork model of Peale and the other was the man himself. Besides the experimental imitation of nature in the moving-pictures exhibition, Peale had recreated the natural setting from which his exhibits were taken, using soil, trees, turf, rocks, and an artificial pond and shore to create an appropriate setting for his stuffed animals, birds, and reptiles in the "most romantic and amusing manner." When Peale used glass cases, the insides were painted to represent appropriate scenery—mountains, plains, or water—and the birds were placed on branches or artificial rocks (Peale 1988, 761). The visitor concluded: "Mr. Peele's Animals reminded me of Noah's Ark" (Peale 1983, 485).[9] In a later bid to attract the public to his museum, Peale sent his black servant Moses Williams out in a feathered dress on horseback, preceded by a trumpeter, to distribute broadsides for the museum (Peale 1988, 379 n. 1). And in a self-portrait from the last years of his life, Peale appears as the biped on display, bearing a curious resemblance to the stuffed birds in their cases, while a turkey does obeisance to this latter-day Noah (fig. 2).

Even before the finding of the mastodon, Peale had been involved in other projects on a mammoth scale. The triumphal arch commissioned by the Pennsylvania Assembly to celebrate peace with England in 1783, probably the most elaborate celebratory edifice of the century, was to be embellished with illuminated paintings by Peale. In a denouement worthy of Laurence

Fig. 2. *The Artist in His Museum,* by Charles Willson Peale, 1822. Oil on canvas, 263.5 cm × 202.9 cm. Courtesy of the Museum of American Art of the Pennsylvania Academy of the Fine Arts, Philadelphia. Gift of Mrs. Sarah Harrison (The Joseph Harrison Jr. Collection).

Sterne, the paintings were accidentally set alight by one of the rockets which were fired on the occasion, killing one member of the public and injuring several others; Peale himself was hit and had to be confined to bed for three weeks (Peale 1983, 405–6). It was the excavation of the mastodon and its subsequent display in the museum, however, that enabled him to use his flair for showmanship to the full. The excavation itself, at least as it is described by Rembrandt Peale, was as much a scene of recreation as it was one of hard toil:

> The road which passed through this farm was a highway, and the attention of every traveler was arrested by the coaches, waggons, chaises, and horses, which animated the road, or were collected at the entrance of the field: rich and poor, men, women, and children, all flocked to see the operation; and a swamp always noted as the solitary abode of snakes and frogs, became the active scene of curiosity and bustle: most of the spectators were astonished at the purpose which could prompt such vigorous and expensive exertions, in a manner so unprecedented, and so foreign to the pursuits for which they were noted. —But the amusement was not wholly on their side; and the variety of company not only amused us, but tended to encourage the workmen, each of whom, before so many spectators, was ambitious of signalizing himself by the number of his discoveries. (Peale 1988, 553)

Once the mammoth, as Peale continued to call it, had been reassembled in the museum, a dinner for thirteen was held inside the skeleton. To the accompaniment of a portable piano, the guests drank toasts to man, the American people, agriculture, the U.S. Constitution, the arts and sciences, the brains of freemen, the friends of peace, all honest men, the ladies of Philadelphia, and the present company. The event was delightfully parodied in Samuel Ewing's "Satire on the Mammoth," a rambling ditty that culminates in the exit of the guests in a "second birth" (Peale 1988, 401–7). A few years later, after Cuvier had demonstrated that the skeleton was not of a mammoth but of a mastodon, Peale raised the possibility of reenacting the dinner for thirteen in a christening ceremony, to include musical accompaniment and the poetical talents of his son Rembrandt. He hoped that the second dinner (which never materialized) would result in publicity that in turn would engender profit (1189, 1205–6).

Peale never failed to regard the dramatic potential of the skeleton as a source of financial gain. This is evident in the entries he made in his diary during the excavation. While Rembrandt's later account has filtered out the more down-to-earth, financial side of the affair, his father's diary is more revealing about this aspect: "(22 Sept. 1801) and multitudes of the Citizens came to see them—this exhibition of the Bones might to some appear a disadvantage in the gain of my future exhibition of them but it appeared in different point of view to me—their magnitude surprized many and only served to excite their curiosity to see the intire Skeleton and I doubt not but many of those Citizens of New York will come to Philada. on purpose" (Peale 1988, 369).

In fact, Peale's expenses in purchasing, excavating, and mounting the skeletons, estimated at two thousand dollars, were soon recovered. The exhibition of the mastodon alone, for which there was a fifty-cent admittance charge, grossed more than seven thousand dollars within the next ten years (Peale 1988, 376 n. 4). In 1802 Peale dispatched two of his sons to England to raise extra funds by exhibiting a second skeleton there. He intended to sell this second skeleton once the novelty had worn off (721), but he never did; later he assigned it to his son Rembrandt for the latter's museum in Baltimore (Peale 1991, 597). After displaying the skeleton in London, Rembrandt and Rubens Peale took it first to Reading and then to Bristol, where the exhibition was opened to the public a few days before the start of the Bristol Fair. The choice of time and place was clearly calculated to attract a large number of visitors, but it is also worth noting what type of visitor the Peales were catering to—those seeking the fun of the fair. A song written by the proprietor and manager of Sadler's Wells, "Mammoth and Buonaparte," was sung night after night to the theater audience, "in addition to the other favorite entertainments" (Peale 1988, 590–91). The tastes of the spectacle and the fairground inform a number of Charles Willson Peale's other museum activities as well, such as his account of a Negro who turned white,[10] his interest in *lusus naturae,* such as a cow with five legs and a snake with two heads, his efforts to obtain an embalmed child and a petrified man, and the inclusion in his portrait gallery of a portrait of a man who died at the age of 108 years and 4 months and of a lock of hair from a certain Miss Harvey, an albino Englishwoman;[11] all testify to a predilection for objects that would not be out of place in a freak show.

Interest in popular entertainment and recreation the realm of "popular culture"—has often been contrasted with the loftier themes of political and intellectual history. Of course, the distinction should not be treated too rigidly, as the theorists of popular culture are only too well aware. However,

Peale's activities not only raise problems for the definition of any boundary between learned and popular culture; they subvert the very distinction itself, which is confounded by his twin strategy of the popularizing of learning and the edifying of entertainment. Following his lead, we shall be confronted with the need to shift the discussion to a different terrain. His activities also transcend any boundary between the mainstream and the marginal, as these categories coincide in the life and opinions of Charles Willson Peale. After fighting on the revolutionary side in the war, he was commissioned to make a portrait of George Washington, with whom he corresponded on matters pertaining to the museum. Washington sent him some Chinese pheasants to be stuffed. Another of his correspondents was Benjamin Franklin, after whom Peale would name his sixth son.[12] Peale's first (unsuccessful) attempt at taxidermy was on an Angora cat that Franklin had brought from France. The Peales' contact with Franklin dated back to the time of Charles Peale senior; his son Charles Willson Peale renewed the friendship during his time in London, where one of his earliest artistic products, *London Lovers,* was a pencil drawing of Benjamin Franklin with a lady friend (Peale 1983, 52). The links between the personal and the political lives of these men can be illustrated from what at first appears to be a trivial detail: Peale's horse was named Belisarius, after the sixth-century general of the same name, who, as legend had it, had his eyes put out and ended up on the streets of Constantinople as a beggar. Peale gave his horse the name to indicate that his horse was a blind and run-down version of what had once been a noble specimen (it is hard not to recall the similar plight of Yorick's steed in *Tristram Shandy*). Franklin was using the same legend at the same time to symbolize what would happen to Britain if it lost its colonies (171 n. 120).

This blending of the comic, the symbolic, the trivial, and the political is also evident in Peale's relations with Thomas Jefferson. Peale, Jefferson, and mammoths were united in popular ideology by friend and foe alike. The 1,235-pound cheese presented to Jefferson by Republican partisans from Cheshire, Massachusetts, was soon dubbed the "mammoth cheese" (Peale 1988, 409 n. 10). The "Satire on the Mammoth," written in connection with the dinner party given in the skeleton, on the other hand, was the work of a political opponent who shared the Federalists' distrust of natural history (it may have been the seafaring lives of many Federalists that made them favorably disposed to practical sciences like astronomy and mechanics). An interest in fossils, however, might be seen as betraying French sympathies (Kerber 1970); in England, there were similar fears that the new science of paleontology was connected with the new ideas of the French Revolution (Rudwick 1992, 20). The political ramifications of the mastodon followed it abroad: the song "Mammoth and Buonaparte" was composed as Napoleon was preparing his invasion fleet in 1803.

Peale's museum itself was the scene of a remarkable political event in 1796, when two rival Native American tribes accidentally met there. After a wary beginning, the chiefs began to parley, the secretary of war was called in, and, after they received a message from George Washington urging peace and harmony, they solemnly signed a peace treaty there (Peale 1988, 160–63).[13] The presence of Indians in the museum the following year, however, was more disruptive: when a box of snakes collected during a trip to New Jersey was opened, a party of Indians entered and one of the chiefs, seizing the largest snake, which had been destined to be sent to Paris, tore it open and swallowed its heart (75 n. 16).

At the point of intersection of political and cultural chains, the categories themselves seem to cave in. As territorial expansion under Jefferson moved further into the interior, many of the animal specimens collected from this horizontal movement found their way to Peale's museum. Expansion in a different direction—vertical penetration into the interior of the earth—yielded other museum exhibits. At the same time, this transcending of boundaries had a temporal component, for the discovery of the American mastodon was a challenge to the view that the world was still as God had created it, opening up the possibility of inquiry into deep time, just as geographical horizons were expanding with the opening up of the West. The debate on the nature of the American mastodon was a matter of national political importance, for it could be used to counter the arguments of Buffon and others on the degeneration of natural kinds on American soil, as well as to bolster pride in the exceptional nature of the new American institutions.[14] The discovery in the 1850s of towering sequoia trees in the West, which soon earned the name "Mammoth Trees," was likewise promptly interpreted as a botanical correlate of heroic nationalism (Schama 1995, 188).

Not only did the circumstances of acquisition of the museum items intertwine with national politics but their exhibition within the museum was itself governed by both the politics and the poetics of display.[15] For instance, by hanging each of the ninety-two pages of Rembrandt Peale's *Disquisition* separately in gilt frame, in an act of "democratic diffusion" (Rigal 1993, 25), the knowledge it contained was made accessible to all. However, preserving the pages from human touch in their gilt frames altered the representational status of the book. It was now something that could be viewed rather than handled, a curiosity like many of the other *Wunderkammer* attributes that adorned Peale's collection. Some idea of the latter can be gauged from the contents of the Model Room, as described in the 1804 *Guide to the Philadelphia Museum*. In addition to fourteen hundred casts of antique gems, the room contained

> a silver Salt Seller, which belonged to Oliver Cromwell, presented by Mrs. Washington; Antique Pot, Household Gods and bas reliefs, from the cities of Herculaneum, and Pompei;—Curiously fabricated Earthen Pots found in South America. . . ; Chinese instruments and ornaments, and a considerable variety of such as are used by the Aborigines of North and South America, such as wrought tubes of Stone, Chrystal Hatchets, &c.
>
> Around the Room are displayed some Paintings, and a number of Indian curiosities, models of canoes, spears, bows and arrows, clubs, paddles, baskets, the Phoonka or great Chinese Fan, Chinese Match Gun, and antient Bow-gun, &c.
>
> Here is the beginning of a collection of Models of useful foreign and domestic Machinery—such as the Chinese Plough and Wheel-barrow; Cottle's Thrashing Machine; a Dry Dock; improved spinning-wheel, &c. —On the floor stands a Throne of curious workmanship, said to be executed by the King of the Pelew Islands, out of a solid piece.
>
> In cases 2 and 3, are models in wax, the size of life, of the following characters, drest in their real and peculiar habiliments, viz. —Chinese Laborer and Gentleman; Inhabitant of Oonalaska; a Kamskadale; an African; a Sandwich Islander; an Otaheitan; a South American; and Blue-Jacket and Red-pole, celebrated Sachems of North America. These cases likewise contain a great variety of articles of Indian dress and ornament of extraordinary workmanship. (Peale 1988, 761)

In the Mammoth Room itself, beside the skeleton of the mammoth and Rembrandt Peale's gilt-framed *Disquisition,* were "the Skull of an unknown Animal of the Ox kind," various small skeletons (monkey, greyhound, parrot, ibis, groundhog, etc.), and the skeleton of a mouse "as an object of contrast with the Mammoth" (Peale 1988, 761).[16] The walls of the room were hung with engravings of the megatherium that had been mounted in Madrid, and the door was framed by the lower jawbones of a whale (764). What is here commemorated is not just the archaeological object itself but the archaeological act of disinterring objects (as represented in *The Exhumation of the Mastodon*), and with it the act of collecting. In this respect, the painting occupies a midway position between the dissociated mastodon bones in the marsh and the recreated mastodon in the museum, focusing on Peale and the Peale family as the instruments by which the bones are raised from beneath the earth (in a movement that mimics the ladder of evolution), transported to the museum, and then reassembled as valuable items within the collection institutionalized as a museum.

Finally, we must mention the way in which the man and his work become implicated. Perhaps Stewart is right in seeing Peale's museum activities as an antidote to his enormous personal losses, as Freud was to interpret mourning as an antidote for wartime losses (Stewart 1994).[17] After the death in 1804 of his second wife, who, ironically, died in childbirth after a pregnancy of twelve months, unable to deliver an oversized baby boy (Peale 1988, 636–37), Peale deliberately played on the ambiguity of looking for bones: not just animal fossils but a member of the sex created from Adam's rib (826 n. 1). In *The Exhumation of the Mastodon* (fig. 1) the leg of the mastodon, drawn on a scroll held by Charles Willson and Raphael Peale, may be a pun on the idea of the leg that supports both the mastodon and the Peale family (Rigal 1993, 30). And in the complex punning of his self-portrait in the museum (fig. 2) Peale himself looms, larger than life, as gigantic as a mastodon by comparison with the miniature human figures in the background, gesturing with his left hand towards both his own leg and the leg of the mastodon beside it. This typically self-reflexive joke opens up a vista of endless recession within the skeletal structure of the museum, in which the living and the dead engage in a seemingly endless pas de deux.

IN THE BELLY OF THE WHALE

Many of the themes we have been exploring here crop up again on the other side of the Atlantic in a dinner given in the belly of an iguanodon. On New Year's Eve, 1853, Benjamin Waterhouse Hawkins and twenty-one guests enjoyed a luxurious and elegantly served dinner in the body of an iguanodon, "whose ancient sides there is no reason to suppose had ever before been shaken with philosophic mirth," as the *Illustrated London News* reported at the time.[18] With the assistance of the anatomist Richard Owen, Hawkins had been commissioned to design a series of life-sized reconstructions of prehistoric animals to be displayed on the grounds of the Crystal Palace in Sydenham. As in Peale's museum, the emphasis was on display amid appropriate vegetation: the iguanodon was placed among the rushes, while the megatherium appeared in the act of climbing an antediluvian tree. Like Peale's skeleton, the Crystal Palace exhibits were intended to exert enormous popular appeal, drawing in the crowds from London after the grounds had been opened by Queen Victoria in 1854. Like its American counterpart, the spectacle offered fare to the cartoonists of *Punch* and other magazines. Here too political considerations played their part, for the strategy of occupying the minds of the lower classes with edifying entertainment, backed up by reminders of the power of the ruling class at home and in the empire, was deliberately used by some of the powers that be as an instrument for keeping the minds of the masses off thoughts of political change. This function was clearly in evidence towards the end of the century in the preoccupations of A.H.L.F. Pitt Rivers. Whereas the collection housed in the Oxford museum bearing his name resembled the ethnological collection of the British Museum and was intended primarily for scholarly purposes, the restored medieval building, exotic zoo, and Sunday concerts on his estate in Farnham conformed to his ideal of a popular museum that could educate the lower classes and hereby make them less amenable to social revolution (Chapman 1985; Coombes 1994, 120–21).

But there are parallels to Peale's mammoth closer at hand. In 1827, the very year in which Charles Willson Peale died, a blue whale was brought to land in the southern Netherlands, near Ostend. Whales and mammoths were closely associated in both popular and learned tradition. Peale had at first assumed that the mastodon bones belonged to a semiaquatic carnivore, arguing that its tusks (which he wrongly supposed to have curved downwards rather than upwards) were used to turn up crustaceans and other forms of aquatic life in marshy ground;[19] the "Dialogue between the Skeletons of the Mouse & of the Mammoth" referred to a diet of sea lions, seals, and giant oysters (Peale 1988, 713). In his *Disquisition*, Rembrandt Peale even speculated that the mastodon was able to submerge under water, using its nostril in the same way that a whale uses its blowpipe (569). And although the author of the "Satire on the Mammoth" connected the huge creature with the behemoth of *Job* 40:15–24, which is clearly depicted as a terrestrial herbivore in the biblical account, Dibdin in his "Mammoth and Buona-parte" presented it as an aquatic creature:

> Some say 'tis this, some say 'tis that, and some say 'tis a
>   *Whale,* Sir,
> And most folks, since the Little Man has such odd capers
>   shewna,
> They wish the Mammoth was a whale and Buonaparte was
>   Jonah.

(Peale 1988, 590)

Fig. 3. Dancing a quadrille in the jawbone of a whale on the birthday of the Dutch queen. FM 6279, courtesy of State Printroom, Amsterdam.

Perhaps this affinity between the mastodon and the whale paved the way for the other resemblances between the circumstances of the display of the mastodon in the United States and England and those of the display of the blue whale in continental Europe. At any rate, on the latter occasion too the skeleton of the beast was the scene of spectacular dramatic and musical entertainment: the quadrille was danced in and around it (fig. 3)—as it was to be danced a quarter of a century later on the stumps of the giant sequoias discovered in the American West[20]—and concerts were given in the belly of the whale, although the selections performed do not appear to have had a pronounced nautical character.[21] The national importance of the event was underlined by its being held it on the queen's birthday. Moreover, a representative of King Willem I was addressed from the belly of the whale, and on behalf of the Dutch monarch he accepted the skeleton as a gift for the museum in Leiden.

The carcass of the blue whale had been purchased by the highest bidder for the price of three thousand guilders. This was a certain Herman Kessels, an inspector of port duties in Ostend since 1824 and a former military adventurer who had served in the Dutch and French armies as well as under Símon Bolívar in Colombia. After the whale had been on display for a week in Ostend, Kessels arranged for the carcass to be cleaned, concluding the operation with a celebration for the sixty-two men who had worked day and night to remove the rotting flesh. He sold sixty-six tons of blubber and commissioned a special pavilion to be built in Ostend. Like Peale, Kessels intended to exhibit the skeleton in a number of countries in order to recover his investments; it had been agreed that the transfer of the skeleton to Leiden would not take place until six years later. After being displayed in Ostend, the skeleton was shown to the public in Antwerp and Brussels and then was taken on a tour of the northern Netherlands—Rotterdam, The Hague, and Amsterdam.

The tide turned for Kessels in 1830 with the outbreak of the Belgian Revolt. Leaving his whale—which had reached Paris by this time—he joined the Belgian rebels and resumed a military career until 1842. He died nine years later.[22] Hostilities between the North and the South put an end to the plans to transfer the skeleton to Leiden, and none of the twenty-four articles of the Peace Treaty of 1839 refers to this promise. The blue whale never reached its destination in Holland.[23]

This was the first blue whale to be sighted on the North Sea coast since 1 March 1594, so it is hardly surprising that it caused such a commotion and was the pretext for large-scale festivities. Some idea of what this meant for ordinary people can be gauged from the text of a song by Jakob Hendrik Arens entitled "Farce of the Whale in Ostend."[24] The song tells the sorry tale of what happened to some girls who went to see the whale. One of them broke her wooden clog; another fell from the dike and ended up in the mud with a torn petticoat and sprained ankle. During their journey home they were beset by "the worst perils." The singer remains silent on the nature of these perils, but the insinuation is that the mystery was cleared up nine months later. The stranded blue whale was thus at the center of a popular spectacle with all the fun of the fair and formed an excellent pretext for carnival-like excesses.

Although this market song can hardly be regarded as a reliable source for the number of visitors (it gives the figure of seven hundred a day), we know from more creditworthy sources that some eight thousand people visited the exhibition of what had been dubbed "The Royal Whale of Ostend." Like the display of Peale's mastodon, this was also an occasion for satire, sometimes of a political kind: Herman Kessels' combination of a politico-military career with the activities of an enterprising showman could hardly fail to elicit the presence of both facets in political cartoons (fig. 4). Another spectacle that aroused popular interest at this time was the visit of a few members of the North American Osage tribe to Europe.[25] The Brussels weekly L'Industriel published a lithograph entitled "The Whale of Ostend Visited by the Elephant, the Giraffe, and the Osages."

The stranded blue whale was not just a source of popular amusement. It also attracted collectors with an interest in natural history, such as J. van Huerne (1752–1844), who had brought together a collection of natural curiosities in his Cabinet d'histoire naturelle in Bruges, and L. Paret (1777–1859), whose large collection was housed near Ostend. Soon after the whale was brought to land, J. van Breda, a professor of botany, zoology, and comparative anatomy in Ghent, hastened to the spot in the hope of acquiring the whale for scientific purposes. In his lament at the loss of this unique opportunity for science he complained that "an unfortunate accident caused the whale to fall into the hands of persons who were unaware of the scientific worth of the creature" (Moens 1977). All that was left for the professor and his students was a piece of whale skin.

If we were to interpret Van Breda's intervention in terms of a conflict of interests symbolized by the rival laments—the song on the whale and the learned professor's complaints—the conflict would seem to have been re-

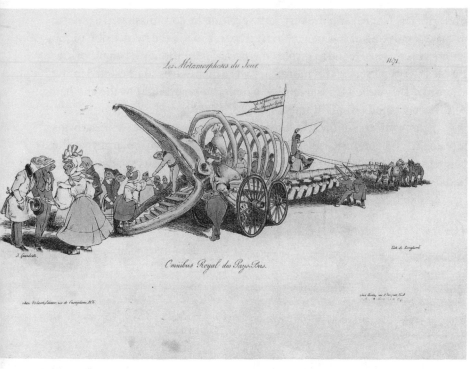

Fig. 4. *Omnibus Royal des Pays Bas,* a print satirizing Herman Kessels' exhibition tour with the whale stranded in Ostend. Lithography by Langhume after J. Grandville. FM 6330/2, courtesy of State Printroom, Amsterdam.

solved in favor of the entrepreneurs and showmen, for it was agreed that the blue whale of Ostend would be widely exhibited for six years before it could enter the scientific collection in Leiden. But Van Breda's version comes from the mouth of one who himself had a stake in the issue. As we have seen, academic interests and showmanship were not as clearly demarcated from one another as he would have us believe.

IN THE PAGES OF THE "FISH BOOK"

Almost three hundred years earlier, on the same North Sea coast, two adventurers bought a *poelomp,* a large squid, and made a handsome profit from displaying it. They were not the first buyers, however, for the creature had previously been purchased on the fish market in Scheveningen for two stuivers by one Adriaen Coenen in October 1546.[26] He had it taken to his house in The Hague, and the very same evening he commissioned a painter to make a painting of it. Coenen's next step was to ask the permission of the authorities in The Hague to display the *poelomp* for money. The authorities granted permission; what is more, they were themselves so interested in the affair that they called for the marine wonder to be brought to the city hall so that they could admire it there.

Coenen's interest in the *poelomp* was not just financial; he was clearly interested in the creature itself, as can be seen from his complaint that the painter was unable to paint the creature properly because its strangeness defied representation. Twenty years later Coenen obtained his second *poelomp*

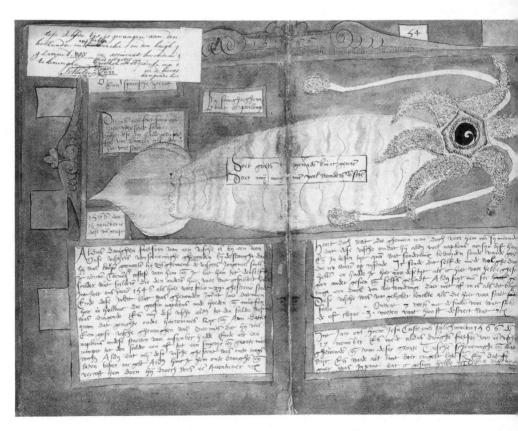

Fig. 5. The *Geuzenvis* (beggar fish) that Adriaen Coenen bought from a Scheveningen fisherman on 15 November 1566. From Adriaen Coenen, "Fish Book," fols. 53v–54. 78E54, courtesy of Royal Library, The Hague.

in a similar way, buying it from a Scheveningen fisherman who had come across it while fishing for shrimps. This time the event attracted even more interest, as this *poelomp* turned out to have a political significance into the bargain. While the *poelomp* was at the painter's, rumor spread that it was a *Geuzenvis*, or "beggar fish." This was indeed the year in which the *Geuzen*, "beggars," were operating in Holland, and one of the symbols of the *Geuzen* was the beggar's purse (Van Nierop 1991). The *Geuzenvis* turned out to have similar excrescences all over its tentacles (fig. 5). The painter's house was soon filled with a crowd, every member eager to procure a piece of the *poelomp*. Coenen wryly concluded that "this fish was sent to me to be displayed for money." He dried this specimen too and sold it to an adventurer, but he felt it necessary to add the following comments to his account of the *Geuzenvis:* "Hear what the common folk thought about it. They imagined that this fish—because it had so many suckers on its body and arrived right at this time—must signify something special, related to the *Geuzen,* who were now in revolt. I myself might have thought the same if I had not seen and even owned another *poelomp* quite some time before, as I have mentioned."

Coenen's interest in the *poelomp*, which, despite its apparent triviality, could still have major political ramifications, was thus marked by a combination of pecuniary motives, showmanship, and curiosity about the wonders of the natural world. The same combination emerges from his encounters with beached whales, which were more frequent than usual on these shores in the second half of the sixteenth century. When three sperm whales were washed up near the Hook of Holland in November 1577 (fig. 6), Coenen decided to join the crowd that came from The Hague, Delft, and Leiden to see them the next day. It is tempting to surmise that, like their nineteenth-century counterparts, they sang about the wonders of the sea on the way. Coenen described his day as follows:

> On Sunday, 24 November, after I had left The Hague in the morning for Scheveningen, I was told that three big fish were beached in Ter Heijde. As I have always been very interested in these strange things connected with fish, I thought that I did not want to miss it; I had to go there. I saw a lot of people riding and sailing there. Since fishing was going on in Scheveningen and I could not get a boat to travel to Ter Heijde, I joined the rest of the company on foot. There was a strong southwester blowing, and it was difficult for an old man of 63 years to walk.

By the time he got there it was high tide, which meant that he had to wait until nightfall to view the whales from close quarters.

> All three fish were lying in the water, so that I could not take a good look at them. I waited until the evening, when the tide was low and the fish were lying on dry ground, so that one could walk all the way around them and inspect them from all sides. . . . When I had taken a good look at them on Sunday together with many other people both from Delft and from The Hague and Scheveningen and other nearby towns and villages, I returned to The Hague during the evening in the company of other folk. It was already dark. I arrived in The Hague at about eight o'clock . . . and we were told then that these fish were going to be auctioned next Tuesday by the Receiver of duties on flotsam and jetsam and by members of the Chamber of Accounts of Holland. Placards announcing this auction were also sent to Rotterdam, Delfshaven, and Delft.

The correspondences with the stranding of the blue whale near Ostend three centuries later are unmistakable. Coenen, who had served as an apprentice to the auctioneer of the Scheveningen fish market, had worked his way up to become clerk of the auction, wholesaler in dried and fresh fish, and official beachcomber of a stretch of the Dutch coast in the province of South Holland. Like his nineteenth-century counterpart, Herman Kessels, he was thus professionally interested in the fate of the three sperm whales.

A couple of days later Coenen was back in Ter Heijde waiting in the house of his colleague, the beachcomber for the Ter Heijde strip of coast, for the receiver and members of the chamber of accounts of Holland, who were to hold the auction. As an experienced clerk of the auction, Coenen was asked to help with the proceedings, which took place where the whales were lying. The three whales fetched a total of more than five hundred guilders, and a part of the proceedings was to be donated to the poor of Scheveningen.

Coenen lunched in Ter Heijde with the local government officials, but when they left in the evening, he remained behind so that he could inspect the insides of the whales the next day, when work on the carcasses was due to begin. According to Coenen's brief description of their physical appearance, all three were males, measuring 55 feet, 49 feet, and 43 feet, respectively.

Fig. 6. Sperm whales stranded on the coast of South Holland in November 1577. From Adriaen Coenen, "Fish Book," fols. 47v–48. 78E54, courtesy of Royal Library, The Hague.

All three were black, their whole body as fat as a porpoise, but less fatty or oily, and with more meat. They had short teeth in the lower jaws, which protruded like the horns of a young cow, and there were holes in the upper jaws into which these teeth fitted. They had small eyes for their size, smaller than those of a cow. All three had sheaths. These were near their bellies, as thick as a herring, tapered like a bull's pizzle. A very blunt head, etc.

Whereas the blue whale of Ostend was but an interruption in the polit-ical and military life of Herman Kessels, Coenen's life was marked from be-ginning to end by a lively interest in marine biology. Adriaen Coenensz van Schilperoort was born in Scheveningen to a local fisherman and a fisher-man's daughter in 1514. Like most Dutch children, he attended the village school, but that was all the formal education he received. Like Charles Willson Peale, he obtained the rest of his education in practice. From his youth, when he was sent by his superior to inspect stranded mammals on the shore, it was his custom to carry a notebook to record his experiences. He kept a record of unusual fish and extraordinary meteorological phenomena, he dissected and dried fish, and he collected shells and popular wisdom connected with fishing and the sea. Coenen continued to investigate fish, to collect inter-esting and rare objects of natural history, and to engage in conversation with fishermen, travelers, and merchants into his seventies. His connection with the (emergent) world of the universities began only towards the end of his life, when he made contact with a few professors of medicine and nat-ural science at the University of Leiden, which was founded in 1575.[27]

As a result of the various positions he held, Coenen had both business and personal connections with the local government officials in The Hague and Scheveningen. He also had contacts with the circles of high-ranking civil servants in the service of the Habsburg governors. In fact, his social ra-dius was considerably larger than his geographical radius. He spent most of his life in The Hague or Scheveningen, apart from a spell in nearby Leiden between 1576 and 1582 and a few business trips to Flanders, Brabant, and the district of Cologne.

Adriaen Coenen wrote three book-length works, two of which are still extant. The fate of his first work, the "Fish Book," which he gave as a present to William of Orange, leader of the Dutch Revolt against Spanish Habsburg rule, is still a mystery. The book was a much-prized trove of information on fish and waterfowl, and as its author and illustrator, Coenen was a popular guest at the tables of certain nobles and officials in The Hague, bringing his book with him and taking part in lengthy discussions on fish and nature in general. Among these interested patrons, Cornelis Suys, lord of Rijswijk (a village near The Hague), jurist, president of the provincial Court of Holland, and first archivist of the charters of the counts of Holland, had a special position. He regularly invited Coenen to visit him, lent him books on natural history, and was very fond of fish himself.

Coenen's second manuscript, which he later called his "Big Fish Book," contains 412 folios and was written between 1577 and early 1579. The bound manuscript has been in the possession of the Royal Library in The Hague since the late eighteenth or early nineteenth century. A third work, on a much smaller scale, is the "Whale Book," the two parts of which, bound in one volume, are now in the possession of the Library of Antwerp Zoo. A slender, unfinished manuscript known as the "Herring Book," which was recently discovered in the Cologne Municipal Archive, consists mainly of excerpts from Coenen's other manuscripts. Typical of all Coenen's manuscripts is the combination of framed textual passages, rich illustrations with a striking use of color, and above all the naive and extremely lively idiom of both the illustrations and the texts. Although Coenen had certainly picked up a considerable number of Latin names for fauna over the years, he wrote in a racy and by no means academic Dutch seasoned with quotations in Latin, French, and German. Almost every page is an individual, self-contained unit, bound by its decorated margins and containing one or more watercolor drawings. The later illustrations are less elaborate in terms of detail, decoration, and use of color. The subject matter ranges far and wide, including details of how to prepare a sole, fishing techniques, legends associated with sirens and mermaids, the migratory patterns of schools of herring in the North Sea, the crocodiles in the Nile, how dolphins give birth to and nourish their young, creatures of the Far East and the Americas, sea monsters, bats and aquatic spirits, and so on.[28]

Coenen's broad interest in natural history and his collection of notes on fish and sea mammals, copies of pamphlets on sea monsters, drawings, shells, and curious fish may have been as important to his career as was his professional expertise as a wholesaler or auctioneer. He certainly attracted the interest of high-ranking officials, as we saw in the case of his first *poelomp*, as well as that of collectors and ordinary townsfolk. An example of how a marine find could mediate between a beachcomber and a nobleman is provided by the story of Coenen's turtle. The appearance of a large turtle on the shores of the North Sea was an unusual event of the first order. After being widely exhibited, it was dried and eventually found its way into the collection of an aristocrat in the southern Netherlands who was the patron of such botanists as Dodoens and De l'Ecluse. According to Coenen, after he had bought the turtle from a shrimper in Scheveningen for six carolus guilders,

> it stayed alive in my possession for a long time. I sent out someone with it in order to show it for money, and he brought it home to me dead, and I removed its entrails and dried it. Its entrails and intestines were like those of a bird. I had kept it alive for a long time in a tub filled with water, but it did not want to eat. When I had thus dried it, I gave it to my lord of Moerken, alias the lord of Renouteren, a noble man in Flanders. This good lord was a great lover of rare and curious things to do with fish and birds.[29]

It was natural to want to earn some money on the side in this way. The turtle was caught in 1565, the year before the so-called Dutch Revolt broke out, and Coenen must have been aware that the turbulence of the times could well affect his financial situation as well as his personal safety and career. Coenen referred to the threat of bankruptcy on at least one occasion. During the summer of 1573 he had to flee from freebooting Spanish soldiers and leave his house in Scheveningen, fully expecting to find only the ransacked ruins upon his return. His wartime losses included a four-foot shark, which he had dried and stuffed himself, together with the twenty-four young sharks found in its belly. It had been left hanging in his garden when plundering Spanish soldiers approached. Ten years later he was still putting his curiosities on display for a fee: an archive source detailing the day-to-day agenda of the Leiden local government contains Coenen's request to display both his "Fish Book" and his collection of dried fish on the market in Leiden for a fee of "one oortgen" in September 1583.[30] On display in Peale's Mammoth Room, it will be recalled, were the fossil remains of a mastodon, a text on the subject (the *Disquisition*), and a painting of its excavation; on display on the Leiden market were the dried remains of certain fish, a text on fish (the "Fish Book"), and Coenen's watercolor paintings of fish contained therein.

It would be hard to imagine a better place for the exhibition of the "Fish Book," which was itself a rambling collection.[31] Like the Renaissance *Wun-*

derkammer, it was marked by a preference for the singularity above the universal. Many of the wonders of the sea described by Coenen featured in the curiosity cabinets too. The *Kunstkammer* of Prince August of Saxony in Dresden contained a dried octopus, as well as shells (Menzhausen 1985, 70). The petrified teeth of snakes or sharks, coral, sawfish or swordfish, and "Jenny Hanivers" (dragonlike curios made from the dried bodies of skates and rays)[32] were on display in numerous Renaissance collections. In fact, the "Fish Book" was literally what many of the collections were figuratively considered to be: a *liber mundi* or *theatrum mundi.*

In the urge to display the wonders of nature, whether financial considerations served as an additional motive or not, Coenen was very much a man of his time. In the winter of 1576, for example, he purchased the "sword" of an almost ten-foot-long swordfish from a fisherman in Scheveningen for a number of rounds of beer. The man had eaten some of the fish, pickled the rest, and nailed the fish's "sword" to the outside of his house. Another fisherman had fastened a crab above his front door. Interest in and display of marine wonders, however, was not confined to humble fishermen. During the sale of the three sperm whales in 1577 the tail and jawbones of the largest of the three were requisitioned by the Court of Holland (of which Coenen's patron, Cornelis Suys, had been president until 1572), not for any commercial reason, but to hang them in a very conspicuous position indeed: on the outer wall of the main hall of the Court of Holland in the center of the Binnenhof, where they remained until a major cleaning-up operation in 1801. As the former seat of the counts of Holland, the center of Habsburg government in the northern part of the Netherlands, the seat of the Court of Holland, and the seat of the Dutch parliament and government from the days of the Dutch Revolt, the Binnenhof was at the core of political, administrative, and judicial power. The Hof was not the only Dutch public building to be decorated with whalebones.[33] A gigantic whalebone was suspended from the outer wall of the old Amsterdam City Hall; clearly visible in seventeenth-century drawings and paintings, it was certainly in position by 1600, though we do not know how long it had been hanging there. Not a whalebone but a model of a complete whale was on display during the triumphal entry of William of Orange into Amsterdam in 1580: "In the water floated a whale, driven by the sea-god Neptune, and on which was seated an attractively attired virgin, surrounded by all kinds of Oriental wares, and at every corner a column painted with the princely coats of arms of the capitals of the Orient" (Moes 1897, 4–5).

The presence of the whale is especially appropriate in this royal context, for, like the lion and the eagle, the whale was widely regarded as the kingly apex of its hierarchy (Thomas 1983, 60). Stressing this symbolic aspect, Simon Schama has interpreted the spate of illustrations of beached whales that appeared between 1570 and 1650 as a reflection of the preoccupation of the young Dutch nation with all kinds of threats from outside.[34] Although he points out that "it would be misleading to suggest a simple chronology by which whale imagery evolved from moral allusion to dispassionate classification" (1987, 136), he suggests that allegorical treatments of whales were predominant during the critical years of the Dutch Republic and that they were gradually replaced by a more naturalistic element, especially as the whaling industry, particularly the Northern Company, got under way. In Schama's opinion, it was not until the eighteenth century that increased insight into anatomy yielded the classification of whales as mammals. "And if learned culture was somewhat uncertain about their anatomy and habits, we may be sure that popular culture still regarded their appearance, especially out of their natural element, as an exceptional and ominous event" (134). May we? The best refutation of Schama's argument is provided by the writings of Coenen himself, for the interpretation of the stranded whales as divine portents in no way excluded a detailed interest in the physiology and habits of these creatures[35]—which, incidentally, dates from long before the foundation of the Northern Company. As a corollary, the decline in supernatural interpretations of these and related phenomena did not necessarily result in improved insights into cetacean physiology.

In short, if Coenen is to be situated in relation to popular culture, it is not to a popular culture conceived as the opposite of learned culture. Indeed, as we have seen from his comments on the *Geuzenvis,* he distinguished himself from what he called "the common folk." On the other hand, he was by no means a full-fledged member of "learned culture" either. Distinctions blurred. The culture to which Coenen had access included elements that derived from elite culture as well, as his references to chroniclers and other written sources make clear.[36] Like Carlo Ginzburg's Menocchio, who experienced a relativistic shock after reading the *Travels* of Sir John Mandeville (Ginzburg [1976] 1980, 41ff.), Coenen drew on various authors from late antiquity to the Middle Ages, as well as on works closer to his own time, such as the *Cosmographei* of Sebastian Münster and Gessner's works on animals and fish (which Coenen read in a vernacular abridgment). All the same, it is not what he read but how he read that matters. He read, not as a scholar, comparing text with text,[37] but as a person with an unremitting interest in the wonders of nature as reminders of divine mercy and providence and an urge to get to the bottom of them.

A HORSE NAMED BELISARIUS

The mastodon with which we began seems to have little in common with the squids, turtles, crabs, and swordfish with which we have ended. Yet at each step in the presentation it has been possible to move from one link in the chain to another on the basis of affinity even though the extremes of the chain have no obvious points in common. The transitions were effected by means of family resemblances, and the similarities that have emerged are morphological likenesses. But what right do we have to take such giant strides? And are they not taken at the expense of faithfulness to the historical context?

By privileging patterns and configurations while putting the question of the historical context aside for the time being, we have discovered certain features that crop up in at least two, and sometimes all three, of the cases under discussion. For instance, the relation to war and revolt: Peale's excavation, following upon his period as a revolutionary soldier, has been interpreted by some commentators as an attempt to compensate for war losses; the outbreak of the revolt of the southern Netherlands against the North in 1830 had far-reaching consequences for the fate of Herman Kessels' blue whale; and Coenen's collecting and writing took place under the shadow of marauding troops during the Dutch Revolt of the second half of the sixteenth century.[38] Another thread connecting the lives of Peale, Kessels, and Coenen is their relation to famous men: Peale communicated with and painted George Washington, Thomas Jefferson, Benjamin Franklin, and many other prominent figures of his day; the display of Kessels' whale was orchestrated to include monarchical ceremony, and Kessels' politico-military career was at least prominent enough to make him the target of political satire; and Coenen was on speaking terms with William of Orange as well as with a number of other notables of his time. Native Americans crop up in each of the stories: Peale's museum was the scene of the conclusion of a treaty between rival Amerindian groups, and it housed life-sized waxwork models of Native Americans; the spectacle of the Ostend whale coincided with the spectacle of Osage Indians visiting Europe; and Coenen included in his "Fish Book" an illustration of an Inuit woman and child he had seen in The Hague (Sturtevant and Quinn 1987).

One could go on, though at the risk of trying the reader's patience. After all, not all of these affinities can be expected to be regarded as equally important to the historian. Indeed, some of them might seem downright trivial. This is a crucial point: a method that involves deciding beforehand what is and what is not significant would be bound to exclude a good many of the details discussed in this chapter. Yet such a method, by ruling out discussion of the name of Peale's horse, for example, on the ground that it is purely anecdotal, would miss the way in which certain elements of the political ideology of the time could permeate all levels of culture, even to the extent of affecting the naming of a horse. Conventionally, the naming of a horse is trivial. However, to apply this criterion as a *protocol*, as a way of distinguishing between appropriate and inappropriate contexts, is tantamount to writing history first and investigating it afterwards.

As pointed out in the introduction, the process at work here is one of *recontextualization*. Certain details have been detached from the context of the selected papers of Charles Willson Peale; other details have been detached from the pictorial and textual record of a brief interlude in the activities of a Belgian military adventurer; still other details have been detached from the context of the colorful manuscripts of a Dutch beachcomber, as well as from the less colorful Dutch archives. Yet there is nothing primary about any of these particular contexts. Peale and Kessels could just as easily appear in a history of men with large families; Coenen and Peale could both feature in a history of painting or in a history of turtle collectors; Coenen and Kessels could occupy a place in a history of whaling; and so on. Once one is obliged to specify a "historical context," it fragments into a multiplicity of different projects. This, according to Revel, is one of the characteristics of microhistory: that it lacks a unified, homogeneous context within which and as a function of which the actors define their choices (1994, 561).

Finally, we are bound to say something more about the nature of the new, provisional context in which the stories of Peale, Kessels, and Coenen now find themselves. What are the affinities we have been trying to delineate? The stories of Peale, Kessels, and Coenen can all be viewed within the perspective of a kind of knowledge that is easier to characterize by what it is not than by what it is. In the cases of Coenen and Peale, both of whom display considerable intellectual activity, this activity is situated outside the university; Coenen worked at a time when the university as an institution had only just come into existence, and Peale worked when the natural sciences had barely been institutionalized in the university. Hence, the kind of distinction that Professor Van Breda was drawing in the nineteenth century between the University of Leiden, on the one hand, and "persons who were unaware of the scientific worth of the creature," on the other, can hardly be applied to situations in which there was no material or institutional support on which the distinction could be based. On the contrary, as we have tried to demonstrate, both Peale and Coenen combined aspects that, though distinct for Van Breda, were unlikely to have been viewed as such in their own time. Intellectual curiosity could be combined with showmanship. In this sense, Peale has a place in two histories: the history of the natural historical museum in the United States as a precursor of bodies such as the Smithsonian Institution and the history of the public display of curiosities, best represented by Phineas Barnum.[39] Likewise, the knowledge compiled by Coenen in his various books makes him an important figure in the history of the natural sciences, particularly in the history of natural historical illustration (Barthelmess and Münzing 1991), while his activities on the Leiden market and elsewhere make him a precursor of his compatriots who organized freak shows far into the twentieth century (Sliggers and Wertheim 1993).

Indeed, perhaps Van Breda's distinction cannot be applied today either. Dinosaurs have recently been incorporated into the business of showmanship and display, with the film *Jurassic Park* being one of the most obvious signs of their commercial potential, but many of the sites where computer-driven reconstructions have been on display were museums of natural history.[40] In the case of the iguanodon reconstruction in the Crystal Palace, there was the same combination of attention to scientific accuracy and placement within the setting of a commercial theme park.

How is one to characterize knowledge of this kind? Carlo Ginzburg, in his discussion of the knowledge of Menocchio, the Friulian miller, pointed out the need to develop "new criteria of proof specifically suited to a line of research based on so thoroughly a heterogeneous, in fact unbalanced, documentation" ([1976] 1980, 155). And new criteria of proof imply a new terminology. *Academic* would be aiming too high; *proletarian knowledge,* the term used by Frank Lestringant (1991b, 34) to describe the knowledge of such self-taught *hommes nouveaux* of sixteenth-century France as André Thevet, Bernard Palissy, and Ambroise Paré, would be aiming too low. Gramsci's term *organic intellectual* comes nearer the mark, suggesting a natural link between the knowledge produced by these individuals and the work to which it was applied; however, the notion of organicity is hardly adequate to characterize an epistemological field marked by so many breaks, fresh starts, and interruptions. Perhaps, *faute de mieux,* Foucault's *le savoir des gens,* which he characterizes as "a particular, local, regional knowledge" (1980, 82), has more to recommend it, as long as we take the genitive to be a double one. In that case, the dual reference is to that knowledge which is the possession of *les gens,* their own specific relation to knowledge; and to the knowledge about people that is an essential prerequisite of any showman. The stories of Peale, Kessels, Coenen, Menocchio, Thevet, Paré, and so on, imply a resistance that is refractory to the efforts of academics to incorporate "popular culture" within their own discourse and framework. In this they suggest a vital resistance to "popular culture" *by* "popular culture."

PART II

POINTS OF
DISTINCTION

Subjecting the manifold to tabulation does
not ensure any actual understanding of what
lies there before us as thus set in order.

Heidegger, *Being and Time*

CONTEXT AND COMPARISON AND THEREFORE THE QUESTION OF HOW
to select and define what can be compared are the main themes of part
II, and they extend their tentacles far into part III as well. In its emphasis on
formal connections the morphological method has obvious parallels with
structuralism. Indeed, Ginzburg confesses to having been pulled in a structuralist direction for a time under the influence of the writings of Claude
Lévi-Strauss, specifically his *Structural Anthropology.* However, the ambi-
tious project of studying basic anthropological categories in different cultural settings ended up by, in Ginzburg's words, "giving birth to a mouse"
(Ginzburg [1986] 1990b, ix).

Ginzburg singles out two important divergences from structuralist method. The first is the limited and marginal function accorded historiography
by Lévi-Strauss. The second is that Ginzburg locates the series of long-term
phenomena analyzed in *Ecstasies* in a sphere "situated between the abstract
depth of structure . . . and the superficial concreteness of the event" ([1989]
1990a, 22). It is in this intermediary space, according to Ginzburg, that the
real contest between anthropology and history is probably played out.

To gain some idea of what this means, it is instructive to compare the
various positions taken on a single, identifiable cultural phenomenon by
Ginzburg and by the anthropologists Françoise Héritier-Augé and Rodney

Needham. The phenomenon in question is the theme of the unilateral figure: the (usually masculine) image of a human being who has been bisected
vertically, leaving him with one eye, one arm, and one leg. Faced with the
problems connected with any attempt to define phenomena such as kinship
or marriage in a way that is useful for comparative purposes (Needham
1971), Needham focused on one object of study that seemed to be relatively
free of this defect—the human body. The human body has a more or less
clear form, implying wholeness and symmetry. On the basis of this premise
Needham proceeded to explore a particular image of the human body: that
of the half-man or half-woman resulting from a longitudinal bisection of
the body. This figure turns out to be distributed on a global scale, independently of social structure; nor is it confined to narratives or visual images
of a particular kind (Needham 1980, 17–40). Criticizing Needham's diffusionist theses, Héritier-Augé (1992, 9) argues that the real question is a *different* one, namely, Why is this motif not found everywhere? Her reply is
that it is one possibility among others; that a whole range of mental figures
could be substituted for it; and that all these figures are capable of being
identified and classified.

In introducing difference Héritier-Augé makes it impossible to continue
tracing isomorphic series, for it is precisely what is allomorphic that interests her. Despite the theoretical sophistication of her argument, it is hard to
see how it could be implemented as a program: How is one to identify what
is different from the object of investigation? More importantly, how is one
to establish that that difference has any pertinence? It is here, we would
argue, that the distinction between morphological and structural methods
emerges most clearly. Héritier-Augé's project is ultimately a reductionist
one, aiming to bring a vast array of disparate data into relation to one particular motif—that of the unilateral figure. Or it is an imperialist one? The
structures of opposition and inversion are extrapolated on an ever-increas-
ing range of phenomena in order to bring them too under the domination
of those very structures.

In *Ecstasies* Ginzburg devotes a whole chapter to the widespread theme
of the human figure marked by an unusual form of locomotion ([1989]
1990a, 226–95). However, he rejects Needham's belief in self-evident, universal symbols or archetypes whose significance can be grasped intuitively.
The object of the research conducted in *Ecstasies*, by contrast—like that of
the present work—is not given but must be reconstructed on the basis of
formal affinities; its significance is not transparent but must be deciphered
by examining the context, or, better, the pertinent contexts. Recognition of

the isomorphism of the features that are discovered does not mean uniform interpretation of so disparate a complex of myths and rituals. And the series that includes these units is, by definition, open-ended (240–42).

These parallels between the two "morphologists" Needham and Ginzburg in their recourse to the human body as a primal signifier indicate both a strength and a weakness of the method. The weakness is the weakness of all comparative research: the problem of comparing entities that a posteriori may well turn out to be disparate, heterogeneous, and thus incommensurable. The strength is the firm sense of conviction that reference to the human body is presumed to convey: we all have one, we all know what it is (or at least we think we do), and we therefore have no difficulty in comparing different representations of the human body as variants on the same theme, bearing a "family resemblance," rather than as disparate entities.

Perhaps we all know what the human body is, but there is nothing self-evident about any other phenomenon—as Needham had already underscored. That applies to honor as well, a phenomenon that is often rooted in a notion of corporeal integrity but in fact has much wider ramifications. Starting from a sixteenth-century case of litigation in the Netherlands, we argue in chapter 2 that whatever heuristic value the comparison may initially have had, the notions of honor of largely pastoral and agrarian village communities in the Mediterranean have as little relevance to early modern urban society in western Europe as does the hackneyed anthropological model of "shame" and "guilt" cultures. Instead, the projection of such a binary division onto the long-term development of societies is shown to be a means of articulating difference and distance: dividing us from them. Moreover, by calling into question not only the distinction between "shame" and "guilt" cultures but also their insertion within a chronological framework, we hope to demonstrate what might be called the "chronocentric" character of such constructions, that they take the modern period as their starting point, just as analyses of a "Eurocentric" character take Europe as their starting point. We hope that the tracing of morphological chains will offer a way of escaping from the implicit teleology and unilinearity of chronological lines of development. (The implications of this challenge to periodization are worked out more fully in part III.)

The idea of a unitary phenomenon "culture," whether it is labeled as a "guilt" or a "shame" variety, has come under attack from anthropologists. As Nicholas Thomas points out (in a critique of the influential work of Clifford Geertz, among others): "Both human attributes that might arguably be universal (at cognitive or linguistic levels, for instance), and differences that arise from age, gender and a plethora of other considerations, are marginalized by this privileging and essentialization of ethnic or cultural difference" (1994, 96).

Questions of identity, definition and comparison arise in a different connection in chapter 3. This time the context within which an "appropriate" comparison is made is at issue. New comparisons imply new contexts of comparison, and with them different forms of recontextualization. This phenomenon has been studied within a number of disciplines. For instance, the anthropologist Nicholas Thomas has discussed the ways artifacts from islands in the Pacific could be reinserted into a variety of different contexts, each of which differed from their Pacific setting (1991). In the field of literary theory, it has become something of an axiom that texts can be grafted from one context to another. In philosophy, J. L. Austin (1975) in particular stressed how some utterances may be "out of context," thereby raising the question what the notion "appropriate context" actually means. Curators of ethnological museums have puzzled over whether artifacts from the regions traditionally investigated by ethnographers should be displayed in recreations of the "original context" or whether their very presence in a Western museum is not itself constitutive of a new context, suggesting possible juxtapositions with "primitivist" work by twentieth-century artists, for example (see Karp and Lavine 1991). And to return to historians, whereas Ferrari (1987) stressed the parallels between the popular features of the anatomy theater and the grotesque side of carnival treated in Bakhtin's famous study of Rabelais, Lazzerini (1994) resorts explicitly to the morphological method to bring out the relevance of a different and more sinister set of contexts: anatomical dissection, sacrifice, and capital punishment.

Starting from the parallels between shamanistic practices in medieval Europe and those in areas that are the traditional preserve of anthropologists, some striking parallels are drawn that cut across the traditional ones; in some cases, it is suggested, the closest European parallel to a South American shaman may in fact be a saint; within other contexts, the shaman may have witchlike aspects; and there are even contexts in which it may be most relevant to compare a South American shaman with a shaman. Touching on the field of historical anthropology, chapter 3 ends by putting questions to both historical anthropology and anthropological history.

Definition and identity return in yet another shape in chapter 4. Ginzburg's preoccupation with the human body not only was part of his dialogue with structural anthropology but also formed a crucial element in the method introduced by Giovanni Morelli of distinguishing original works of art from copies. Morelli recommended that the critic concentrate on ear-lobes, fingernails, and shapes of fingers and toes as those details most likely to escape the notice of a copier. In his famous essay "Clues: Roots of an Ev-idential Paradigm" Ginzburg traced the parallels between the methods of Morelli, Sherlock Holmes, and Sigmund Freud back to early hunters' ability to read animal tracks ([1986] 1990b, 96–125). Not only early hunters pos-sessed this skill: this ability on the part of Amerindians, celebrated in James Fenimore Cooper's *Last of the Mohicans* (1826), also exerted a considerable influence on Sherlock Holmes' creator, Arthur Conan Doyle (Caisson 1995, 118–19). In the bold and imaginative leaps of *Ecstasies* such microscopic at-tention to detail is combined with the tracing of resemblances on a grand scale. This combination of microhistory with morphology explains why the research cannot be situated at the abstract depth of structure or in the su-perficial concreteness of the event.

Chapter 4 draws its inspiration from the work of Morelli, with its stress on vision and the importance it attached to distinctive visual marks. In the case of Jews in the early modern Netherlands, it demonstrates the advan-tages of focusing primarily on external markers such as name, language, physical appearance, dress, occupation, and address. Surface and appear-ance—the margins of the body—may be just as relevant to questions of group, individual, or personal identity as are less clearly visible factors such as beliefs and convictions. Contending with the metaphysical modern no-tion of identity as something that is internal, located (or even locked) in the innermost ranges of personality and mind, means contending with lan-guage, which equates profundity with truth and surface with shallowness and triviality. As in the preceding chapters, it is not only the concept of what we are trying to study but also the method of studying it that needs to be reassessed.

2

POINTS OF HONOR:
THE LIMITS OF COMPARISON

A MORALITY TALE

THERE WAS NO POINT IN TRYING TO HIDE THE FACT ANY LONGER: friends, relatives, and neighbors, perhaps the whole town, knew that the marriage of Cornelis Kelou and Geertruyd van Berckenrode was near the breaking point. According to her, Cornelis squandered her money in dubious business adventures; he played at dice and spent his time in bad company. Cornelis countered that his wife's so-called friends drank far too much, gave her bad advice, and incited her to challenge his authority. In his version of the conflict she was continually nagging and badgering him, calling him names, insulting him in the worst of terms, and generally behaving in an insolent way. Even in public she humiliated him. After about ten years of marriage and the birth of several children—we do not know exactly how many—the time had come for legal action.

The references to playing dice and, perhaps, to the challenge to the husband's authority might make us suspect that this is not a description of a modern marital crisis, but in every other respect it is hard to tell whether this story belongs to the twentieth, the nineteenth, the eighteenth, or an earlier century. In fact, we are talking about the 1560s and about a couple living in the Dutch town of Haarlem, not far from Amsterdam. Their controversy had its roots in the early years of their marriage, but it came into the open around 1568 and remained a matter of public discussion until 1571. There was talk of divorce, both spouses sought legal assistance, and legal proceedings got under way amidst an increasingly alarming political, religious, and military situation. It was the first and in many ways the most violent phase of the Dutch Revolt against Spanish Habsburg rule.[1] Just a few years earlier, in 1566, iconoclasts had sent a wave of destruction through Roman Catholic churches in many parts of the Netherlands, and Adriaen Coenen, as we saw in chapter 1, had had a portrait painted of his *poelomp,* or beggar fish, which seemed to herald further disasters. At the end of 1572 the Spanish armies would begin their long siege of Haarlem, bringing famine and death to many citizens. The conflict between Cornelis and Geertruyd was first dealt with by the local town court, but it eventually reached the highest judicial level: the Great Council of Mechelen (Grote Raad van Mechelen), which had been acting since the late fifteenth century as the supreme court in the as yet undivided Netherlands. The records of the Great Council do not reveal how the controversy ended; there is no verdict among the documents.[2] Perhaps there never was one. Geertruyd and Cornelis may eventually have decided to settle out of court. Given both the acrimony of their dispute and the rapidly changing political situation in the spring of 1572, however, it is more likely that their personal problems were overshadowed by the general turmoil. By that time it may no longer have been expedient to continue proceedings in a court that was increasingly coming to be regarded as the judicial representative of an enemy government.[3]

More interesting than the final conclusion of Cornelis and Geertruyd's controversy are the questions how and why such a relatively minor conflict was taken to the highest national court and what the remaining documents, fragmentary and one-sided though they are,[4] can tell us about male and female honor and shame in the circles of sixteenth-century Dutch citizens. In order to interpret the statements about honor and reputation contained in these documents, as in chapter 1, we must focus on contexts in the plural. As Jacques Revel puts it, microhistory does not assume that national history can only be written at the level of the nation or that personal history is only attainable at the personal level; instead, "from nearby or from afar, every historical actor participates in processes—and is therefore inscribed in contexts—with different levels and dimensions, from the most local to the most global" (1994, 561). None of these contexts is simply given. However, proceeding from one question raised by the archival records to the next and circling around the central case helps to expose aspects of honor and shame that are obscured or even obliterated by more linear approaches.

We will start with the smallest circle, that of the controversy itself, as it can be reconstructed from the remaining judicial records. In order to understand how and why the pair were fighting, we need to know about the protagonists of this story: What was their background? To which families did they belong? What was their position in Dutch society? The latter question naturally requires some information about the local setting, and thus the context slowly widens from the individual protagonists to the urban setting and the particular characteristics of the town of Haarlem. After that a big leap follows, but first we will concentrate on the local level.

This brings us to the sources. Although the court records that provide most of the information used here are incomplete and full of tantalizing gaps, they do allow us to catch glimpses of a dramatic "private" history developing against a background of even more dramatic historical events. This private drama reveals ordinary, everyday preoccupations as well as unusual characteristics and circumstances. It is dramatic too in the sense that the records show us the unfolding of a story, episode by episode, whose structure is reminiscent of a tale, with interludes, repetitions, farcical elements, tragic phases, and so on. There are even small pieces of dialogue. The comparison between literature and judicial records is not a new one. Many scholars have shown both the liveliness and the dramatic potential of judicial records and the difficulties posed by them. They require as much careful analysis and attention to style, gaps, and so on, as do strictly literary sources.[5] Perhaps some other similarities between fiction and judicial records, however, have not yet been given the attention they deserve.

The use of literary representations always raises questions about the relation between representation and historical practice and about the social and regional origins of the views expressed. Do we read what the authors believed, what their readers wanted to hear, or what the authors imagined that their readers wanted or needed to hear? The same applies to judicial records. The fact that they were not meant as fiction does not mean that we should read them as if they were simple accounts of "reality"; nor should we forget that every statement is colored by the intentions, wishes, and goals of the respective parties. This seems simple enough, but in civil cases (even more than in criminal ones) it means that the number of "authors" involved multiplies drastically. Instead of one author trying to shape the text, we have two, theoretically equal parties doing the same, as well as a third, apparently neutral one who influences the texts at least as much as the others do. Nearly every statement that we are allowed to read—they are all part of the official records—comes to us in a heavily censored and rephrased form that reflects legal categories and juridically correct forms of presentation. Both parties in this case were instructed by their counsels to couch their depositions in the form that would be most advantageous to their case while still adhering, however tenuously, to the rules of the legal game.[6] Like many forms of fiction, then, such depositions are consciously stylized representations of reality—a similarity that need not prevent us from recognizing that the relation between representation and reality differs in the two cases and that it is a far from simple one in either case.

Finally, fiction and judicial records have one more thing in common: both address a public. This is more easily recognized in the case of the criminal records, which were so closely connected with the theater of public executions, the announcement of new ordinances by town criers, and the nailing of sentences and proclamations to church doors for every inhabitant to see. But court proceedings in civil cases were public affairs too, and judges who pronounced verdicts in such cases realized very well that their decisions had more than just a legal import. They were continually creating precedents in the widest sense of the term. By their verdicts they demonstrated the norms. They were well aware that their decisions could be taken as social guidelines. Even if there was no decision but only a settlement out of court, such disputes were still very public affairs. It is inconceivable that the inhabitants of any provincial town would have let slip the chance to discuss and gossip about causes and consequences for all the parties involved. A conflict that had reached the stage of going to court was by definition no longer a private affair—if anything ever was in the sixteenth century. The judicial records thus not only provide ambiguous and often hard-to-interpret clues to contemporary views and norms; by their public character court cases also helped to shape these norms, which is why their records can be read as morality tales.

THE CASE IN POINT

What exactly were Cornelis Kelou and Geertruyd van Berckenrode fighting about? To avoid becoming immediately entangled in their contradictory statements, it may be helpful to introduce this couple briefly and to sketch the chronology of their marital problems. They were married in 1559 and lived for several years in King's Street, near the central market square of Haarlem. Mid-sixteenth-century Haarlem was an important and fairly rapidly growing manufacturing town of about fifteen thousand inhabitants.[7] The local economy depended largely on the expanding textile production. Brewing and exporting beer had been the principal backbone of the urban economy in the past and still remained an extremely important source of urban income, but it was slowly coming to occupy a secondary position behind the textile business.

Both Cornelis Kelou and Geertruyd van Berckenrode belonged to a segment of the urban elite that included members of both the lower nobility and the upper echelons of the bourgeoisie. Geertruyd is especially interesting in this respect (see Thierry de Bye Dolleman 1958). A contemporary account of events in Haarlem between 1572 and 1581 does not mention Geertruyd herself but is full of references to her numerous and generally wealthy kinfolk (Verwer 1973). They occupied crucial political, judicial, and administrative positions as mayor, alderman, or treasurer of Haarlem for most of the sixteenth century.[8] The Van Berckenrode family did not belong to the group of noble families with large landholdings, but most members of the family seem to have followed the noble precept not to engage in manual labor or commerce (Van Nierop 1993, 42). Geertruyd was born around 1527, the fourth of five children. Her father, Willem van Berckenrode, several times held the offices of alderman and mayor of Haarlem during the 1520s and 1530s. Her only brother, Gerrit, who died young in 1559, likewise acted as alderman. In 1544 the eldest of her three sisters married a certain Adriaen Claeszoon, who was treasurer of the town of Haarlem from 1552 until his death. During the last years of his life this Adriaen Claeszoon acted as a go-between and peacemaker in the conflict between Geertruyd and Cornelis. Geertruyd herself married late, when she was thirty-three. Her dowry was considerable, amounting to several thousand guilders. Marriage in community of property was fairly common in the Netherlands, but the size of the dowry in this case was probably the main reason why a marriage settlement was drawn up stating "that no other community of property would exist between them than that they share equally in the profits and the losses."

We know far less about Geertruyd's husband.[9] Apparently Cornelis was also relatively well off. His family too contained men who occupied high positions in local government. They did not belong to the local elite of Haarlem, however, but came from the southern part of the province of Holland. One of Cornelis's uncles, for instance, was a burgomaster of Rotterdam. About Cornelis's professional activities we know only that he was somehow involved in commerce, but no further details can be found in the dossiers. As we shall see, he tried to obtain prestigious (but by no means always remunerative) posts in local government and administration like those his wife's relatives held, so we must assume that he had some independent means. Brief references to a considerable amount of leisure also suggest that he either lived on his private means or had delegated most of his business activities to subordinates. Perhaps, however, he simply expected continued access to his wife's family capital. He was in for a shock.

Cornelis's status was lower, though perhaps not very much lower, than his wife's, a point that should be kept in mind as we more closely examine the theme of honor. Geertruyd may be regarded as continuing a family tradition in this respect, since she was by no means the only woman in her family to marry down, into the higher bourgeoisie, rather than up, into the higher ranks of the nobility (Van Nierop 1993, 69).[10] As a married woman, Geertruyd occupied herself first and foremost with management of the household and with the children. She was also involved in the manufacture of linen and woolen cloth, important branches of the local textile industry. From the deposition of a woman living in the same neighborhood we may infer that Geertruyd was not a large-scale manufacturer. It is more likely that she acted as a middlewoman in an urban putting-out system that involved the processing or finishing of quantities of raw material or cloth in private workshops and homes: "And, further, that the same housewife was engaged in a certain trade having woolen cloth manufactured and flax spun." In a statement produced by Cornelis Kelou's counsel, the same neighbor (who owned a grocery shop) declared that Geertruyd actually worked at a loss and that her commercial activities brought her in close—too close?—contact with lower-class women—one more point of honor to which we shall return.

Even if Geertruyd had married below her station and did not conform to all of the noble standards of behavior, she could still rely on the support of powerful relatives who occupied strategic positions in local government. Her husband had his own connections, but these belonged mostly to the world of education, the professions, church, and science. Among the men who came to his support during the long-drawn-out legal conflict with his wife were several notaries, some church officials, such as a priest and a vicar of the Saint Bavo Cathedral in Haarlem and the dean of Haarlem and its environs, the principal of the renowned college of Haarlem, the apothecary Maerten Adriaensz, several "town skippers," and the famous physician and humanist Hadrianus Junius.[11] Cornelis could also enlist the support of several influential local politicians, such as Dirck Jacobs de Vries, who had been alderman of Haarlem seven times and burgomaster eight times between 1542 and 1572. In the course of the 1560s Kelou himself several times came close to being appointed to a government sinecure. According to one of his acquaintances, Kelou had "made a great effort . . . to obtain some office in order to drive away his free time" and "all these applications must have cost Cornelis quite a number of pots of wine." On one occasion he was formally promised the post of steward of the abbey of Egmond; on another he was in line to succeed the town sheriff, Gerrit Pieters Berkhout, who had actually offered the job to Kelou when he resigned. Former sheriff Berkhout also appeared as a witness testifying in favor of Kelou, but we may well ask whether the recommendations of a man who, in spite of being the town sheriff, was described by the city fathers as "negligent and incompetent" would not have been more of a liability than a help.[12] We cannot completely exclude the possibility, however, that Cornelis's attempts to obtain these offices were thwarted by his marital troubles, which had become public knowledge by then.

Relations between Cornelis Kelou and Geertruyd van Berckenrode came under severe strain within two years of their marriage. Certainly by that time Cornelis was asking two women neighbors to testify in writing to his blameless conduct. By 1568 the situation had deteriorated to such an extent that the couple were looking for help from outside. Cornelis had left the house and moved in with his mother. It seems likely that he threatened to take legal action against his wife. Geertruyd may have supposed that it would be expedient to be the first to take legal action. It was she, in any case, who submitted a request to the burgomasters and aldermen of Haarlem to place her husband under guardianship and thus deny him the right to use their joint property as he saw fit. That step was a drastic one but one that is slightly easier to understand in light of the fact that the town government consisted largely of her relatives, friends, and friends (or clients) of friends. Cornelis reacted immediately. Relatives from both sides were asked to intercede and help bring about a reconciliation; at the same time, Cornelis turned to a higher court, the provincial Court of Holland (Hof van Holland), in order to protest formally against Geertruyd's attempt to take away his powers. We may speculate that this step not only was inspired by procedural motives but also helped to put pressure on his wife to revoke her request.

An attempt at arbitration by the burgomaster of Rotterdam (an uncle of Cornelis) and the treasurer of Haarlem (a brother-in-law of Geertruyd) during the autumn of 1568 resulted in a pause in the conflict, but in the course of 1569–70 the controversy flared up once more. In August 1570 the town court of Haarlem formally decided to place Cornelis Kelou under guardianship. There was worse in store for him, however. The provincial Court of Holland did not find in his favor either. Soon after the decision of the Haarlem court, the Court of Holland ordained that the joint property of Cornelis and Geertruyd be administered by a trustee. Although this looked like a more equitable decision, it very much favored Geertruyd. After all, until that moment their joint property (which did not include either Geertruyd's capital or Cornelis's probably far smaller funds) had been mainly his to use as he saw fit, since women could only conclude financial transactions with the permission of their husbands or male relatives. That power was no longer his, and everybody knew it. What is more, the trustee appointed could in no way be regarded as impartial. It was a clever choice. Who, after all, could object to the town treasurer? But Cornelis can hardly have been pleased to see Geertruyd's sister's husband, Adriaen Claesz, in this role.[13]

Again Cornelis sought legal help, going even higher this time, to the supreme court in the Netherlands, the Great Council at Mechelen. He appealed the sentence of the provincial court and requested a new verdict against his wife. Until the spring of 1572 he continued to submit new documents and amplifications, but the Great Council seems not to have heeded his requests, as no verdict has been found. Many of Cornelis's friends and acquaintances testified in his favor. Even some of the very highly esteemed former burgomasters of Haarlem came to declare that to their knowledge *no man* had ever been placed under guardianship in their town without being heard first. In other words, there was a very peculiar smell to this case. It looks as if Geertruyd had employed her influential kinsmen to exert pressure not just at the local level, which must have been easy enough, but also in the provincial court at the Hague and perhaps even in the supreme court at Mechelen. Of course, at the local level there may have been other motives as well. For instance, Kelou's de facto removal from public life—for how could a man be appointed to any public function who could not manage his own business or his wife?—must have been a godsend to rival claimants for the public functions he had coveted. However, Cornelis himself never explicitly adduced such arguments in his defense, and they are not strictly necessary to understand the notions of honor and shame that were of such importance in this case.[14]

POINTED REMARKS

Thanks to Cornelis's persistence in taking the controversy to ever higher levels of justice, we have access to documents that allow us to probe some of the complexities of concepts of honor in sixteenth-century Holland. What did a husband, neighbors, or relatives think or say about the honor or virtue of a sixteenth-century housewife who belonged to one of the upper strata of local urban society? How was a husband supposed to behave in these circles if he wanted to be regarded as an honorable man? What did a woman have to do—or, even more important, not do—if she wanted to keep her good reputation? What strategies did men and women in this Dutch town deploy to maintain their honor? Could honor once lost or blemished be restored, and if so, how? How big were the differences between men and women in this respect, and what about the famous double standard with respect to sexual behavior? In which terms, finally, did the parties concerned—including witnesses, jurists, and relatives—discuss notions of honor and shame?

We shall start with Geertruyd's point of view. She said that her husband "is living in a very dissolute way and is badly governing his affairs and diminishes and dissipates his property in various kinds of disorderly company and otherwise, whereby she and her children are doomed to misery and poverty." The burgomasters of Haarlem investigated her complaints, or so they said, and found that Cornelis's property had indeed diminished and that there was some mention of "disorderly behavior." The remaining documents do not give us any details. Their findings may not seem much to us—and we suspect that they were not much then—but for these hardly impartial magistrates they clinched the case against Cornelis. The provincial Court of Holland does not appear to have done anything but copy their findings. It did not order a new "investigation" or check the accuracy of the earlier account. The verdict of the provincial court likewise calls attention to Kelou's (unspecified) dissolute way of life but puts far more stress on the fact that he "squandered by useless means wealth and merchandise." What was worse, he squandered not only his own money but also the property that had come with his wife. That in particular was the reason why the verdict of the Court of Holland reproached him for not behaving as "a man of honor was bound to do." Would provincial magistrates always have been so concerned about the morals of a member of a local elite, or do these statements echo the worries of Geertruyd and her influential relatives about their family fortune?

The exasperated Cornelis responded within a few weeks to this verdict of the Court of Holland. He appealed to the Great Council van Mechelen, complaining, through his counsel, that his wife "as well as some of her consorts ... through their false and sinister statements" had obtained a decision in their favor from the provincial court. Cornelis of course denied emphatically "that he had behaved in an unseemly way, shown signs of prodigality or dissipation, or contributed to the dilapidation of his possessions." He was, moreover, extremely distressed about the impending public proclamation of the decision to place him under guardianship, "which would not only bring him more injury, damage, and defamation by everybody but also rob him of his good name and reputation [*name ende fame*], which (once lost) could not be recovered or remedied . . . which proclamation was going to bring him, Cornelis, even more shame [*schande*] and desolation [*desolatie*]." Publicity, in other words, would be fatal to his reputation and would bring him infinite disgrace.

Even statements from a much earlier phase of the controversy throw some light on local opinions about what was proper or improper behavior for a married man or woman. As early as 1561 the fights between Cornelis and Geertruyd had attracted some public attention. According to some women neighbors, Geertruyd in particular misbehaved. They stated that some of the marital altercations—described as "injury and strife"—were triggered by Geertruyd's (too) close contact with a certain Lijsbeth Everts and her daughter Anne, women of bad repute about whom two other neighbors also had nothing good to report: "Lijsbeth and Anna, her daughter, are commonly reputed to cause strife between husband and wife." If we may believe the reports by these neighbors, this Lijsbeth had told Geertruyd several times not to suffer her husband's rebukes, since it had been she, after all, who had brought in most of the capital: "And do not allow your husband to chastise or judge you; the property has all come from you." According to the neighbors, not only did these two women incite Geertruyd to rebel against her husband's authority but they invited her to drink, and Geertruyd was seen in their company on several occasions when they ordered "jugs and tankards" of wine and beer to be brought to Lijsbeth's house. After these convivialities Cornelis was confronted by a drunken wife shouting insults. On such occasions she was also known to call her mother-in-law a "sorceress," among other "evil and villainous words." At those times neither Cornelis nor anyone else could stand Geertruyd. The same neighbors also agreed that "Cornelis has always treated Geertruyd as an honorable man is bound to behave and should behave towards his wife."

As Cornelis explained several years later, it had been Geertruyd's close connection with these two "unequal and improper females, both inside and outside the house . . . that had made him consider that this was going to cause great blame and scandal to the said Geertruyd and her kin." It had been mainly for this reason that he had left the house and moved back into his mother's house. The point is clear, of course. Whether Cornelis's report about his wife is true or not does not matter much in this respect. He apparently felt that the judicial authorities would immediately understand that he had had to distance himself from a wife whose unsuitable friends and depraved behavior would threaten to blemish his own reputation. As mentioned earlier, relatives on both sides tried to mediate during their informal separation. It was for them—and at first for their eyes only—that Cornelis wrote down his views on the intolerable situation and tried to formulate a compromise. Later, during the final phase of this controversy, when his case was being considered by the Great Council at Mechelen, he presented this revealing document as evidence:

> Further, that she has frequently beaten me and at various times ... has threatened me and tried to stab me, which would give cause to a good man to lose his temper. . . . That she is also daily calling my mother a sorceress [*toveressche*], which I could not suffer. . . . That she calls me every day a bloodsucker, a rogue, a thief, a villain, and a thousand similarly abusive names. . . .
>
> She is hanging around all the time, both inside and outside the house, with whores, dishonest women, and women who foster discord. . . . She holds slanderers, gossips, whores, and servant girls in more esteem than her own husband, so that I, when sharing a table with these people, could not admonish her or the house would be in uproar. And a thousand more matters that could easily make people regard a good man as a villain.[15]

Cornelis was clearly desperate. He thought he had tried every possibility to improve matters, but he could see no solution unless Geertruyd was prepared to subscribe to the following conditions: "First, that she would sever contacts with all slanderers, gossips, second-hand dealers, and neither speak with them inside my house, outside in the street, or in other houses, nor keep them company, nor let other friends take her to visit such folk." Second, that she would converse in a friendly way with the friends and acquaintances they had in common and no longer badger him about his friends. Third, that she would leave the management of their common finances completely in his hands, while he would give her what she needed for household expenses, and "that I will have an account at all times." Further, she would have to cease her commercial activities in the textile business, which only caused losses and encouraged contact with the wrong kind of womenfolk. "Honorable people and their friends," on the other hand, she might visit as often as she wished, within reason. Cornelis concluded with the following, hardly optimistic words: "If she does not want to firmly promise all of this and regulate her behavior accordingly, it will be more necessary for us two souls to divorce from each other before more evil consequences ensue."

Arbitration did indeed produce some results. A neighbor, the woman who owned a small grocery shop nearby, later declared that "during their separation Cornelis's wife had begged her [i.e., the neighbor] to . . . induce Kelou to come back to her, so that they would be joined again in love and devotion, to which Kelou had at the same time kindly agreed and consented." Geertruyd and her representatives realized very well, moreover, that legal proceedings might easily lead to a shameful and disgraceful public exhibition, and they prayed "that they would repair matters in friendship without shaming each other in court."

Geertruyd seems to have promised that "she would relinquish the disorderly company she continually kept and would pay more attention to her household and children. That she would also give up her activities in the textile business since she served no purpose there." The new understanding was short-lived, however, and soon matters took another turn for the worse—that is, if we may still rely on Cornelis's statements. He declared that he had not seen a penny of the profits of their joint property, which was administered by Geertruyd's brother-in-law. Moreover, he accused Geertruyd of literally forcing the lock of his front door—it is not clear whether he was living in his mother's house at that moment—and taking away everything she wanted: "Whenever she did not have any money, she was scolding and abusing him, and taking her jewelry and silverware to the pawnbroker's . . . continuing her old dissolute way of life, and . . . she reproached the appellant [i.e., Cornelis] every day for not being a good guardian for her and her possessions any more, defaming [*diffamerende*] him in the streets."

Cornelis's document tells us clearly how a good wife was *not* supposed to behave in these social circles. Her public connection with lower-class women, the shouted insults, her discourteous behavior to well-bred and highly placed friends and (business) acquaintances, and her public display of insolence to both her husband and her mother-in-law were regarded as extremely serious breaches of decorum. Hardly less grave were the losses incurred by her apparently ill-considered commercial activities, her slipshod way of managing the household, beating and threatening her husband, and the public display of drinking. Once more, it is not relevant here whether Geertruyd actually behaved in this way. Cornelis must have been convinced that his description of this type of behavior would persuade the magistrates that she had far exceeded the boundaries that circumscribed a good wife's conduct. In that sense his catalog of complaints reads very much like an inverted manual. We only have to invert again and we have a wonderful, stereotypical description of the ideal housewife: subservient to her husband and mother-in-law, respectful in her conduct towards her husband's friends, discerning in the choice of her own friends, who should belong to the right social circles, demure and restrained in her behavior in public, prudent in commercial undertakings, competent in household management, and so on.

Various other points about Cornelis's grievances are significant as well. The most intriguing point is perhaps an absent one: sex. The only sin Geertruyd is not accused of is cuckolding her husband. Drinking, yes, but with female friends. There is not even a hint of irregular male companions. Did Cornelis omit such a complaint because it would do too much damage to his own honor? It is hard to imagine, for by the time his case had reached the Great Council he cannot have had much "face" left to save. He had already been placed under guardianship, and it was by his own statement, dating back to the period of mediation, that he was described as a husband beaten and publicly insulted by his wife, a henpecked husband, in short. Or would he have balked, after all, at calling himself a cuckold?

A second point likewise hints at the partly hidden theme of female power in this controversy. Geertruyd publicly insulted not only her husband but also her mother-in-law. That she chose to strike out at her husband's mother and the terms Geertruyd used to abuse her are particularly interesting. Mothers-in-law were commonly known to make a nuisance of themselves, or even worse, to tyrannize their daughters-in-law and dominate the joint households as long as they could. That was not precisely the situation in the present case, but it may have come close. Cornelis's mother did not share Geertruyd and Cornelis's house, but she must have lived nearby. As we have seen, Cornelis moved back in with her during an especially bitter phase of the controversy. His mother was a widow by then, and her four unmarried daughters probably lived with her. It is not hard to guess how this materfamilias, who probably felt protective of her only son, living with his "difficult" wife, handed out well-meant advice to Geertruyd and silently (or not so silently) compared her with her own daughters. This would have ruffled the feathers of Geertruyd and perhaps made her behave in an (even) less restrained way when her mother-in-law was present, ending up by calling her a sorceress to her face. But who can say that the mother-in-law did not actually resort to sorcery in a situation that was fast getting out of control and threatening to bring serious harm to her son and her whole family? The situation certainly called for special measures—the law, or sorcery, or perhaps both (see Ruggiero 1993).

Cornelis did not confine his complaints to topics like keeping up appearances and publicly throwing away one's honor and good reputation. Nonetheless, the public dimension of honor shines through at almost every moment. It is no coincidence that apparently irrelevant references to the location of incidents—"both inside the house and outside in the street"—recur again and again. That a man was insulted by his wife's friends was bad enough; that it happened in his own house, at his own table, was execrable. Nor were the words "in the street" a meaningless addendum to Cornelis's charge that Geertruyd abused him: it was public abuse, and so much the worse for that. It is equally clear that Geertruyd's behavior had consequences not only for her own reputation but also for her husband's name and, by implication, for the name of his family. If she did not show him respect, nobody would. That at least is implied in Cornelis's references to her lack of deference towards himself. Even the simple rumor that she tried to have him placed under guardianship was, as Cornelis correctly remarked, enough to damage his honor and to make him lose credit in both the literal and the figurative sense.

It seems clear that Cornelis was not alone in his views of what was suitable or unsuitable behavior for a married upper-class woman. We should expect a large degree of congruence between Cornelis's statements and public opinion if we are correct in assuming that he and his counsel knew what they were doing when they phrased their complaints for presentation in court to conform to more or less generally shared opinions about women's behavior. It is less self-evident that their statements do not appear to have represented a typically male point of view. Cornelis's complaints about Geertruyd included many of the same topics remarked upon by the women neighbors who belonged to the urban (lower) middle classes. They too had pointed out Geertruyd's too close contacts with lower-class women of bad repute, who encouraged drinking and fomented dissent between husband and wife; they too had commented upon Geertruyd's neglect of her duties in household management and her unprofitable business ventures; and they too had said nothing about sex.

A similar consensus seems to have reigned across the sexes and across the middle and upper classes about how a married man was supposed to behave. As we have seen, Geertruyd's main grievance was money. She said that Cornelis squandered their joint property, and possibly her private capital as well, on dubious business ventures, thereby endangering the livelihood of his wife and children. It seems doubtful that there was ever any

chance of Geertruyd's going without food, but it is clear from the neighbors' reactions that they too thought that a married man's first duty was to
provide and safeguard the family's income. Of secondary importance, both
in Geertruyd's complaints and in the neighbors' comments, was his way of
life. A married man of good position should not gamble, go to whores, or
spend his nights away from home, in taverns or in brothels. His conduct had
to conform to the standards of behavior for a man of honor. The woman
with the grocery shop, for instance, declared "that she has never heard that
. . . Kelou has been involved in any bad deals, nor has played at dice, gam-
bled, gone to the whores, or spent his nights in taverns, but that he has always acted honestly [eerlijken] as a man of honor is supposed to do and has
always consorted with other honorable people [luijden van eeren]." This
final sentence is particularly revealing, for it shows how the word eerlijk
could be used at the time both in its (current) meaning, "honest," and in the
more usual contemporary meaning, "honorable," referring to conduct be-
fitting a particular social status, to respectability, and to the association with
what was described in a later century as "men of quality."

In the depositions made by several male inhabitants of Haarlem in favor
of Kelou we may detect similar notions, even if the phrases have been stan-
dardized by notarial clerks. These men had known Cornelis for a very long
time, if not since his youth. Hadrianus Junius, who had known Cornelis for
eighteen years, said that he had "always conduct[ed] himself in all piety,
honor [eerbaerheijt], and virtuous association," that he was "of good name
and reputation and always commonly reputed to be an upright [oprecht]
man of honor." He had never "seen or heard anything about this same man
that contradicted his honor, nor had he [Cornelis] ever involved himself
with light and disgraceful company, shown a tendency to playing at dice,
adultery, or prodigality."

That the word honor was continually used by both men and women, notaries and witnesses, to describe Cornelis but not Geertruyd is less significant than might seem. The available documents primarily reveal the point
of view of Cornelis, according to whom Geertruyd had behaved in a shameful and disgraceful way. A very intriguing document in this dossier shows,
moreover, that women were by no means only of negative import in matters of honor in these social strata. Nor did they only function as subservient
appendages to their kinsmen where honor was concerned.

As we have seen, Cornelis was hurt, offended, and exasperated by his
wife's attempt to have him placed under guardianship. He felt dishonored,

not because his wife had deceived him with another man but because she had attacked his reputation, his respectability, in a way that was perhaps considered even more damaging in these circles. But Cornelis was not the only one who felt hurt and insulted; five female relatives—his mother and his four sisters—were so distressed and aggravated that they themselves decided to take legal action against Geertruyd and her "consorts." Honor—both Cornelis's and their own—and the good name of their family played a big part in their decision. As these women declared, Geertruyd's actions had "tarnished his and their honor, name, and reputation, . . . all of which causes their infamy [*infamie*] and a decline in their honor, name, and reputation, which is enormously and excessively injured hereby."[16] In the original Dutch the word for "their" in this quotation is in the feminine form, *haerluijden;* there is no mistaking the fact these women were referring to their own female honor and not just to joint family honor. What these women did *not* do, then, was leave matters in the hands of male relatives, who must have been available. The women took action themselves; they apparently regarded themselves as competent representatives of the family and acted independently as guardians of their own honor and reputation.

Considering the fact that all women in early modern society were formally incompetent to take legal action or perform any other legally binding deed unless they had the formal permission of a male guardian (or were represented by him), the quick and easy recourse these women had to legal means is astonishing.[17] This applies to Geertruyd as well. Even when we take into account the complicated background of the controversy between Cornelis and Geertruyd, that there had been attempts at mediation, and that the town court must have been strongly prejudiced in favor of Geertruyd, it is still extremely significant that she resorted to legal means and that her female opponents did the same. It shows us that women as well as men could use the courts and the attendant publicity under certain circumstances as instruments in family and marital conflicts, instruments that may have been especially important to women because they had fewer means of power than men. In this case, for instance, Cornelis stood to lose far more than Geertruyd did by the negative publicity entailed by her request to place him under guardianship, and she probably was well aware of this. It is also important to acknowledge that all parties concerned apparently shared the opinion that legal means could indeed help to restore or repair honor. In spite of Cornelis's statement that a "good name and reputation . . . (once lost) could not be recovered or remedied," he tirelessly took his case from one court to another. He did this not just to recover his financial powers, for his credit was intimately bound up with his honor. In any case, not only Cornelis but also his mother and sisters apparently thought that they could repair their damaged honor by legal means.

Summarizing some of the points of honor that arise from the case, we find that a considerable consensus existed among the sixteenth-century urban middle classes and elite about how honorable men and women were supposed to behave. Both men and women seem to have agreed on which types of conduct were particularly damaging to a good reputation. For both sexes *public* behavior was very important. Men and women were supposed to behave in accordance with their station in life, especially in public; to exercise self-restraint; to show discernment in their choice of friends and associates; and to manage their affairs, whether professional, business, or household, competently. The first concern of a married man should be the livelihood of his family, and his bearing should be dignified: there was no room for profligacy or ribaldry, and he should not be overfamiliar with members of the lower classes.[18] The same rules applied to married women, but in their case the care for household and children replaced the male duty to maintain the family. Moreover, they should always treat their husbands respectfully.

THE POINT OF COMPARISON

In an orderly procedure we should now advance to the broader context of studies about Dutch honor. It is perhaps significant that, with only a few exceptions, the theme of honor has been ignored in Dutch historiography until very recently. This obscurity tells us a lot, not about the early modern Netherlands but about the remarkable preoccupation of Dutch historians— and of other historians as well—with modernity.[19] Honor has long been regarded as the hallmark of an archaic way of life and thus as irrelevant to (the study of) modern society. That was true in the Dutch Republic as a whole and even more so in the province of Holland, which epitomizes Dutch modernity in early modern times. It is no coincidence, therefore, that most of the small number of publications pertaining to honor and shame in the Netherlands deal with the Southern (Burgundian or Habsburg) Netherlands, that is, with regions regarded as fairly distant from the heartland of the Dutch Republic and, consequently, more "Continental"; with a period (from the thirteenth century to the fifteenth) regarded as premodern and, rightly or wrongly, as culturally distant from the Dutch Republic; with the nobility, which has always been regarded, again rightly or wrongly, as culturally irrelevant to the Netherlands; or, finally, with literary sources, which for a long time have been neglected by historians as irrelevant to the serious study of history.[20]

In the context of historiography, then, the topic of honor could be regarded as a means by which (Dutch) historians have articulated cultural distance from their own past. Honor has been relegated to periods, regions, classes, or documents seen as peripheral to the Dutch nation. This dialectic of production by exclusion has been well discussed by Stallybrass and White (1986), who document a number of cases in which the observer, although purporting to describe a different setup in time or place, is actually constructing his or her own antithesis. This process can be seen at work in the representation of domestic others, such as the bourgeois spectator's image of the slum (128), the medieval European image of the Wild Man (Mason 1990a, 43–50), or the Dutch courts' image of criminals (Egmond 1993b, 195). As we shall see in chapter 7, it also operates in the production of representations of exotic others, such as Brazilian Indians. In all of these cases what is at issue is not the historical or ethnographic accuracy of the representation but that those who see themselves as the bearers of culture are defining themselves and the culture they defend by antithesis. In portraying what they are *not* they create an implicit image of what they *are* (or would like to be). The function of this labeling reflects the preoccupations of the labeler— is the phenomenon under consideration to be placed on the side of the labeler's culture or relegated to a location that is distant in time or place?[21]

Let us therefore take a big leap in our search for illuminating contexts, from the local setting of Haarlem to the Mediterranean and to anthropological theories. Many of the topics discussed in the preceding paragraphs sprang from the confrontation of the Dutch archival records with questions deriving from anthropological literature dealing with a Mediterranean context.[22] What is the principal basis of honor? To what extent is honor (only) a matter of public behavior? What is regarded as an insult? How about physical violence, sexual behavior, differences between men and women, and the question whether women can have honor at all? Most anthropological studies of twentieth-century Mediterranean societies discuss honor as a male concept. Although it is hardly ever explicitly stated that women do not have honor, women figure mainly as potential threats to the honor of their kinsmen.[23] In the Mediterranean, male honor, if we follow Anton Blok's description for the moment, is predicated on the capacity to command and enforce respect, which requires and presupposes both physical strength and social prowess. Both self-control and the capacity to control property (including women) are crucial. According to this way of thinking, women are weak—meaning that they lack self-control—and are therefore easily seduced. Consequently, they need permanent, external (i.e., male), supervision. The best one can expect from them is that they, owing to their virtuous conduct, will not bring shame upon their kinsmen and husbands, their family (Blok 1974, 1981). References to this anthropological model of Mediterranean honor can be found in nearly every historical publication about honor in Europe—with respect not only to Italy, Spain, or Greece but also to France, Germany, the Netherlands, and England.

This model is closely connected with the classic distinction between *shame cultures* and *guilt cultures* and the transition from the former to the latter. In shame cultures public reputation is crucially important; the emphasis is on presentation and the show of control. Social gaffes, blunders, and other unseemly behavior cause shame, the loss of honor or "face," but no feelings of guilt. Honor is about public reputation, not private morals. The concept of shame cultures has been linked with societies having a fairly strict separation of public and private spheres and, concomitantly, of male and female domains. In contrast, guilt cultures are characterized by internalized notions of guilt and virtue. Briefly, in such societies it does not matter whether unsuitable behavior is publicly known or not: one feels guilty about it anyhow. The transition from shame culture to guilt culture is seen as a process of internalization and conscience formation. It has been linked with the rise of modern states since the late Middle Ages and with the changing interdependencies between citizens themselves and between public authorities and citizens.

Should we regard all of this as a relevant theoretical context for our Haarlem case? It has become increasingly clear in recent years that the model of shame and guilt cultures involves major problems. These can be solved neither by regarding both shame and guilt cultures as extremes of a continuum nor by other forms of toning down the distinction. One of the worst problems results from the fact that a basically analytical and static distinction between shame and guilt cultures has been transposed to a model of the long-term development of societies. Grand nineteenth-century evolutionary theories may have gone largely out of fashion among historians, but they have not disappeared. The implicit strategy of distancing by means of honor in (Dutch) historiography, described above, is a case in point.

It is here that we return to the question whether we should compare early modern western European urban notions of honor with modern Mediterranean concepts of honor. The principal basis for such a comparison seems

to be the idea that these societies display a similar stage in their development: in western Europe state formation and centralization progressed more
rapidly than in the Mediterranean; concurrently a "modern," more internalized concept of honor developed sooner north of the Alps (Blok 1981).
According to this view, studying (parts of) Mediterranean societies in which
state formation had as yet had very little influence—which includes most
of classical antiquity as well as twentieth-century peripheral regions—could
shed light on notions of honor in early modern western Europe.

Put this way, it is not difficult to see that nearly everything is wrong with
such a comparison. For instance, if we compare honor in classical Greece
or Rome, in sixteenth-century Italy, and in twentieth-century Greece, we do
so first because the phenomena look similar, then because they belong to
the same region, and finally because we assume (or try to trace) historical
links between them. In such an approach morphology comes first, and what
follows is the search for historical connections, for genealogy, as Darwin
preferred to call it in his discussion of genealogy as one of the principles underlying the "mutual affinities of organic beings" ([1859] 1985, 397). Cross-
space comparison, given the sources, is not radically different from cross-time
comparison, but the "genealogical" links of succession in time within one
region have to be replaced by even wider-ranging cross-regional (as well as
cross-temporal) connections, as is demonstrated in Ginzburg's *Ecstasies*.
This is only the case if we find it necessary to actually demonstrate that similar forms are historically linked by either genealogy or mutual contact. We
might, on the other hand, disregard both and concentrate on morphology,
stepping or jumping from one link to another in chains of family resemblances, whether within one European region, across Europe, or across time.
In such a method differences are at least as relevant as similarities, and there
is no built-in tendency to force historical phenomena into the mold of their
ideal types. The approach in terms of shame and guilt cultures, however,
confuses morphology and genealogy, offering the advantages of neither. It
looks for formal similarities but does not go on to search for historical connections. Nor does it restrict itself to morphology, since it assumes that formal similarities derive from the fact that the societies concerned find
themselves in roughly the same phase of development. The existence of
such a general process of social development is, of course, no more than an
asumption, even after more than a century of attempts to pinpoint it. Moreover, the very connection between internalization—conscience formation,
the transition from shame to guilt, or whatever we may call it—and state

formation is speculative as well. If anything, these processes would need to be proved, not assumed. The whole model linking shame and guilt to state formation, therefore, should be left where it belongs: among the complicated stratagems devised by modern social scientists, psychologists, and historians to distance themselves from what they (would like to) regard as nonmodern, as "other" in time or place.

If we look once more at the Dutch case and its implications, we may see how a comparison between Mediterranean and Dutch honor based on such a model would not only direct us towards a useless and eventually circular argument but also deflect our attention from crucial points of honor. One context that would have to be studied if we followed the "old" model is the degree of "modernity" of sixteenth-century state organization in the Netherlands, which should ideally correspond to the degree of internalization of shame or guilt. In the decades preceding the beginning of the Dutch Revolt the Habsburg government had been trying very hard to develop a more "modern," more efficient, more centralized bureaucracy and to increase its grip on life in the Netherlands. This policy was successful up to a point, even if there were many (partly conservative) backlashes. Against that background the social position of Geertruyd, Cornelis, and their kinsmen gains a new significance; after all, they belonged to the social strata directly implicated in local and provincial politics and influenced by Habsburg policy. It is precisely in these circles—which were numerically, economically, politically, and culturally influential in Holland—that we should expect to find a relatively "modern" and at least partly internalized concept of honor. That is not at all what we have seen, however. Terms like *guilt* or *virtue* are never used in this case, and among the many accusations made by Cornelis and Geertruyd there is not a single reference to immoral behavior.[24] Unseemly, undignified, unsuitable, dishonorable, yes, but not bad. Honor in this society was a preeminently public matter and was directly linked to standards of behavior determined by gender and class.[25]

In this respect, then, sixteenth-century Dutch and Italian citizens would have had no problems in understanding each other. But in terms of women, the divisions of public and private spheres, violence, and sex the situation is quite different. Both the Haarlem case and the scattered publications dealing with honor in the northern Netherlands make clear that the combination of women and honor was far more usual in Holland than in southern Europe. In Holland as in the Mediterranean, women could pose a threat to the honor of their husbands or kinsmen by adultery or other types of licentiousness, and many Dutch men and women may have thought that women needed male supervision. Yet, that women had their own honor, that they themselves could even defend their personal honor and that of their family—as shown by Cornelis's mother and sisters—should be emphasized. This is not to say that men and women were equal in Dutch urban society, but perhaps the division between private and public spheres was less closely linked with a male-female division of domains than in the Mediterranean. That possibility would fit in well with the fact that many women who belonged to the lower and middle classes in the early modern Netherlands had relatively easy access to life outside the household and family. It is probably no coincidence, then, that female honor in the sixteenth-century Netherlands included aspects that were linked with public behavior and not only with sex.[26]

The public role of Dutch women certainly made it much harder for men to supervise and control them.[27] References to women as part of a male patrimony are largely absent, and the whole theme of physical violence, male bravado, or male competition for women as a form of male honor is extremely subdued in the Dutch context, though this may apply to a lesser extent to the highest circles of the nobility. In these Dutch circles male honor and power were expressed and symbolized not by physical force but by stability and reliability in financial matters. Of course, it could be argued that a public show of disrespect to a Dutch husband was comparable to adultery in Italy or that male control of property and finances represented a more general control of all possessions, including women, but that would be a worse than useless type of reductionism. It would obliterate precisely those details and characteristics that enable us to recognize these ideas as the peculiarly Dutch sixteenth-century ideas of people belonging to the urban elite. As the microhistorians repeatedly point out, it is often details that reveal crucial characteristics.

The considerable emphasis on finances, on the control of (family) capital, the management of commercial affairs, and the reliability of a husband and a business partner in matters of finance, which recurs in many other Dutch court cases from the same period, shows how intricately marriage and business, male power and financial control, were interconnected. In that sense Geertruyd's steps to have her husband placed under guardianship—we might say to have his powers taken away—must have been understood at the time as more than a mere practical measure to safeguard her capital: it was a straightforward attempt to dishonor him. As in the case of female public roles and their relevance to female honor, the emphasis on the capacity to handle finance in male honor reflects the crucial importance of money—not land, flocks, or even women—to male reputation in these urban circles.[28]

Finally, the importance of legal action should not be overlooked. In spite of formal regulations, women as well as men had recourse to court action. Both apparently regarded the courts as an arena for settling conflicts, as a forum that might (up to a point) restore or repair blemishes to their honor, and as a means to be used in their private battles. This familiarity with legal action and the completely self-evident way in which Geertruyd, Cornelis, and many of their contemporaries sought legal advice in family matters once private attempts at mediation had failed reveals a lot about early modern urban society in the Netherlands. After all, in a different society or a different period Cornelis might have beaten his wife, locked her up, sent her back in disgrace to her relatives, demanded more money as compensation for staying married to her, divorced her, taken the boat to America, or revenged himself violently on Geertruyd's kinsmen. These Dutch citizens do not appear to have even considered violence, and it may well be that any recourse to violence would have been regarded as dishonorable. Here we can usefully compare and contrast the early modern English situation described by Lawrence Stone. He locates a shift from the use of violence to the use of legal means and the compensation by monetary damages, which accompanied a shift in attitudes towards honor and "was in part a product of the growth of the nation state," in the late seventeenth century; notions of honor among the landed elite shifted from "a moral code based on honor and shame to one based also on the rights of property by a husband in the body of his wife" (1990, 280–81, 302). Although Stone's emphasis on this shift seems to derive mainly from an equally binary model of early modern violence versus modern litigation and monetary compensation, it seems clear that the use of violence was an option in many English circles, whereas it seems to have been much less of an option, if it was an option at all, in the circles with which we have been concered.[29]

THE MORAL

The points of honor in the Haarlem case demonstrate, then, how aspects that would have been regarded as incompatible according to the model of shame cultures and guilt cultures easily blended in practice.[30] There is no point in replacing the model of the break in time with one that stresses long-term continuities within each region but points to a cultural rupture between northern and southern Europe. That would only result in the same type of problems we have already encountered, but now in space instead of in time. Cornelis was neither "Mediterranean" nor "antique" in his view of honor as being primarily a matter of public reputation. Nor were Geertruyd and her mother-in-law "West European" or "modern" on account of their relatively public role and insistence on female honor. Once we abandon the idea that societies develop in accordance with a unilinear cultural pattern, whether from shame to guilt or in any other respect, the use of labeling certain traits as either "ancient" or "modern"—and a fortiori "postmodern"—disappears as well. Perhaps precisely because it is not concerned with genealogy or other types of historical connection, morphology helps us to bypass the conceptual gaps posed by such binary models.

3

POINTS OF COMPARISON: SAINTS, SORCERERS, AND SHAMANS

BETWEEN HISTORY AND ANTHROPOLOGY

As we saw in the previous chapter, when events threaten to get out of hand, one may have recourse to the law or to sorcery. Cornelis Kelou and his wife, Geertruyd van Berckenrode, turned to the law; in the present chapter it is to sorcery and shamanism that we turn. As in the case of honor, historians have repeatedly turned to anthropologists for illumination when faced with particularly puzzling aspects of magical or religious practices in a European setting. Anthropologists, for their part, have cited the work of historians to buttress their own speculations about witchcraft in traditional settings. As we shall see, this relationship of mutual admiration is not without its problems.

Something else we came across in the previous chapter was the way discourse about others often takes the form of constructing an antithesis to oneself. Thus, magico-religious phenomena can be exoticized, rendering religious representations held by other cultures as something occult, supernatural, extraordinary, and mysterious in terms of one's own culture. Alternatively, they can be familiarized, for example, by using everyday terminology to describe them (Olivier de Sardan 1992). The degree of strangeness or familiarity of the object of analysis is in the eye of the beholder. "Shamanism," like many other phenomena conventionally labeled "exotic" (Mason 1996b), is as strange and exotic as we choose to make it.

Problematizing the attempt to define "shamanism" raises the question of comparison itself: if the fixity of both A and B is called into question, how can the operation of comparing A with B be carried out at all? In the light of the discussions in the previous chapters, it will come as no surprise that the question hinges on the issue of the plurality of possible relevant contexts. In the course of the present chapter, the bizarre, the unfamiliar, and the irreducibly different will be shown to be as much a part of European practices and conceptions as they are of the Amerindian worldviews and their implications.

Shamans and shamanism have played an increasingly important part in a number of works of European cultural history from the last few years. Duerr's *Dreamtime* ([1978] 1985) frequently draws on reports of Asian and American shamans to illuminate the practices attributed to the European witches. Klaniczay (1984) has drawn attention to shamanistic elements in Central European witchcraft,[1] and similar shamanistic features have been found in some cases of seventeenth-century witch trials in Finland (Heikkinen and Kervinen 1990, 329). One of the most striking claims made by some of these historians is that the analogies between the magical practices of the cultures traditionally studied by anthropologists and those of European witchcraft are not purely formal. For instance, in a study of anatomical dissection, sacrifice, and capital punishment, Lazzerini stressed that the links between these three phenomena are not simply based on analogy: "They are derived from folklore and have spread in such a capillary way that *there can be no doubt about their reality*" (1994, 226, emphasis added). Bertolotti, in a discussion of the magical practices consisting in killing an animal, preserving its bones, and resurrecting it through the agency of a divinity, uses the instruments of philological criticism to support the claim that "this correspondence points to a *historical* connection between a specific popular belief that is incorporated into witchcraft in the Christian era and the hunting cultures that developed in the European region in the archaic era" ([1979] 1991, 49).

In his study of the ecstatic fertility battles of the Italian *benandanti* Ginzburg had already pointed out the links with shamanism ([1966] 1983, 28–32). In his more recent *Ecstasies* he argues that relations of analogy, isomorphism, or even identity link Eurasian shamans with the protagonists of the battles fought in ecstasy ([1989] 1990a, 170–73), and he enlarges the complex of related practices even further to include werewolves and European beliefs connected with the nocturnal goddess known under a variety of names, including Diana.[2]

One must surely welcome these historians' receptiveness to anthropology. In particular, it is worth stressing that, unlike many of their colleagues, they are not unaware of *recent* developments in anthropology, such as the influence of the so-called linguistic turn. In what follows, their references to shamans and shamanism will be reconsidered in the light of other theoretical developments in anthropology and in light of a case study of shamanism—Michel Perrin's study of Guajiro shamanism (1992)—in which these considerations bearing on the definition of shamanism come to the fore.

BETWEEN THE EXOTIC AND THE FAMILIAR

Perhaps starting with Lévi-Strauss's demolition of the construct "totemism" (1962), attacks have been launched by various scholars on the possibility of studying topics such as "kinship" (Needham 1971), "marriage" (Rivière 1971), "myth" (Vernant 1980; Detienne 1981; Magaña and Mason 1986) as isolated fields of study at all. Each of these clusters of phenomena drawn from different domains seemed to tell us more about the workings of the anthropological imagination than about some purported ethnographic "reality."

The question therefore naturally arises, To what extent are we justified in talking about something called "shamanism"? Very simply, the existing ethnographical literature can produce an exception to any universal definition of it. There may be certain elements in these constructs that can be found with striking regularity all over the world. Thus, Needham analyzes a synthetic product—the particular case of European and non-European representations of the witch—as a set of variable combinations of what can be discriminated as primary factors of experience. He finds that opposition, inversion, darkness, color, animals, flight, and nocturnal lights are variously and sporadically combined into the synthetic image of the witch in a wide spectrum of cultures (1978, 41). Nevertheless, it is the sporadic nature of the distribution of these elements that makes definition impossible.

In a similar vein, Michel Perrin lists a few of the many definitions of *shamanism* that have been produced by anthropologists and then points out that in their attempt to embrace both the intellectual system and the social function, these definitions combine the vaguest terms drawn from psychology—*trance, ecstasy, extraordinary psychic state*—and the science of religions—*charisma, prophet, mystic*—with arbitrary elements drawn from specific societies (1992, 103–4).

This blurring of the edges of "shamanism" is in line with Wittgenstein's injunctions to talk about "family resemblances" if we cannot arrive at a crystalline purity of definition. For Ginzburg, Wittgenstein's notion of "family resemblances" seemed to offer a way of dealing with striking parallels in the myths and rites of Siberian shamans to two components of the European witches' sabbath that could not be accounted for by the strictly historical study of the late medieval origins of the stereotype elements: their ability to transform themselves into animals and their ability to fly to their nocturnal meetings.[3] These long-distance resemblances, which were so striking and so hard to prove in a way that would convince fellow historians,[4] could be seen as "distant relatives" of the compromise cultural formation found in Europe.

Ginzburg also isolates a different ensemble of elements—the tale of Cinderella, the myth of a missing bone, and the ritual of divination based on the scapular bone of sacrificed animals (scapulimancy)—to draw far-reaching conclusions. In contrasting the presence of these elements in a geographical area stretching from the British Isles or even the Bering Strait to Asia or even China with their almost total absence from continental Africa, Ginzburg suggests that this pattern of distribution is correlated with the dominance of possession and the absence of shamanistic phenomena in continental Africa, concluding that "behind this sharp contrast we perceive a presumably very ancient cultural differentiation" ([1989] 1990a, 249). However, as Perrin remarks, the dichotomy between shamanism and possession once advanced by Luc de Heusch is the result of a dogmatic structuralism; the specific characteristics of shamanism are by no means so clear-cut (1992, 104 n. 1).[5] Thus, although Ginzburg uses the Wittgensteinian notion to compare "distant relatives" in time and space in terms of a central concept[6]—shamanism—it is important to realize that the very concept itself is no more than a loose, poorly defined, and indefinable cluster of elements.

This uncertainty about what we are to understand by the construct "shamanism" applies equally to the term itself. Since the work of Marc Bloch, historians of Europe have been familiar with the debate whether *feudalism* can be extended beyond the confines of Europe to, say, Japan. *Shamanism* is an equally awkward term, requiring us to follow Wittgenstein's injunction that "we must plow through the whole of language" (1993, 131). The anthropologist Joanna Overing, for example, states: "I did not understand Piaroa statements about the world as they did until I changed the labels through which I was looking at their statements, i.e. when I dropped 'magic,' 'religion' and 'shamanism' to look instead at 'ontology,' 'cosmology,' 'epistemology' and 'power'" (1987, 85). As Overing points out elsewhere, this changing of labels has both emotional and intellectual consequences. Thus the use of *wizard* and *god* instead of *shaman, culture hero,* or *demiurge* has an "uplifting" effect (Overing 1985, 249). This effect should be seen as an attempt to counteract the effects of the process of labeling with terms like *kinship-based, shaman, taboo,* and so on, which tend to denigrate the other to a lesser status. The tension between these two approaches, reflected in the choice between an "uplifting" and a "scientific" terminology, can be seen in Michel Leiris's various attempts to present the results of his experiences during Marcel Griaule's famous mission from Dakar to Djibouti in 1932. On the one hand, he sees possession and magic as microsociological phenomena related to manipulation; on the other hand, the dimension of the sacred to which they provide access opens the way to the experience of the transcendental Other, which is resistant to analysis (Reichler 1989, 90–95).

That anthropologists do not share the same basic representations as do those whom they are describing can lead to an exoticizing of the other culture and the reinforcement of existing stereotypes of unfamiliarity (Olivier de Sardan 1992, 20).[7] Probably one of the areas in which this process is most apparent is that of magic and religion—the domain of "shamanism" itself—where the very choice of terms used to translate magical and religious terms reflects a greater or lesser degree of exoticizing of the other. Michel Perrin makes this difficulty explicit when he states that Guajiro shamans become *pülasü* when they officiate. How is one to translate this word? In listing a series of qualifications that might approach it in certain contexts—"prohibited, taboo, dangerous, occult, disturbed, strange, etc."—he notes that none of these terms is adequate to render what is a single word in Guajiro. *Sacred* is not satisfactory either, in view of its connotations of stasis, human control, and so on. Finally, *supernatural* can hardly be applied in a society in which the categories "nature" and "natural" are thought of in terms of the category "supernatural" (Perrin 1992, 100 n. 1). Perrin even goes so far as to coin a neologism, *chamanerie,* to translate native expressions referring to the function of the shaman and to his or her altered state. This term makes it possible to avoid some of the connotations of the term *shamanism* as it is used by anthropologists and enables the author to stress some of the paradoxical relations between illness and what he calls *chamanerie* (109 n. 1).

As is evident from Perrin's remarks, there can be no "proper" or "adequate" translation of these Guajiro terms. Indeed, there is much to be said for the view that "radical translation [is] a 'red herring,' a false problem that if taken too seriously impedes investigations into the diversity of systems of thought and knowledge" (Overing 1987, 78).[8] In coining new terms, these anthropologists are not aiming at a "better" translation, at a "more perfect" fit. Instead, these neologisms impart a particular emphasis that the worn-out coinage of standard terminology can no longer convey. As Wittgenstein noted, "An entire mythology is stored within our language" (1993, 133).

In trying to familiarize practices that are apparently strange, however, Wittgenstein assumes a fundamental agreement between cultures regarding their knowledge of nature: "The nonsense here is that Frazer represents these people as if they had a completely false (even insane) idea of the course of nature, whereas they only possess a peculiar interpretation of the phenomena. That is, if they were to write it down, their knowledge of nature would not differ *fundamentally* from ours. Only their *magic* is different" (Wittgenstein 1993, 141). But the thesis that European and, say, Amerindian views of the world share certain basic propositions is untenable. A worldview like that of the Wayana of Surinam, in which men are represented as the children of their wives (their father is the Moon) and kinship has more to do with gardens and food than with anything else (Magaña 1992, 107–8) is surely beyond our grasp. Such a case serves as a reminder of the ultimate incommensurability of cultures, the impossibility of comparing worldviews based upon totally different premises. But the impossible can have its uses too. The advantage to be gained from such an enterprise has been aptly described by Needham: "Well, a real and even charitable view of the course of anthropological theory over the past century and more is that it has traced a sequence of failures, and that our advantage consists in being in a position to recognize these more readily as such" (1985, 41). In other words, following the principle of "pessimism of the intellect, optimism of the will," it might still be useful to engage in attempts at cultural comparison even if we know beforehand that the lesson to be learned is that such a comparison is impossible. The (ultimately futile) attempt at description of systems that are to a greater or lesser degree incommensurable with our own is required to demonstrate that very incommensurability. Paradoxically, it is the very thwarting of the desire to capture the otherness of the other that gives us glimpse of that very other, what Jacques Derrida refers to as "the experience of the other as the invention of the impossible" (1987, 27).

BETWEEN AMERINDIA AND EUROPE

The dialogue between history and anthropology in which we are engaged is a dialogue between two partners in conversation who share the same preconceptions. History and anthropology, after all, are both members of the family of Western human sciences. Anthropology is by no means the voice of the other. At best, then, such a dialogue is an exchange between the self talking about self and the self talking about its production of the other.

In introducing his work on the Guajiro, Michel Perrin is aware that he is translating another culture into terms that will be familiar to a European readership: "[The ethnologist] must carefully translate what has been entrusted to him, and then say in our languages what he thinks the others are thinking. As a kind of intermediary, he bears witness to the richness of a different culture by rendering it accessible to our understanding. That implies respect for complexity, paying attention to others, and modesty. When he writes, he should incessantly imagine that these 'others' he is talking about will read it one day, and that he will not find this embarrassing" (1992, 10–11). The familiarity for European readers is enhanced by the fact that almost every chapter begins with a citation from a well-known, mainstream European writer: Freud, Durkheim, Valéry, Lévy-Bruhl, Bastide, Molière, Aron, Bourdieu, Barthes, Mauss, Lacan, Breton, Lévi-Strauss . . .

On the other hand, the bulk of each chapter consists of material from the Guajiro themselves, including extensive citations from myths. Moreover, the arrangement of the material, Perrin claims, conforms to Guajiro practice: "Shamanism, dreams and sickness are the main themes of this book. Starting with dreams, it reveals the background against which shamanic activities take place. At the same time *it follows the Indian logic* according to which, in order to avoid misfortune or to combat it, one appeals to dreams before calling the shaman, this veritable 'dream practitioner'" (9, emphasis added). On the one hand, then, we have the European frame of reference, provided by European literary and academic authorities.[9] On the other hand, we have the words and (reported) actions of the Guajiro, presented in accordance with the Guajiro worldview. The mediating figure between them is the author-ethnologist himself, explicitly present in the ethnography through the narration of personal anecdotes and experiences.

The flow of the text—from France to Amerindia and then back to France—follows the pattern inaugurated by a figure whom Lévi-Strauss (1982) has claimed as one of the founding fathers of French anthropology: Jean de Léry, the sixteenth-century Huguenot whose account of his voyage to Brazil and his stay there, first published in 1578 (Léry 1990), has been called "the ethnologist's breviary" (Lévi-Strauss 1955, 89). As Michel de Certeau has stressed in a seminal article on Léry (1975, 215–48), the structure of Léry's text mirrors his own voyage. Starting from the familiar, it moves towards unfamiliar ground, accommodating strange practices and terms, before returning to the point of origin. In its power both to retain the past and to expand it, writing demonstrates its ability to encapsulate orality, and this is as true of Perrin's text as it is of Léry's.

The same directional flow—from Europe to America and back again—is also evident in many of the works of Lévi-Strauss (Mason 1986, 46). For instance, the reflections on psychoanalysis in *La potière jalouse* (Lévi-Strauss 1985) take Freud as their starting point, proceed to an analysis of the concepts of anality and orality at work in *la pensée sauvage* of Amerindia, and then return to apply these insights to the original premises. Michel Perrin follows the same trajectory with regard to psychoanalysis: after setting up a distinction between the field usually reserved for psychology and psychoanalysis and the terrain covered by his account of dreams and shamanism among the Guajiro, he expresses the hope that the analysis of what eludes those disciplines may help them to strengthen their interpretations (1992, 10).

However, the reader can also find the reverse flow in the Lévi-Straussian corpus. Starting with his analysis of the Oedipus myth "American-style" (1958, 227–57), Lévi-Strauss has also tried repeatedly to show how a starting point in Amerindia can be used to gain insights into historical European material before the argument resumes its course back to Amerindia again. Thus when he returns to the myth of Oedipus in a later publication Lévi-Strauss proceeds from Amerindian myths to the myths of Perceval and the Holy Grail (1973, 31–35).

The latter strategy, starting from *la logique indienne* and then applying the insights gained to historical European material, is rooted in alterity. Beginning with the voice of the other, it sets up a dialogue between different sets of others—those remote from us in terms of space, those remote from us in terms of time—whose aim is to expose the familiar to the impact of the other. At this stage, instead of going into the potential and limitations of such a strategy in detail, it may be more illuminating to present an example from which they emerge by themselves.

Our starting point, then, is the Guajiro worldview as elucidated in Michel Perrin's monograph on the "dream practitioners." Every being in the everyday world has a counterpart in the otherworld *(le monde-autre)*. To dream is to come into contact with a double from this otherworld, which is inhabited by deities, ancestors, specters, spirits, and fantastic creatures. Though it is associated with death, this otherworld is not an afterworld, for one can gain access to it in this life by means of dreams. At the same time, this means of access to the otherworld is a guarantee of the distance separating it from this world: a failure to dream implies approaching death, that is, the end of that separation.

Besides the otherworld, there is a third world, the world beyond the world of the dead. As the Guajiro themselves put it, "we die twice, and we bury our dead twice." Immediately after death the human soul passes into one of the imprecise, invertebrate spectral forms *(yoluha)* that live on a peninsula to the northwest of Guajiro territory, where they enjoy unlimited food and sex. At the end of the period between the first and the second burial these specters lapse into anonymity and become ready to dissolve in the world beyond the world of the dead, where they are assimilated to one of the two opposite and complementary figures by which that world is dominated, Pulowi and Huya (Rain). As emissaries of these two powers, they can return to the earth as rain or as deadly spirits called *wanülüü*, which appear in a variety of guises: as seductive women, giant snakes, white deer, and others. These various emissaries guarantee the persistence of the cycle: rain preserves the life on earth, which is itself a tributary of the dead; the deadly emissaries ensure that the living die and thus that the cycle is perpetuated (Perrin 1992, 31–39).

Guajiro dream interpretation is based on the correspondence between events in dreams, that is, in the otherworld, and events in this world. The existence of a temporal disparity between the two orders enables dreams to have a predictive force (66). Despite the existence of this temporal disparity, however, the otherworld is structured as this world is structured: the rich in this world are the rich in the otherworld, and the poor in this world are the poor in the otherworld. It is this homology between the two worlds that makes a two-way communication between them possible (102). A Guajiro shaman is designated by the otherworld and can be said to belong to it. Dreams emanate from the otherworld. Since illness involves falling into the grip of the otherworld, it is the shaman who can bring about a cure by restoring the general cycle of exchange between the two worlds (173).

To turn to historical material from Europe, medieval Latin literature contains many stories of visions and wanderings in the otherworld. There are tales of people who found themselves in another world in sleep or after death and then returned to life to tell what they had seen and experienced. These tales betray such a thematic monotony and traditionalism that the historian of medieval popular culture Aron Gurevich claims, "All in all, in spite of some development of the genre, the stories from the sixth to the thirteenth centuries are essentially products of one and the same mode of thought" (1988, 20).[10] If we examine Gurevich's analysis of these popular notions of the European otherworld before Dante (104–52),[11] many features can be seen to resemble the characteristics of the Guajiro otherworld. To start with, in medieval European beliefs too the homology between the two worlds facilitates communication between them. Paradise as a hierarchical realm of order displays the same social structure as the medieval world itself. Visions of the Virgin or of the archangel Michael are verified because of the correspondence of the figures seen in the visions to images seen in churches and cathedrals (126). In some cases, it was believed that those who died wandered around in the bodily appearances of "doubles" in deserted places near the village. Only with time, after expiatory sojourns around the village of the living, do the settlers of the village—like the Guajiro *yoluha*—die for good.

The medieval otherworld was not exclusively a hereafter, for it was widely believed that the earthly world and the otherworld were in direct communication. In fact, at least up to the fourteenth century the dead continued to lead an existence and were engaged in mutual relations with the living (Geary 1994). Thus, the dead could figure in lawsuits and run up debts. Despite attempts to ban them by the Christian authorities, meals for the dead, in which the nourishment of the dead occupied a central place, were held throughout the Middle Ages. The centrality of the nourishment of the dead likewise implies acceptance of the dead among the living, a continuity that was not dissolved until hygienic measures were taken to counter the Black Death in the fourteenth century (Oexle 1983).

There was also speculation about the whereabouts of the otherworld. Volcanoes figured prominently as entrances to it in southern European traditions, whereas some of the northern European traditions located it in Ireland. Moreover, unlike Dante's polar dichotomy between paradise and hell, the medieval visions of the otherworld before Dante are much vaguer and include a varying number of different places, often assembled in an irrational topography (Gurevich 1988, 130–35). Time in the otherworld elapses differently from time in the earthly world. One day in the earthly paradise is equivalent to a year in this world. All the same, time is marked in the same way in both worlds. Thus, in the otherworld too the canonical hours are marked (by birdsong), candles light themselves with the onset of the time for liturgy, and church holidays, including Sunday, are observed (134). As in the Guajiro case, there may be a temporal disparity between the two worlds since the otherworld is the future, though it is at hand in the present through visions. Communication between this world and the otherworld could be effected in visions, which were most commonly experienced by monks in the early Middle Ages. However, a special class of individuals had privileged access to both worlds: the saints as miracle-workers and healers, the "very special dead," as they have been called. Thus saints who needed to prove the legality of their rights could produce witnesses from the otherworld if necessary (49). Like the Guajiro shamans, the medieval European saints were bound up in a generalized cycle of exchange that began with the gifts they received during their lifetime. The principle that a gift demands a gift in return ensured that the saints would continue to provide their services after their death as well. If they failed to do so, their relics could be subjected to humiliation in order to rouse them to action; in such popular practices the peasants beat the saints as they would beat a disobedient beast of burden to rouse it and force it to perform its work (Geary 1994, 95–124). Saints, in turn, could be vindictive if they were neglected; go so far as to break the limbs of those who were lax in observing the liturgy (Gurevich 1988, 47).

To pass from these formal similarities between the Guajiro worldview and that of the European Middle Ages to a more structural level, we can note the tension between dual and tripartite systems in the medieval European worldview. According to Gurevich, "In contrast to Dante's strict tripartite division, the visions of the preceding period resemble church art, insofar as they display a dichotomous structure." The symbolic topography of the visions is divided dichotomously into right and left, east and west (132). The introduction of purgatory turned the dual system into a tripartite, though it is a matter of scholarly debate exactly when this introduction is to be dated.[12]

Perrin refers to the presence of a dual principle governing Guajiro thought connected with the two mythical beings Pulowi and Huya, the masculine symbol of life-giving rain and the female symbol of deadly drought, respectively (1992, 35–36). Yet this dual organization of the Guajiro otherworld is articulated with tripartite structures: the triad of body, soul, and bones and the existence of three worlds, this world, the otherworld, and the world beyond death.[13]

Perrin mentions two special cases in which the otherworld is bypassed. First, shamans who carry out rites to invoke rain during their lifetime do not pass through the stage of the otherworld of the specters but are immediately transformed into rains *(juya)*, which are associated with the third world, the world beyond death. Second, warriors who meet a violent death are transformed directly into *wanülüü*, the deadly spirits. The native logic is the same as in the case of the shamans: those who act as hunters of men during their lifetime continue to perform the same function as *"wanülüü* archers," who kill and thereby perpetuate the cycle of life and death (8–39).

Although these cases are exceptional in that they bypass a sojourn in the otherworld, they still adhere to the native Guajiro logic. Whether mediated by the otherworld or not, it is still a three-tier system that is operative. However, if we can call this system a vertical one, uniting this world to the otherworld, on which it depends, there is also a horizontal system that does not share the bipartite conception according to which a serious misfortune stems from the otherworld. This horizontal system is sorcery (101). In sorcery the relation between the source of affliction and the victim or healer is a horizontal one in that they are both situated within this world and do not depend, or depend only indirectly, on the otherworld.

Perrin's theses on sorcery are especially interesting in that he associates the rise of sorcery with the internal evolution of Guajiro society. From the beginning of the present century, there has been an increasing tendency in Guajiro society to accumulate goods. In the sixteenth century, it should be noted, the Guajiro were unusual among the lowland Indians of South America in that they kept livestock instead of hunting and gathering or raising crops.[14] The more pronounced hierarchical nature of Guajiro society, based on associations of large and powerful lineages at the expense of the smaller ones, has led to a decline in the status and power of the shaman.[15] At the same time, however, this increased inequality has led to more allegations of sorcery. Jealous rivals are now thought to be behind changes in the shifting power constellations. The source of a misfortune can now be accounted for if the healer manages to find a packet of charms or can show that someone has cast the evil eye (242). The otherworld, by contrast, is assumed to be impartial to such social tensions.

If the parallel between the Guajiro otherworld and shamanism, on the one hand, and medieval European conceptions of the otherworld and the role of saints, on the other, is sustainable, can we detect a European parallel in which the decline of the European "shamans" is connected with the rise of European "sorcerers"? In the European Middle Ages, as we have seen, contact with the otherworld could take place through visions and also through the mediation of a saint. Moreover, the dues and obligations of the saints helped to maintain a generalized circuit of exchange. The cult of the saints had much in common with paganism, and the use of holy relics sometimes recalled the use of pagan talismans (Flint 1991, 240–53; Gurevich 1988, 44–45). The rise of accusations of witchcraft and of the European witch hunt, however, belongs to a later period. It has been shown to coincide with the early modern period, first emerging in Renaissance Italy. Moreover, if one were to follow the functional interpretation advanced by Keith Thomas (1971), belief in witches can be seen to have helped to uphold the traditional obligations of charity and neighborliness at a time when other social and economic forces were conspiring to weaken them. In other words, the rise of witchcraft accusations both among the modern Guajiro and in Renaissance Europe appears to have been connected with an increase in individual possessions and a growing tendency towards hierarchization.

The period in which witchcraft accusations were on the increase also appears to have witnessed a change in the notion of dreaming, marked in French by the transition from the word *songer* to the modern *rêver*. Documentation spanning at least twelve centuries indicates the existence of a widespread European belief that dreaming involved the departure of some element (often represented in the form of a small creature like a fly or a lizard) from the body of the dreamer. At some point in the seventeenth century, this notion of dreaming as a literal *transport* outside the body, opening up the possibility of encounters with other beings from other worlds, was replaced by the notion of dreaming as a physiological activity situated within the body. It may have been under the impact of witchcraft accusations that nocturnal wanderings became internalized in this way: from now on, the bridge that shamanism had effected between this world and other worlds was closed, the sabbath was only a dream . . . (see Fabre 1996).

From the above discussion it emerges that Guajiro shamanism—"an example of shamanism"—is conditioned in two respects. First, it is an integral part of a cosmovision in which this world is dependent on an otherworld. It therefore cannot be studied in isolation from the investigation of the worldview of the Guajiro and the premises on which that worldview is based. Second, shamanism among the Guajiro entails specific social and economic relations, such as the absence of large-scale accumulation. It is therefore historically circumscribed by changes in these relations over time.

BETWEEN TRANSLATION AND COMPARISON

We have compared the Guajiro and medieval European worldviews in terms of formal similarities (morphological comparison), structural (bi- or tripartite) homologies, and genetic historical processes. It should be stressed that these comparisons have no explanatory value. It is therefore impossible on the basis of particular points held in common to fill in other gaps in our knowledge by a process of analogy, for there are no a priori grounds for supposing that any analogies beyond the data analyzed here exist. Indeed, it is even questionable whether these comparisons have any value at all. After all, how can we be sure that the objects of comparison *are* comparable? To what extent are these comparisons forced, that is, to what extent have some awkward factors been left out in order to make the argument more compelling?

At this point the question of the "proper" comparison comes to resemble that of the "proper" translation with which we began. Every comparison is forced to some degree or other; if there were not *some* difference between the objects of comparison, there could be no comparison at all. To seek for exact comparison is thus wrongheaded. To paraphrase Overing's comments on translation, the problem of comparison is not a problem of comparison as such but one of relevant emphasis and, more importantly, of knowledge, experience, and creativity (Overing 1987, 76). Within a certain context the relevant emphasis might lead one to view the shaman as a wizard; within a different context it might be tempting to see the shaman as a saint; and in yet other contexts it might even be most relevant to consider the shaman as a shaman.

The question of "improper" comparisons is relevant not only to the comparisons anthropologists and historians make between different fields of study but also to the metaphors they use to describe them. Many anthropologists have had recourse to the metaphor of the anthropologist as translator. Ginzburg (1990b, 156–64)[16] and Rosaldo (1986) opted for the darker metaphor of the anthropologist as inquisitor. After all, the way in which many anthropologists have attempted to fit other cultures into a familiar Western grid cannot help recalling the way in which the inquisitors tried to get their suspects to make confessions in line with learned stereotypes of the witches' sabbath (Ginzburg [1986] 1990b, 1–16). Indeed, in his analysis of the trial of a number of Jews on a charge of ritual murder in Trent in 1475, Hsia refers to "an ethnography of blood" (1992, 81ff.).[17]

Although Perrin still refers to the anthropologist as a translator, he does not consider this to be enough: "If the object of ethnology is to understand societies different from ours, the ethnologist must not only 'translate' them into our languages and discover the laws that govern them but also compare them with one another and with our society, find the right distance to appreciate the points in common and the divergences, and, finally, appreciate the alternatives for which they offer the model" (Perrin 1992, 184). On the one hand, one could attempt to *translate* a Native American culture into "our languages." But if native ontologies are to be taken seriously for what they are, it is hardly admissible to subject them to the intrinsic violence of the act of translation. On the other hand, one could *compare* different Native American cultures, in particular, their conceptions of the otherworld, as has been done, for instance, by Cipoletti (1983). But this would imply a privileged position for the agent performing the act of comparison, who chooses which cultures are to be compared with one another, the terms of comparison, and the fact that, comparable with one another, they differ from his or her own culture. The confrontation between the Guajiro worldview and that of medieval Europe is hardly an act of translation, for they are compared, not translated. At the same time, a comparison that starts from "the Indian logic" at least reverses the usual flow of cultural comparison.

Perrin's *Les praticiens du rêve* is not a simple reversal of Eurocentrism into Indiocentrism, for it contains the germs of a polycentrism. The author briefly considers the possibility of taking as one central point the displaced Guajiro living in Maracaibo, mixed up in a world of crime and violence. The disorder of their homes was a symbol of the breakdown of indigenous ways of thinking under pressure of acculturation. It is in this discrepancy between traditional and national culture that hybridity breeds. Seen from this angle, the attempt to reconstitute a native worldview seems more of an intellectual or aesthetic pastime than an attempt to grasp some kind of reality (Perrin 1992, 253–54).

This emphasis on hybridity has received particular attention in the work of James Clifford, who celebrates it in the impure, "inauthentic" productions of past and present tribal life. Yet it is this very empathy for the impure that is suspect. When Clifford states that "intervening in an interconnected world, one is always, to varying degrees, 'inauthentic': caught between cultures, implicated in others" (1988, 11), he is expressing an enthusiasm for those cultures that mirror the anthropologist's own hybridity.[18] In other words, the cultivation of the hybrid for its conformity to postmodern taste is a peculiarly rarefied form of Eurocentrism.[19] After the anthropologist as translator, as inquisitor, we have the anthropologist as hybrid—all metaphors that imply a degree of violence towards the other.

BETWEEN YOU AND ME

"To approach the other, when the other is so distant, one has to love that difference and admit that it will never be reducible" (Perrin 1992, 189). Perrin is referring here to how a Frenchman approached the culture of the Guajiro. One of the most endearing qualities of his work is precisely the love of difference that it reveals. He certainly encourages us to like the Guajiro. But there is nothing to stop one from reading the message in reverse: for a Guajiro to approach the other, it is necessary to embrace difference and to admit that the other will never be reducible. Another possible reading is: for one to approach *Les praticiens du rêve,* if the act of reading is not to be an act of violence, then we readers too must welcome that difference. And if we recall the passage in which Perrin envisages the possibility that his future readership will include the Guajiro themselves (10–11), the situation is conjured up in which Guajiro readers might approach the otherness of a book written about them as others. To untangle this skein of refractions would take the patience of a saint or the skill of a shaman.

4

POINTS OF IDENTITY:
SKETCHING A JEWISH PROFILE

IDENTIFICATION

ONE OF THE PROBLEMS RAISED IN CHAPTER 3 WAS THE PROBLEM OF definition: how can we be sure that the phenomena we are comparing are comparable at all? This question is all the more urgent when we are comparing phenomena taken from widely different cultural contexts and distinct historical periods. But do things get any easier if we confine our attention to a more historically circumscribed case? And what clues should we be searching for?

In a pamphlet printed in Amsterdam and dated 26 August 1773 the anonymous author relates the events accompanying a burglary committed only a few days earlier. Several men had broken into an inn and farmhouse in a village near Amsterdam. They had arrived by boat, entered the house, and threatened and trussed some of the inhabitants. The gang had had to leave, however, without taking anything because a woman had managed to escape and raise the alarm. Early the next morning all of the men had been arrested as they waited patiently in their boat for the city gates to open. In a postscript to the pamphlet the author lists some of the perpetrators:

Goesman Gossen, 42 years old
Jacob Gossen, 28 years old
Simon Gossen, 24 years old   Three brothers born in East-
    Friesland
Frans Scholts, quack, 42 years old, born in Scotland and said to be
    a city soldier
Bastian Welter, captain of this band, 40 years old, born in Germany
Elias Cohen, German Jew, 34 years old, born in Silesia
Barend Meyer, 33 years old, born in Westphalia

Jan Hendrik Nijhaus, 33 years old, born in Osnabrück
Levi Moses, alias Lypje Topje, 24 years old, born in Amsterdam.[1]

These brief personal descriptions raise a number of questions about the identification of individual Jews as members of a minority group in the Dutch Republic. Did Jews usually present themselves as Jews, or were they immediately recognized as such? Did they regard themselves as members of a separate group, an ethnic minority, to use a modern term? And if their Jewishness was important to them, in what did it consist and what was Jewish group identity about? It is striking, for instance, that the author of the pamphlet designates Elias Cohen as a "German Jew," whereas any such qualification is lacking in the cases of Levi Moses and the three Gossen brothers. It might be argued that there was no need to say that Moses was a Jew, but Gossen was not immediately recognizable as a Jewish name. Should we presume, then, that the author considered the link between Jewishness and crime of only marginal interest to his readers? Was he unconcerned with ethnic background, or did he just forget to mention it in a few cases? Each option sounds more unlikely than the preceding one, considering the prominent role of Ashkenazim in both urban and rural property crime at the time and the increasing concern of eighteenth-century established Dutch society about the large numbers of poor immigrant Jews from Poland, Germany, and other parts of eastern Europe.[2]

Poor Ashkenazim constituted the majority of Dutch Jewry. Most of them had settled in Amsterdam immediately after their arrival in the Netherlands. Quite a few, however, remained on the move, spending much of their time in cheap urban lodging houses and living for weeks on end in Amsterdam between trips to Germany and the northeastern Dutch provinces or tours in the Dutch countryside. Most of these men spent the winters in the big cities of Holland. Several of the unfortunate burglars described above belonged to this sector of Jewish society in the Netherlands. They did not belong to the established Jewish communities, they lacked money as well as professional training, and some had only recently arrived in the Netherlands.

Because of the sources available, and probably for reasons of respectability as well, historical research has concentrated largely on established Jews and Jewish communities and on issues such as internal politics, Jewish legal status, and emancipation. If the poorest sector of Dutch Jewry was discussed at all, it was usually in quantitative terms in the context of immigration, demography, housing, and so on. We know very little of their way of life, their beliefs, their customs, their relations with established and more well-to-do Jews, or their social contact with their Christian counterparts. And we know nothing about the extent to which they identified, if at all, with established Ashkenazic communities in the Netherlands.

These questions are all the more intriguing in that Dutch Jewry itself was strongly divided. During most of the seventeenth and eighteenth centuries Sephardic and Ashkenazic communities in Amsterdam existed separately. Especially from the 1670s onwards, when each community had its own synagogue, relations were marked by typical boundary conflicts about the right to slaughter ritually and sell kosher meat and about intermarriage—a Jew who married "a woman from another Jewish nation" lost full rights of membership in his own community (Kaplan 1989b, 43–44). The Spanish and Portuguese community of Amsterdam "had formed a stereotype of the *tudescos* and *polacos*. That image identified them with poverty and beggary, moral corruption and degradation, and even deviation from the ways of Judaism and the observance of the Torah. This negative image provided legitimation for the need seen by the leaders of the Portuguese community to set themselves apart from the Ashkenazi Jews and refrain from all intimate contact" (39).

Distinctions were made not only between Ashkenazim and Sephardim, however but within each community as well, in particular between the elite and established middle classes, on the one hand, and the lower classes, on the other. In 1660 newly arrived Polish and Lithuanian Jews, including several well-known scholars, established a separate community in Amsterdam. Such separatist tendencies among the eastern Europeans were encouraged by the Sephardic community (Kaplan 1989a, 38). Class antagonism went beyond group boundaries:

> The heads of the Talmud Torah community did not of course seek the removal of the entire community of "polacos" from Amsterdam. . . . The leaders of the Sephardic community sought the departure of the masses of poor Polish Jews, and they invested great efforts in sending these undesirable beggars beyond the borders of the Dutch Republic, apparently with some assistance from the heads of the local Polish community. Once again we see how the very same hand which offered protection to the Polish community as it gained a foothold in the city, was the one which repelled those Polish Jews

who, because of their social status or economic condition, threatened the tranquillity of the well established veteran Jewish population. (41)

Such class distinctions may have been even more important among Jews than among Christians. In Amsterdam, as in most smaller Dutch as well as German towns, the very existence of the established Jewish community depended on the capacity of its leaders to guarantee and enforce the good behavior of all of its members. Understandably, respectable Jews attempted to distance themselves as much as possible from "undesirable" elements even while they professed the unity of Jewry and diligently applied themselves to poor relief and other forms of assistance (Glanz 1968; Kaplan 1989a, 1989b). Considering these circumstances, the question whether poor, semi-itinerant, and generally despised German Jews nonetheless identified with established Jewry becomes even more interesting. On the face of it, as outcasts twice over they had excellent reasons not to want to be Jews at all.

CONTOURS OF JEWISH IDENTITY

The question whether these poor Ashkenazim were recognizable as Jews is immediately connected with the way they (re)presented themselves in different settings and to different groups, ranging from fellow Ashkenazim to non-Jewish associates or Christian members of the judiciary. It pertains directly to their self-image. Was Jewishness always an important aspect of their identity, or did they regard themselves first and foremost as members of the poor and semi-itinerant classes? And if it was important to them to be Jews (which is not self-evident, as we have just seen), how was their Jewishness constituted? In attempting to trace the outline of a Jewish identity in the case of poor Ashkenazim in the Netherlands in the seventeenth and eighteenth centuries we will skirt some of the more obvious aspects, such as learned traditions, religious beliefs, and the (supposed) strong adaptation of Dutch Jewry to the Dutch national character (Michman 1989). Nor will we discuss the theme of a shared history of persecution. Surprisingly, perhaps, this motif never figures in the statements of either the Jewish defendants on whose interrogations this chapter is largely based or their interrogators, the Dutch criminal courts. Topics that do present themselves are religious observances, clothes, language, names (including both personal and group denominations), residence, (inter)marriage, and professional forms of cooperation. The focus is therefore on external appearances; we approach the issue of Jewish identity from the outside.

This circuitous strategy is dictated partly by the sources that can tell us most about this sector of Jewish society: the records of Dutch criminal cases against Ashkenazim who were tried for property crimes ranging from buying and selling stolen goods to theft, picking pockets, burglary, and armed robbery. None of the defendants was ever asked to state his views on Jewish identity or religion or to recount his religious convictions or (lack of) affinity with Dutch society in general. Any information pertaining to Jewishness has thus to be gathered from descriptions of criminal activities, journeys to and from houses that were broken into, depositions of witness-accomplices, and casual remarks by the defendants themselves.

All the same, we have adopted this roundabout approach as much by choice as by necessity. Even if eighteenth-century Jewish defendants had been asked to define and describe their Jewishness, we could not take their statements at face value, let alone completely rely on them without checking them against actions and indirect references. Moreover, it would be extremely naive to assume that learned traditions, religious beliefs, or any other element regarded as essential to Jewish elite culture should also be a fundamental component of Jewish identity among lower-class Jews, who were despised not only by the Christian Dutch population but also by the established Jewish communities. After all, no one would try to define the Christianity of the lower classes in western Europe by the standard of biblical scholarship.

Besides, an oblique approach that touches upon the outline of a Jewish identity—upon a Jewish profile that may, after all, turn out to be nothing but a presupposition—allows us to set aside, at least temporarily, the modern notion of identity as an internal phenomenon, as something that can be approached only by uncovering inner convictions and invading the innermost ranges of personality and mind. In this endeavor we have to contend with language itself, which reflects as much as it enforces this implicit link between core, truth, importance, and profundity, on the one hand, and surface, deception, triviality, and shallowness, on the other. Metaphors such as "focus," "crucial," "pivotal," "central," and "superficial" are almost impossible to avoid when describing the search for identity that proceeds from margin to core, a search that involves the removal of (by implication less true, deceptive, and irrelevant) masks, shells, or layers in order to arrive at a true core.[3]

The philosophical critique of this metaphysical notion of identity was conducted by Nietzsche, but in the eighteenth century too—or in the sixteenth or the seventeenth, for that matter (see Greenblatt 1980 and Biagioli 1993)—there was a profound awareness of how identity is *constructed*. Perhaps this is best exemplified in the long letter in Laclos's *Les liaisons dangereuses* in which the marquise de Merteuil describes the process of self-fashioning, which extended from manners to physiognomy: "I might say that I have created myself. . . . Once sure of my demeanor I attended to my speech. I regulated both according to circumstances or simply as the whim took me. . . . This experiment in self-mastery led me to make a study of facial expression and of character as it is displayed in physical features" (Laclos [1782] 1972, letter 81, 223).

Shifting the course of inquiry from the inner to the outer, to the seemingly superficial, to outward appearances and external boundaries, to morphological points of resemblance and difference, blends two approaches that address the problem of identity from rather different perspectives. Focusing on rituals and symbolic boundary markers, anthropological studies of local communities of the type outlined by Cohen (1985) increasingly pay attention to the ways communities define who belongs and who does not.[4] Here the boundaries between self and others, the ways in which distinctions are made between us and them, the gradations of alterity, and what alterity tells us about identity constitute a principal theme (Mason 1987, 1990a, 1990b, 1993, 1995; Stallybrass and White 1986). Identity can only be conceived in contrast to alterity: if no differences are perceived between us and them, it cannot be easy to put a finger on what *we* have in common either. It seems appropriate, then, to look for important aspects of group identity in a group's contacts with those perceived as others. (This approach is elaborated in terms of iconographical markers of self and other in chapter 7.)

In "Clues: Roots of an Evidential Paradigm" Ginzburg advocates a method of reasoning from apparently irrelevant external details to the main points of a criminal problem, the singularities of a specific illness, or the identity of a painter as epitomized in his style ([1986] 1990b, 96–125). If an artist's identity or individual style can be expressed most clearly in such apparently unimportant details, there seems no reason not to try and trace a group's identity from the routine aspects of its everyday existence and its contacts with members of different cultures.[5] Not only the concept of what we are looking for but also the method of looking for it has to be revised.

TELL-TALE TERMS

Returning to the robbers whose personal descriptions gave rise to these reflections, we may compare the pamphlet's descriptions with those found in the records of the Amsterdam city court, which prosecuted and sentenced these band members, who had committed several more burglaries and armed robberies in the province of Holland. The Amsterdam proceedings are fairly typical of the proceedings in Dutch criminal cases against Jewish and other defendants suspected of property crimes or a combination of violence and property crimes. Since identification of the suspect was (and still is) of primary importance to a criminal court, interrogation invariably started with questions of personal identity: name, sex, age, place of birth. Questions pertaining to address, profession, relatives, and so on, followed later, if at all. The Amsterdam court describes the above-mentioned suspects as follows:

> Cosman Gossels, German Jew from Oostfriesland, 42 years old.
> Simon Gossels, German Jew from Oostfriesland, 25 years old.
> Jacob Gossels, German Jew from Oostfriesland, 28 years old.
> Berent Meijer, German Jew, 33 years old.
> Elias Cohen, German Jew from Silesia, 34 years old.
> Sebastiaan Welter from Alarock in the county of Berg, 40 years old.
> Francis Schols from Herzfeld, 34 years old.
> Jan Hendrik Nijhuijs from the Osnabrück area, 33 years old.[6]

Characteristically, the designation *German Jew* preceded the description of any other personal characteristics. The Dutch judicial authorities clearly regarded ethnic identity as one of the most relevant aspects in the identification of a suspect, to be mentioned directly after his name.[7] This does not reflect a special type of criminal procedure in the case of Jews, as Jews were not subject to special criminal legislation in the Netherlands; nor were they treated differently from other suspects by the criminal courts (Egmond 1993b, 106–26), though civil law was another matter. The main reason for this special interest, then, must have been the considerable influx of poor Ashkenazim from the late seventeenth century onwards, an interest that probably intensified around the mid-eighteenth century, when the courts began to get a clearer picture of the prominent role of itinerant Ashkenazim in certain types of organized property crime. Some of the courts not only used the formal designation *Hoogduitse* (High German) or *Duitse Jood* (German Jew) but also resorted to the colloquial and pejorative term *smous* (sheeny), with its connotations of thief and vagrant.[8]

Even more important from our perspective is the way Jewish defendants referred to themselves and to their Jewish and non-Jewish associates. Understandably, they never used the term *smous,* but they referred to both themselves and their colleagues as *Joden* (Jews) or, more particularly, as *Hoogduitse Joden* (German Jews). The term *Ashkenazim* was never used by either Dutch courts or Jewish defendants. Since Portuguese Jews were nearly completely absent from the criminal circuit in the Netherlands, we do not know how they would have been designated. In any case, there was no need for Ashkenazic suspects to distinguish themselves from their fellow Jews. Both Dutch court members and Jewish suspects employed the terms *natie* (nation) and *Joodse natie* (Jewish nation) in order to distinguish Jews as a group from Dutch society in general. Without further evidence this cannot, however, be taken as a sign that poor German Jews felt they actually belonged to this nation, let alone that they considered themselves respected members of it.

That Jews did indeed call themselves Jews may seem self-evident. But is it a banal observation if we take into consideration both the general and the specific circumstances? After all, these men were suspected of involvement in serious property crime, and their statements were made during interrogation by the Dutch courts. Precisely because immigrant German Jews already had a bad reputation, they might have tried to deny any connection with their Jewish associates, as indeed they did, as well as with (German) Jewry in general, which they did not. Furthermore, their general position as itinerant and often extremely poor men on the fringe of established German Jewish society in the Netherlands offered few prospects. As indicated above, itinerant Ashkenazim were excluded twice over: by Dutch society and by the established urban communities of Ashkenazim. If they nonetheless and unreservedly held on to their Jewish identity, they must have done so either because they were so unmistakably Jewish that their identity as Jews could not be denied or because they did not wish to deny it, or both.

A clue might be found in the way they referred to their non-Jewish associates. Did they use a negative term, defining these people as non-Jews and thus revealing a positive self-image? Or did they employ more neutral, descriptive language? The criminal records do not mention any such negative terms with respect to either their Christian or their Gypsy colleagues, but this may only reflect the particular character of these sources; after all, could defendants really be expected to use pejorative terms for Christians during criminal interrogation by a Christian court? As we shall see, other indications of Jewish self-confidence and cultural predominance in their relations with Christian and Gypsy associates can indeed be found in the records.

Terminology thus provides some quite important clues to Jewish self-perceptions and the boundaries between "us" and "them." *We*, for these poor Jews, meant the nation of German Jews with whom they identified, although they remained on (or even outside) its fringes in terms of social interaction with the respected members of this nation. Explicitly regarding themselves as Jews, they defined the difference between themselves and others mainly in terms of the opposition between Christian and Jew. Terminology by itself thus indicates that we may indeed speak of a Jewish group identity, but we do not yet know whether the opposition between Jew and Christian points to a group identity based on religious denomination or more general cultural distinctions.

A JEWISH PROFILE

Again a circuitous approach, starting at the meeting point between a Jew and a Christian, seems appropriate. How would a Christian inhabitant of eighteenth-century Holland be able to recognize a poor German Jew when he saw one? Or to phrase the question differently, which signs of Jewish identity would a German Jew display?

Jews appear to have been easily recognizable. In the Dutch Republic they were not required to wear special marks or signs on their clothing (see Kisch 1979, 2:115–62). Nor were they distinguished by exotic dress, hair styles, or headgear. If Jews had indeed worn sidelocks or long black robes, we might expect to find these mentioned in the personal descriptions recorded by Dutch criminal courts for the purpose of tracing suspects, but in fact the only reference we have come across to Jews wearing conspicuous dark garments, black curls, and earrings stems from the eastern provinces and may refer to recent immigrants. With respect to external appearance, there is a clear contrast between different types of sources. Whereas eighteenth-century popular tales refer to the large noses, long beards, and awful smell of Jews,[9] all of these characteristics, with the possible exception of the noses, are generally absent both from contemporary personal descriptions recorded by the Dutch courts and from the far more extensive (and often published) German lists referring to exotic personal appearance.

A list of suspects drawn up in 1769 by the provincial court of Holland at
The Hague provides some good examples:

> *Nathan Focks,* alias Nathan Gannif, born in Amsterdam, 24 years
> old, rather tall and good-looking, light-skinned and round-
> faced, wears a black wig, uses coarse language, has a cut across
> the palm of his hand, speaks Dutch, and has been in prison in
> Amsterdam for the last five years.

> *Joseph Hamburger,* born in Hamburg, lives in Amsterdam, about 34
> years old, tall and slender, round-faced and white-skinned, black
> eyes, a thin line of black beard round the chin, wears a wig.

> *Nathan Beellte,* born in Amsterdam, 50 years old, tall and thin, dark-
> skinned and gaunt of face, wears a little black goatee, an old
> wig, and an old coat; his wife lives in Rotterdam; he lives in Am-
> sterdam; has been in detention in Rotterdam.[10]

A later German list includes the following:

> Gumpert Meyert, vulgo Isriil also called Tall Mosche; is 43 years
> old, has black hair, a clear brow, black eyebrows, brown eyes, or-
> dinary nose and mouth, rather long chin and face, pale. . . .

> Haium Koppel . . . is 20 to 22 years old, 5 feet tall, has black hair,
> black eyebrows, a round brow, black eyes, a rather snub nose, a
> narrow chin, relatively long face and healthy color. (Schwencken
> 1820, 123–24)[11]

Neither the Dutch archival records nor the published German lists mention
long black garb or sidelocks. In fact, references to the clothes worn by these
people point to similarities between the dress of Christian and Jewish poor
rather than to a distinctive Jewish costume. Dark eyes and dark hair or wigs
are frequently mentioned as typical characteristics. But in the Netherlands
recognition as a Jew—by non-Jews as well as by the German Jews themselves—seems to have depended more on the combination of such aspects
of outward appearance with the use of easily recognizable names and of the
"Jewish" language (the term *Yiddish* is never used in the records). Such
immediately visible and audible indications were usually corroborated by
information about occupational activities and, especially in Amsterdam, ad-
dresses.

Names in particular were typical (Beem 1969). Nathan, Hertog or Hertz, Salomon or Schlomme, Jacob, Meijer, Aaron, Juda, Levi, Abraham, Moses, David, and Isaac were among the most common first names. Ashkenazic Jews had no fixed surname: they used their father's name (Jacob Isaacs, Moyse Daniels, Isaac Samson, etc.), or added their place or region of birth (Polak, Hamburger, Bamberger, "from" Kinsbag, Elsasser) or their occupation (e.g., Hooijbinder, meaning "hay binder," or Visschoonmaker, "fish cleaner") to their first name. Some of these additions eventually became established family names. The same occasionally happened to the fixed nicknames and aliases characteristic of Jewish thieves. Often such nicknames referred to physical characteristics: Black Mortje Derbach, or Kromme (Crooked) Borach. Others mentioned professional specializations, and many referred to occupations and personal qualities at the same time. In a few cases we may still guess at double meanings and allusions. Ongeslepen Diamant (Rough Diamond), for instance, was the nickname of a very young thief. It may have referred to his (still) unpolished technique as well as to his exceptional, though (as yet) hidden, qualities. Since diamond cutting was a typically Jewish occupation, it may also have hinted at his own (or his father's) training and professional knowledge of jewelry.

If these poor German Jews had desired to deny, get rid of, or just hide their Jewish identity, the use of such names would have been unthinkable. Nor would they have continued to use the "Jewish" language when cooperating with non-Jewish colleagues during robberies. When questioned by the Amsterdam city court, a non-Jewish member of the Gossels band stated that he had not heard anything about the transport of the booty "since they spoke 'Jewish' with each other the whole time." Asked whether he more or or less understood "Jewish," he answered, "No, not at all." Another non-Jewish band member, Jan Hendrik Nijhuijs, confirmed that "while drinking several glasses of wine with them, he had not understood what the others said, since they did not speak High German or Low German, but 'Jewish,' which he did not understand."[12]

Occupations were just as telling. In the Dutch Republic, as in the neighboring countries, Jews were excluded from most branches of agriculture (by being barred from owning land) and from nearly all activities controlled by the guilds, which included artisanal occupations as well as some types of retail trade. Among the relatively small number of activities still open to them were cutting and polishing diamonds, drying and cutting tobacco, selling books, engraving (of seals, etc.), cattle dealing, moneylending, cleaning and selling fish, and many types of unskilled labor and retail trade. They sold in particular haberdashery, spectacles, textiles, jewelry, lottery tickets, fish, kosher meat, old clothes, scrap, and various other types of used materials. Some made a living as itinerant musicians (mostly as fiddlers); many were employed in a range of unskilled occupations (as barrow men or porters), and a few served as sailors with the East India Company or temporarily joined one of the European armies.[13]

A court case concerning Ysaak Moses and his son provides a good example not only of Jewish occupational activities in predominantly rural areas but also of the vulnerable position of Jews in terms of civil rights and of the bad reputation of itinerant German Jews. Ysaak Moses was born in Geldern (Germany). By 1743 he had been living and working as a butcher in Enkhuizen (North Holland) for a number of years. He was "six feet tall, fat and thickset, round of face, big eyes, . . . 43 or 44 years old; wears a brown coat and a wig when in Enkhuizen but has been seen in Amsterdam wearing the outfit of a gentleman."[14] Together with his nineteen-year-old son, Moses Ysaak, he frequently toured the countryside of North Holland and visited farmers to buy sheep. In 1743 Ysaak Moses and his family were ordered to leave Enkhuizen on account of their frequent contacts with poor and itinerant German Jews suspected of involvement in a gang of burglars. After moving to Amsterdam, the son tried to earn a living by selling goat's milk and poultry from door to door; he also worked on a fishing boat or at the fish market.

Members of the Gossels band were involved in typically Jewish occupations and lived or temporarily lodged in Amsterdam. Although the Jewish quarter of Amsterdam did not have a ghetto, street names in this area referred (and some still do today) to the numerous Jews who occupied the northeastern section of town.[15] The non-Jewish band members—and this was typical—lived in quite different parts of Amsterdam that also were known as poor working-class neighborhoods. Their occupations were different as well.

CUSTOMS

Identification of a Jew in the early modern Netherlands, whether by a Jew or by a non-Jew, depended primarily on a combination of names, language, external appearance, occupational activities, or address. But there were other, less immediately noticeable characteristics as well, such as particular forms of Jewish-Christian professional cooperation, the near absence of Jewish women from the public sphere, and the observance of specific religious customs.

Since occupational restrictions kept Jews from joining in most Dutch occupations, organized crime must have been one of the few professional activities in which Christians and Jews actually worked together doing the same jobs. The small Gossels band was typical in this respect. Contacts between Jews and Christians remained businesslike. When the men shared a few glasses of wine, it was during the planning of a theft, not during a leisurely chat in a tavern. As we have seen, the Jewish band members continued to speak Jewish during the robberies, thus excluding the Christians, who remained separated from their Jewish associates not only by language, names, and regional background but also by different types of family connection, religious orientation, and occupational history. In this respect, whether Jews or Christians constituted the majority did not matter. The much larger band of Captain Calotte, which operated during the 1760s in the southern province of Brabant, consisted predominantly of Christian men and women. On certain occasions they were joined by a contingent of about twelve German Jews. The Jews largely kept to themselves, joined as a group, and left again together after the robberies. They did not merge with the larger network. Professional cooperation between Jewish and Christian thieves never made the Jews change their way of life, and cooperation did not result in integration. Instead, in the rare cases of prolonged professional association of Jews and Christians, the Christians tended to adopt (some) Jewish customs (Egmond 1993b, 106–46).

One of these customs had to do with the position and role of women. Jewish women (and children up to the age of fifteen) hardly ever accompanied the men on legal or illegal business trips. Nor were they usually present when the men conducted their business in the public sphere. Most of them stayed at home with their children, and home tended to be one of the towns of Holland. Even if they did have jobs as cleaning women or landladies, the wives and daughters of these poor German Jews, like their counterparts in Germany (see Glanz 1968, 183–97), thus adhered to the traditionally Jewish division of male and female domains: public, outside, and itinerant for the men; private, within the family and household, and static for the women. Women's names, or rather the way in which Jewish men referred to them, reflect their subservient position in terms of contact with the outside world. These women were often designated by their first names alone , or they were defined in terms of their husbands and kinsmen, for example, Sara, wife of

Baruch Meijer, or Gaije, wife of Juda Marcus, or Rachel, widow of Hersch. In public matters they attained a definite identity only by reference to a male person.

In the Great Dutch Band of the 1790s, an international criminal network comprising 120 to 160 men, two-thirds of whom were German Jews, Jewish family connections constituted the infrastructure of the band. Nearly all of the band's Jewish and Christian captains were linked by ties of marriage or kinship with the family of Moyse Jacob, founder of the network, Jewish husband of a Christian wife and father of four daughters. Dinah Jacob and her three sisters spent much of their time at their mother's house in Brussels, waiting for their menfolk to return from business trips, or attending the "staff" meetings, which were held at home. The Jacob women were quite well informed about the men's activities, their plans, and the membership and organization of the band, but their place was primarily at home, and their principal role was to be supportive. In this band, however, it was not only the Jewish women who stayed away from the public domain. The Christian women—who usually played a more public (though by no means leading) role in Christian bands and quite often accompanied their men on journeys—followed the Jewish pattern, not perhaps to the extent of actually staying at home, but certainly by not joining the men during trips and by keeping themselves at some distance from the band's business.[16]

This pattern of Jewish cultural predominance is not only evident in the international criminal networks of the late eighteenth century. At the level of the individual it can also be observed in mixed marriages. First, it was not Jewish women who married Christians; Jewish men got involved with Christian and Gypsy women. And in these cases it was not the Jewish men who adapted to their wives' customs but vice versa. The case of the Gypsy woman Fisone is characteristic. Fisone was born about 1700. In the course of the 1720s and early 1730s she married (or lived with) several men of Gypsy or Christian background, bearing five or six children. From the mid-1730s onwards she lived with a Jew called Levi Abrahams or Lijp Diersum, who was at least fifteen years younger than her. Lijp and Fisone had indeed "made grave promises to each other." For most of her life Fisone earned a living by casual rural labor, selling medicines, telling fortunes, and going from one farm to another begging for food. During her involvement with Lijp she did not cease to do so, but "she had become a Jewess . . . and could not eat any meat [i.e., pork] or bacon, and therefore did not beg her food but buys it." Moreover, Fisone's youngest child, called Fockertje, after his Christian father, Focker Jongbloet, was given a new, Jewish name by his stepfather: from then on he was called Afroompje, Little Abraham or Little Afrom (Egmond 1993b, 137–46).

Fisone's relationship with Lijp was not the only such case. Nathan Moses, a Jew born in Germany during the last decade of the seventeenth century who was professionally involved in crime at least from 1735 up to the time of his arrest in the late 1760s, lived for a long time with a sister of Fisone's third husband. This Gypsy woman bore him eight children and actually changed her name from Koba to Rachel (a sign of conversion?). That did not keep Nathan Moses from eventually leaving her, however. After that he had affairs with at least five to ten Christian and Gypsy women (138–48).

Finally, then, we have come to the domain of religion. But it is not religious convictions that are at issue here. The only available evidence concerns religious observances, and the relationship between belief and practice is by no means a simple or indisputable one. The ambiguities are nicely illustrated by a quotation from the interrogations of the Gossels band. When asked how he had first met some of the other band members, Cosman Gossels declared that one of them had wanted to buy a mirror: "This person had come to his room together with another man, a Christian, in the course of the next day's evening, but he had not been able to conclude a deal with him because the Sabbath had already begun and also because he had not had the type of mirror the man was looking for." Later, in the course of the Saturday evening, Cosman had gone out with the Christian man, rowing to some ships that had arrived from the East Indies in order to buy tamarind, but only "when the Sabbath would have ended." Several parts of these statements turned out to be lies or partial lies, but the matter-of-fact way in which Cosman referred to the Sabbath, on the one hand, and to the absence of the right type of mirror, on the other, as more or less equally important reasons preventing the deal is telling, to say the least. Yet it does not necessarily imply a lack of respect for religious custom, and Cosman would not even have mentioned the Sabbath if Jewish religious ceremonies had been totally irrelevant to him.

We know that at least a few poor German Jews did observe the Sabbath and worked on Sundays. During the 1790s Abraham Levi Singer, for instance, worked on Sunday afternoons as a fiddler at a tavern in the capital of the province of Brabant. Moreover, the interrogations of Jewish suspects include occasional references to Passover as a marking point in time, just like the references to Easter or Christmas made by Christian defendants. The least we may infer from these references to the Sabbath and other religious festivals is that they point to a fairly strong and openly displayed adherence to Jewish religious custom. This supports the evidence we found on the non-Jewish women who married Jews, changed their names, and began to comply with Jewish dietary practices, which suggests that their husbands kept to these rules as well. Such findings in turn fit in with the considerable demand for kosher meat, to which the large number of German Jewish butchers, especially in some rural areas, attests.[17] Nicknames or surnames referring to occupations dealing with the production or selling of food might have been revealing in this context, but such names are disappointingly scarce among the people studied here (most of whose nicknames refer to personal characteristics, often of a physical nature, or to criminal specialization); the few names that allude to food mention the butcher's trade, cleaning or selling fish, or selling goat's milk, wine, or vinegar.

Insofar as this fragmentary evidence allows any conclusions, it shows that the everyday aspects of Jewish religion were indeed important to poor German Jews. They might have ignored the Sabbath, Passover, and religious food prescriptions, but they did not. Moreover, they made no secret of their commitment even when they might have had good reason to do so. The observance of religious custom should, then, be listed among the marks of identity of a group that found itself at a considerable distance from the established communities of Ashkenazim and of concomitant social and religious control. At the same time, however, we should bear in mind that the people discussed here only referred to religious ritual in passing and in a very matter-of-fact way. Such references are scarce and cover only a few aspects of religious custom. We do not hear anything at all about, for instance, ritual baths, circumcision, or bar mitzvah, all of which may be listed on the public, social, or ceremonial side of religion. Perhaps the fact that all the defendants were circumcised Jews (we only know this to have been true of Nathan Moses) was simply taken for granted by all those concerned. But their silence on the other aspects cannot be explained by the division between public and private aspects of religion. Should we infer that religion was primarily important to them insofar as it affected their everyday customary behavior? Was it a cultural practice rather than a matter of belief or conviction, or is that a false contrast based on modern distinctions?[18]

In keeping with our assumption that important aspects of group identity should be looked for at the margins, in external details, we may search for clues in situations where Jews felt themselves in danger of losing their identity as Jews. The great significance of a whole range of outward aspects of identity is apparent from the plight of Jews in the Amsterdam house of correction, the Rasphuis, all of them poor Ashkenazim arrested for loitering, begging, and so on, who in the 1640s were forced to violate the Sabbath, eat forbidden foods, and remove their hats when praying (Kaplan 1989b, 43). In 1658 the Amsterdam authorities imprisoned large numbers of poor Jews and forced them "to violate the holy Torah and the blessed Lord, both in eating the forbidden foods given to them in prison and violating the Sabbath and other holy days" (37). Whether religion in the sense of a deep inner conviction was or was not important to these people we cannot know for certain. But religious observance very clearly was, even if it was only one among the many external (although by no means superficial) characteristics that formed important marks of their identity as Jews. It cannot be a coincidence that they felt their group identity to be threatened not by an attack upon their hearts, livers, or stomachs—representing the social body—but by a violation of their individual external boundaries. Could anything be more closely connected with the outward margins of the body than the wearing of hats or the ingestion of certain types of food? In this situation there is nothing superficial about the surface, just as there is nothing marginal about the margins.

Finally, it is not by chance that we have selected the poorest, most stigmatized, and twice excluded category of German Jews as subjects for a discussion of Jewish identity, deliberately keeping away from the "core" of Dutch Jewry, from its social, political, or religious elite, its rabbis, and even from the established communities of Ashkenazim. We have inspected the margins, assuming that the most significant marks of group identity can be found where the strongest effort has to be made to remain part of a group, and where practical considerations might easily have induced people to renounce their Jewish identity. Such a circuitous procedure is not designed to provide definitive answers to the question what (group) identity was all about in the past—or is in the present, for that matter—but skirting the issue may make a change from the more usual invasive attempts at probing the innermost ranges of personality, belief, and mind.

PART III

REINVENTION AND THE RESISTANCE TO CHRONOLOGY

But I can also see the evolutionary hypothesis as
nothing more, as the clothing of a formal connection.

Wittgenstein, "Remarks on Frazer's *Golden Bough*"

THERE IS AN INEVITABLE TENSION BETWEEN THE SEARCH FOR continuities over time and the urge to divide time into periods. In his classic *Die Kunst- und Wunderkammern der Spätrenaissance* of 1908, Julius von Schlosser implied continuity between the Middle Ages and the Renaissance when he demonstrated the lack of any break between medieval practices of collection and the ways in which Renaissance collections of curiosities were put together and displayed (Von Schlosser [1908] 1978). In the continuity for which Le Goff has argued (1985, 7–13) the "Middle Ages" can be taken to extend from the third century to the mid-nineteenth century. In turn, the "nineteenth century" is capable of further expansion: Agulhon takes it to mean "the long nineteenth century that extends from 1789–1799 to the 1940s or 1950s" (1988, 11). Such a periodization would seem to stretch the *longue durée* to the breaking point.

Not all scholars would accept these conclusions or this periodization, of course. After all, they bear an uncomfortable resemblance to Karl Marx's now discredited use of the concept "pre-capitalist mode of production," or the bewildering variety of uses of the term *postmodern* to cover an enormous range of highly differentiated phenomena. What they all have in common is the idea that chronological succession is a homogenous substance;

although opinions are divided on how it is to be chopped up, the underlying assumption is that all of the separate pieces are part of a single fabric.

This notion has come under criticism in the previous chapters, and similar doubts about the application of developmental models to the course of history have been raised in other quarters. For example, in his brilliant analysis of the activities of the Dominican Annius of Viterbo, who forged a fake text by Berosus at the end of the fifteenth century, and of modern responses to them, Anthony Grafton pours scorn on an image of "a train in which Greeks and Latins, spurious and genuine authorities, sit side by side until they reach a stop marked 'Renaissance.' Then grim-faced humanists climb aboard, check tickets, and expel fakes in hordes through doors and windows alike." He goes on to note with satisfaction that a new generation of scholars "has introduced some attractive loops and swerves into this rectilinear and teleological account" before presenting his own analysis, which, he claims, is "even more crooked and complex" (1991, 78–80).

One of the major factors that explain these loops and swerves is the invention of tradition (Hobsbawm and Ranger 1983), "how something comes to be repeated, relocated and translated in the name of tradition, in the guise of a pastness that is not necessarily a faithful sign of historical memory but a strategy of representing authority in terms of the artifice of the archaic" (Bhabha 1994, 35). In relation to the morphological method that we are advocating, this requires that attention be paid to the plurality of pertinent contexts in which the phenomena under investigation can be set as a way of fragmenting the unitary narratives within which traditions are invented and reinvented and of recovering discontinuity behind the facade of continuity that such narratives imply.

Chapter 5 examines a particular anthropological idiom—the so-called Plinian monstrous human races—in the works of the sixteenth-century cosmographers as a preliminary to a more wide-ranging discussion of the question of continuity and discontinuity. The monstrous human races, we argue, are resistant to history: since they are not the same thing under all definitions, any history of them can only be a quasi history and no history can encompass their alterity. All the same, there is more to be said than this, and the rest of the chapter illustrates how visual and textual representations of the monstrous human races can be inserted within a wider network of different contexts, including deformities at birth, collections of curiosities, political pamphlets, and nineteenth-century embryology.

In chapter 6 a similar resistance to chronology is shown to be a feature of a particular ritual punishment, in which the victim was tied inside a sack along with a dog, a snake, a monkey, and a cock and then drowned. Alleged continuities and discontinuities in material stretching from antiquity and Germanic law to the early modern period are called into question. We argue that the study of the history of this particular punishment collapses into the reinvention of tradition at various points in history.

Finally, chapter 7 combines many of the themes of the previous chapters to present three historical moments in the portrayal of the barbarian: in the text of Tacitus's *Germania;* in the text and illustrations of Clüver's work on ancient Germany, *De Germania Antiqua* (1616); and in a series of seventeenth-century Dutch portraits of natives of Brazil. This chapter returns to consider the major theoretical question posed by the combination of microhistory and morphology, namely, what the connection is between morphological chains, sometimes spanning millennia, and the notion of a chronological sequence within a specific historical context. As in chapter 1, visual and textual representations from different periods are drawn upon to indicate some of the ways morphological analysis can throw light on processes of historical change.

Despite the seemingly antiquarian character of these chapters, they have ramifications of a cultural and political nature as well. In the nineteenth century, Renan's Germanism, which is in line with those aristocratic interpretations of French history that sought to provide a Germanic genealogy for the *noblesse d'épée,* can be contrasted with an intellectual tradition sustained by such thinkers as Carlo Cattaneo, who used the *Germania* to argue that it was the urban traditions of Egypt, Phoenicia, and Asia Minor that had created a basis for civilization in the Mediterranean, who rejected Germanism in all its forms, and who dismissed the notion that nomadism was a source of fresh values (Thom 1990). Chapter 6 examines a similar debate between "Germanists" and "Romanists." The debate did not die down in the past century, however. The various ways a text like Tacitus's *Germania* was interpreted in the Third Reich indicate how such writings could be utilized to construct ideological genealogies (see Canfora 1979; and Lund 1995). The question of the collusion of certain influential thinkers with right-wing politics has also been revived in connection with the work of Georges Dumézil, whose popularity among the New Right has given rise to a discussion of the political coloring of the *oeuvre* of Dumézil himself (Ginzburg [1986] 1990b, 126–45). We hope that our undisguised admiration for such historians as Eric Hobsbawm, Carlo Ginzburg, and the late E. P. Thompson will show where our political sympathies lie.

5

THE RESISTANCE
TO HISTORY

THE ORIGINS OF THE SECRET OF HAPPINESS

Towards the end of *THE TEMPTATION OF SAINT ANTHONY*, after the appearance of a sphinx and a chimera, Flaubert introduces a number of figures with human bodies but hardly conforming to the norm. There are the Astomi, like bubbles of air, composed of breezes and scents;[1] the Nisnas, the bisected people we encountered in the introduction to part II, who have only one eye, one hand, and one leg and live comfortably in their half-houses with their half-wives and half-children; the Blemmyes, a headless people with strong shoulders whose face is on their stomach; the Pygmies; the Sciapods, who sleep in the shadow of their enormous feet and have discovered that "keeping one's head as low as possible is the secret of happiness"; and the Cynocephales, dog-headed plunderers of bird's nests. Where do they all come from?

Among the sources consulted by Flaubert during the preparation of the final version of the *Temptation* was a French edition of the famous *Cosmographei* by the German humanist scholar Sebastian Münster (1488–1552).[2] Two years before his death, drawing on the results of extensive additional inquiries at first and second hand, Münster was able to bring out a considerably expanded edition, lavishly illustrated with many more woodcuts than the five hundred or so of the first (1544) edition and issued by Petri, the renowned publishing house in Basel. Enormously popular, the work was widely used in the education of the upper classes;[3] by the middle of the following century there had been forty-six editions in a variety of languages (Burmeister 1964). The lion's share of the expanded edition of the work was devoted to Münster's native Germany. It is only towards the end of book 5, "On the Countries of Asia," that the author comes to describe the more remote regions of the globe. Drawing on the legends associated with Alexander the Great's expedition to India,[4] he offers a description of the peoples

Fig. 7. Plinian monstrous human races. From Sebastian Münster, *Cosmographia* (Basel, 1552), fol. 1240. Courtesy of University Library, Amsterdam.

Fig. 8. Plinian monstrous human races. From Sebastian Münster, *Cosmographia* (Basel, 1552), fol. 1240. Courtesy of University Library, Amsterdam.

who live on the other side of the Ganges: dog-headed people; one-eyed people; one-legged people; people with one huge foot, which they use as a parasol; people with enormous ears, which they use as blankets; and many more (Münster 1550, 1165). The two accompanying woodcuts depict representatives of these peoples: in the first, a figure reclining on his back with his huge foot in the air, a figure with one eye in the center of his forehead, a two-headed dwarf, a headless figure whose face is on his chest, and a figure with the head of a dog (see fig. 7); in the second, a figure with extremely elongated ears and a figure with black pigmentation (see fig. 8). The first of these woodcuts recurs in book 6, "Of the Country of Africa," where a similar list of monsters is presented to give the reader an idea of the inhabitants of the (uncharted) interior of the African continent (Münster 1550, 1225).

The aim of the present chapter, however, is not simply to reconstitute sources in some antiquarian exercise. Although the point of entry is not exactly a front door, we hope that this entrance through a side passage will nevertheless throw light on questions of greater import. In particular, we call into question a simplistic view of history as something that conforms to the traditional linear movement of narrative. Chronology is not synonymous with history; the historical relations delineated below cannot be subsumed within a chronological order. In fact, in view of the way in which we come across various objects from different periods buried in unpredictable contexts, the method followed here might best be characterized as archaeological rather than historical, though with the proviso that none of the strata that are laid bare can claim priority over the others.

Without going into Münster's text and images in more detail at this stage, it is instructive to compare the French edition of the *Cosmographie* published in Paris in 1575 by Nicolas Chesneau and Michel Sonnius for François de Belleforest (1529–83). Author of one of the only two cosmographies to be published in the vernacular in France in the sixteenth century (the other was André Thevet's *Cosmographie universelle,* published in the same year),[5] Belleforest followed Münster's lead in three main respects. First, he devoted a major part of this new edition (folios 161–397) to his native country; second, he obtained much of the material through an extensive network of informants scattered in various regions of the country (Simonin 1987); and third, his work follows the tendency also shown in successive editions of Münster to reduce the number of extravagant illustrations and to increase both the number and the accuracy of town plans. Symptomatic of the latter trend is the nature and distribution of the illustrations accompanying the account of the Americas. In the 1550 (German) edition of Münster, the woodcuts to this section of the work represent a ship (twice), a tree, a volcano, cannibals chopping up their victim on a table, a cannibal roasting a human victim on a spit over a fire, a tree hut, and a city; and the single woodcut of a city is of a nonspecific type. In Belleforest's 1575 edition, which has a much larger section on the Americas, taking into account the conquest of Mexico and Peru, all trace of these colorful details has disappeared, and the only illustrations are the plans of Cuzco and Tenochtitlán (2058–59 and 2138–39, respectively). Belleforest's descriptions of India and Asia conform to the same pattern. The monstrous peoples have been eliminated, and the few illustrations are mainly town plans. In the terminology of the time, Belleforest's edition bears witness to a shift from cosmography to chorography.

This much is child's play—browsing through the pages of old books, counting illustrations, adding "learned" details culled from the excellent biographies of Belleforest and Thevet that have appeared during the last few years (Lestringant 1991a and Simonin 1992). It would be easy to go one step further and advance a hypothesis on the basis of this evidence: that the period between 1550 and 1575 marks a break, a rupture, a caesura in intellectual history. Before the watershed, even people as learned as the Basel professor Sebastian Münster were prepared to believe that the remote corners of the world were inhabited by monstrous human peoples. With the watershed, common sense triumphed over credulousness, even gullibility.

Such a hypothesis has a certain attractiveness insofar as it can be supported by the independent research of other scholars. For instance, attention has been drawn to a certain "progress" in ethnography at the end of the sixteenth century, marked by the elimination of monsters from geographical compilations and from costume books and by an attenuation of their "extravagance" by a transformation of physical incongruity into extravagant dress (Pellegrin 1987, 511 n. 9, 525). The monstrosity of foreign peoples is now reduced to a difference in costume that is not even skin-deep.

Moreover, there is an inherent plausibility in the hypothesis in light of what Lestringant has referred to as "the crisis of cosmography" (1993, 319–40). This crisis, he argues, is the product of three kinds of tension in the cosmographical project. One is the tension between the mathematical theories of Claudius Ptolemaeus (ca. A.D. 90–168)[6] and the empirical practice of travel, as evidenced by the work of Münster, a tension that Janni (1984) has subsumed under the opposition of "ancient cartography" and "hodological space." Another is the tension between the theories of trained scholars, versed in what the classical tradition and its aftermath had to say about the peoples of Europe and the rest of the world, on the one hand, and the charts of sailors, on the other. A third is the tension between the strength of tradition and the value attached to eyewitness accounts.[7] Lestringant has shown convincingly how the work of André Thevet is marked by these tensions. And the period in which Thevet's works saw the light of day—the third quarter of the sixteenth century[8]—was the very period that separated Münster from Belleforest.[9]

Finally, while it has become a commonplace that early woodcuts like those in the first edition of Münster's *Cosmographei* very rarely were realistic representations, the woodcuts in Belleforest's *Cosmographie,* especially the topographical (chorographical) ones, are generally taken to be much more verisimilar. They display a greater differentiation than do most of the earlier illustrations, which have a generic quality.

No doubt any presentation of a tendency as a radical break is bound to be tendential itself. However, our first task will be, not to point out the exaggerations in the hypothesis outlined above, as if it were enough to hedge each statement with a word of caution, but to indicate what is questionable about each and every one of the assumptions. Let us begin by considering another woodcut from Belleforest's *Cosmographie* (fig. 9). It opens the section dealing with the origins of the peoples of Europe, focusing on the population movements associated with the Goths, the Vandals, and the Huns. The outer figures can easily be found in the books of national costume that began to circulate in the second half of the sixteenth century (Defert 1987). What catches our eye here is the pair of figures in the center. The man on the left can be identified as a native of America (Brazil). From the first decade of the century feathered clothing or ornaments around the waist, at the knees, and on the head, nudity, and a bow and shield were all compatible with, or served to mark, the figure of the Amerindian, both male and female. By a process that has been called "Tupinambization" (Sturtevant 1988), the Tupinamba of Brazil served as models for the iconography of the Amerindians *tout court,* no matter from which region of South or North America they came. Though some aspects of this iconography, such as nudity and the use of a bow, overlap with the European image of the Wild Man and his female counterpart (Colin 1987), by the time of Belleforest the woodcut illustrations to Thevet's *Les singularitez de la France antarctique* (1558) had already provided numerous examples of what Amerindians were supposed to look like, so that the figure can be identified without question as an Amerindian.

Fig. 9. "On the Goths and their cruelty." From François Belleforest, *La cosmographie universelle de tout le monde* (Paris, 1575), fol. 868. Courtesy of University Library, Amsterdam.

As for the righthand member of the pair of figures in the center, which appears at first sight to be a birdman, there is no reason to see anything monstrous in his appearance. It is an example of courtly dress, and the figure is in masquerade. Iconographically this pair—the Amerindian and the man in bird masquerade—has a very close parallel in the series of masquerades designed by Jacques de Gheyn II and probably engraved by Zacharias Dolendo at the end of the sixteenth century (Luijten et al. 1993, 388–89); one of the prints in this series represents an Amerindian woman (identifiable by the feathered headgear, skirt, and knee ornaments)[10] accompanied by a figure wearing a feathered suit and a bird mask (see fig. 10).

Incidentally, if this seems an odd assortment of figures to represent the ancestors of the German people, it should be borne in mind that the view of previous generations as primitives encouraged an assimilation of historical and ethnographical iconography in a two-way traffic. As we shall see in more detail in chapter 7, the newly discovered peoples in distant lands were believed to mirror what people had been like in remote times. Seen in this light, the dress of "primitives" in America, national costumes of other countries, and courtly masquerades could all be taken to indicate the appearance of the Goths, the Vandals, and the Huns from centuries before the time of writing.

Fig. 10. *The Masquerade,* by Jacques de Gheyn II, ca. 1592–96. Courtesy of State Printroom, Amsterdam.

Beginning in the time of Christopher Columbus there was a persistent tradition of representing the Amerindians as a monstrous people. The sixteenth-century visual and textual record bears witness to the application of the iconography of one-eyed peoples, headless peoples, anthropophagi, and so on, to the native peoples of the Americas (Mason 1990a). In this light, it is important to note the *absence* of the monstrous in this woodcut illustration from Belleforest's *Cosmographie*. It would appear that by 1575 it had become sufficient to designate the foreignness of other times and other places in terms of mode of dress, without recourse to the idiom of monstrosity. After all, curious though these figures may be, they are not monstrous. If we now turn to the corresponding section in the 1550 (German) edition of Münster's *Cosmographei,* however, we find the identical woodcut (Münster 1550, 296). In other words, instead of a progression from physical monstrosity to superficial body decoration we find a juxtaposition of both kinds of representation in the same work. The thesis of a rupture can only be maintained if we assume serious inconsistency within the 1550 edition itself—a case of multiple hernia.

Let us move on to the second buttress to the initial hypothesis, the neat correspondence with the crisis of cosmography. This would only work if it could be shown that Münster and Belleforest come down on opposite sides of a great divide.[11] Certainly there are some points in favor of such a position. For instance, Belleforest's relatively humble origins and his lifelong attempt to gain acceptance in more charmed social circles (Simonin 1992, 21ff.) would appear to ally him with other *hommes nouveaux* such as Bernard Palissy, Ambroise Paré, and of course Thevet, representatives of what Lestringant has called a "proletarian science" (1991b, 34). On the other hand, the empirical interest in firsthand as well as secondhand evidence is displayed by both Münster and Belleforest. Moreover, it is not the openness to new (geographical) information which is significant but the rhetorical strategies to which it gave rise (see Campbell 1988, 218). For instance, Thevet attempts to oppose his own descriptions, based on his own alleged eyewitness presence, to what he calls Belleforest's "rescriptions," based on a perusal of the literature (Simonin 1987).[12] Within this rhetorical strategy Belleforest plays Münster to Thevet's Thevet. In other words, we should be wary of taking the tropes of the parties involved as indicative of a strict demarcation between conservative, learned tradition and what can only anachronistically be taken for enlightened empiricism.

As for the notion of a steady increase in verisimilitude in representations of nature in the course of the sixteenth century, there is no lack of arguments to the contrary. One relates to the use of the woodcut as a medium, for we may note that there is an enormous discrepancy between the degree of accuracy of printed images and that of, say, da Vinci's contemporary drawings. That is, the choice of the medium used to convey a visual representation partly determines the standard of scientific illustration. All the same, even if we limit ourselves to comparisons within a single medium—in this case the woodcut illustration—clear lines of development are hard to draw, and different degrees of verisimilitude may be juxtaposed side by side. For example, the herbal *Gart der Gesundheit* (printed in Mainz in 1485) contains illustrations copied from medieval illuminated manuscripts as well as illustrations from nature of plants that were not to be found in the ancient sources (Ackerman 1985).[13] In the field of human anatomy, although dissection was expanding knowledge of a "new continent" within the human body (Sawday 1995), artists who illustrated works of anatomy from the mid-sixteenth century were just as likely to draw on classical or classicizing models of the human body as on observation from nature. The same picture emerges with regard to views of cities: both at the beginning of the sixteenth century and at the end interest in verisimilitude seems to have been lacking; the same prints were used to illustrate different phenomena at different times and in different places (Gombrich 1959). Thus Damascus, Ferrara, Mantua, and Milan are represented by one and the same virtually unaltered image in the woodcuts Dürer's tutor, Wohlgemut, made for Hartmann Schedel's *Nuremberg Weltchronik* of 1493. Exactly one hundred years later we still find the publisher Theodore de Bry warning the reader that his engraver, not having a correct image of the town of Sevilla at hand, has instead drawn the town of some seaport or other after his own invention (Mason 1987, 587). As for beachings of whales like those discussed in chapter 1, an engraving produced by an alleged eyewitness to an event in 1601 may simply be based on other engravings of whales beached at different times and in different places (Duerr [1978] 1985, 9–10). The thesis that there was increased differentiation in visual representations in the course of the century becomes hard to sustain.

A ROYAL ROBE WITH AMPLE FOLDS

If this brief survey of image-making in the sixteenth century fails to yield any clear-cut discontinuities, it is not because the break we are looking for belongs, say, in the seventeenth century rather than in the sixteenth. Nor is it the case that we are out to establish that the representations of the period display a striking *continuity*. Rather, we question the value of looking at historical phenomena in terms of smooth or broken surfaces at all. As suggested above, the phenomena under discussion bear more of a resemblance to the disparate artifacts scattered in disorder on an archaeological site.

Given that there *is* a difference between Münster's *Cosmographei* of 1550 and Belleforest's 1575 edition, is this difference simply a question of deferral in time? Surely, mere duration in time is a contingent matter (Osborne 1992); though it may be useful as an instrument for the *measurement* of difference, its use would imply that the objects of comparison are commensurable entities of the same substance, differentiated merely by virtue of an extrinsic delay. Telling the time, after all, tells us nothing about the degree of mutual attraction and repulsion or the degree of mutual contamination by which Münster and Belleforest are both connected and disconnected. Indeed, if one had to find a word to describe the nature of their relationship to each other, a more suitable candidate would be Heidegger's *Entfernung* (Heidegger 1957, 105–7), a term that covers both farness and, paradoxically, the removal *(Ent-)* of farness in proximity. Unlike *Abstand* (distance), which refers to a point located elsewhere in space or time whose distance from self can be measured in an external fashion—in the present case, twenty-five years—*Entferntheit* (remoteness) never gets taken as distance in the sense of a measurable interval; *Entfernung* might be said to evoke both farness and proximity in a much more intrinsic relation.[14]

Rather than trying to impose some kind of external, reductionist grid on the material under consideration, then, it is worth trying an approach that enables the works in question to produce the very criteria by which we judge them. If we turn to the works themselves, one such point of entry is the question of translation. Münster's *Cosmographei* was indisputably translatable, for besides Belleforest's French-language edition it was translated into Latin, Czech, Italian, and English. Translatability, Walter Benjamin posited in the introduction to his 1923 translation of Baudelaire's *Tableaux parisiens*, is an essential quality of certain linguistic creations (see Benjamin 1968, 71). Through the translation process, the original undergoes a change in its continued life *(Fortleben)*, and the mother tongue of the translator is transformed as well. According to the traditional theory of translation, no translation will ever be considered adequate among the totality of its readers because of its secondary, derivative, and consequently impoverished nature by comparison with the original. Benjamin, however, moves away from this common usage to demonstrate that although there is a relationship of affinity *(Verwandtschaft)* between the original and the translation, affinity does not necessarily involve likeness.

Benjamin makes use of a number of figures in his discussion. For instance, "The language of the translation envelops its content like a royal robe with ample folds"; the original and the translation are "recognizable as fragments of a greater language, just as fragments are part of a vessel" (75–76); and unlike a work of literature, "a translation does not find itself in the centre of the language forest but on the outside facing the wooded ridge; it calls into it without entering, aiming at that single spot where the echo is able to give, in its own language, the reverberation of the work in the alien one" (76). Despite these organic, vitalist metaphors,[15] the relation Benjamin proposes is not a genetic but a structural one. The intention underlying each language, he claims, is an intention "which no single language can attain by itself but which is realized only by the totality of their intentions *supplementing* each other" (74, emphasis added).

The supplementary character of this relation goes a long way towards explaining the existence of both continuities and discontinuities. If the original is translatable, it loses itself in the translation; if it is not translatable, it fails to survive at all.[16] Either way, loss is involved, and it is this loss that is both hollowed out and suspended by the supplement. In this sense, Belleforest's *Cosmographie* is a supplement to Münster's *Cosmographei*. It helps to preserve and disseminate Münster's work, but in doing so it threatens to supplant it. It is in bringing Münster's work closer that it distances it.

ILLICIT IMAGES

So far, contrary to usual academic practice, the discussion has been confined to visual representations. One reason for adopting this strategy was to bypass for the time being the question of what authors *say* in order to concentrate on what they *do*.[17] A second reason was that images can be transposed from one text to another. Although in each case they may be embedded within a textual framework, they often lead a life of their own. In fact, it is precisely the ability of images of the monstrous human races to leap across different textual contexts that is crucial to the present discussion. Third, giving priority to image over text is in some cases a reflection of what is actually going on. To illustrate, André Thevet's description of a giraffe in his *Cosmographie de Levant* credits the animal with a small horn on its forehead in addition to the two horns on top of its head ([1554] 1985, 145).[18] This at-

Fig. 11. Giraffe from the menagerie in Cairo. From André Thevet, *Cosmographie de Levant* (Lyon, 1556), fol. 146. Courtesy of University Library, Amsterdam.

tribution of a unicornlike third horn to the giraffe is zoologically inaccurate, but it can be explained by the woodcut illustration of the giraffe accompanying the text (see fig. 11): the animal's rather clumsily executed left ear has been mistaken for a horn, showing that the text at this point depends on the illustration, and not vice versa. Fourth, an attempt to break away from the hegemony of textual domination can be seen as a response to the challenge recently issued by Stafford: "How do we gain visual knowledge and come to imaginatively possess all that cannot be consumed, or subsumed, by words?" (1991, 45).

Not that our aim is simply to reverse the positions of text and image within a hierarchy; rather, we suggest that the sixteenth-century cosmographies under discussion might be regarded along the lines of Derrida's discussion of the postcard: "What I like about the postcard is that you can't tell back from front, here from there, near from far. . . . Nor what matters most, the image or the text, and in the text, the message or the caption" (1980, 17).[19] That being said, we cannot, of course, simply turn our backs on the texts themselves. So let us see whether what Münster and Belleforest say corresponds to what they (say they) do.

After listing a number of monstrous human races mentioned by ancient authorities such as Megasthenes, Solinus, and Pliny, Sebastian Münster notes that although none of these reports is based on firsthand observation, there is no reason to doubt the possibility that such beings exist, for God in his ineffable wisdom and power is perfectly capable of creating anything, no matter how incredible it may seem (1550, 1176).[20] Belleforest, on the other hand, is "astonished that Munster has taken such pains to depict in his work all these monsters as if they really existed" (Belleforest 1575, 1587).[21]

A cursory reading of these texts seems to support a superficial scrutiny of the woodcuts: there is a great divide separating the medieval outlook of Münster from the scientific approach of Belleforest. But this ignores the force of rhetoric. Belleforest's disclaimer is nevertheless accompanied by a full list of the monsters as if they really existed, and by the time he has come to the end of the list he seems to have forgotten its original intent, which was not to endorse but to refute the marvels it contains. He is deploying the rhetorical figure known as *praeteritio:* by listing the monsters in the first place he can have it both ways, since he presents what he denies. The effect on the reader is a double bind, since he or she is forced to read what Belleforest claims to expunge. The elimination of the monsters is effected visually insofar as Belleforest's pages on the Indies do not contain any woodcut illustrations of them; but despite his disclaimer, they are present—indeed, very much so—in his text. In this respect the monstrous human races conform to the general behavior of the *singularity* in the Renaissance, for, as Lestringant has stressed, the *singularity* is transmitted from context to context, whether it is accompanied by refutations and ironical disclaimers or not (1991a, 314; 1993, 17–48). One of the many examples of this mechanism in the work of Thevet is his use in his *Cosmographie universelle* of two woodcuts depicting the cruelty of the Amazons: the images, which themselves testify to the existence of the Amazons, appear on the very page on which Thevet *denies* their existence (Lestringant 1991a, 125).[22] It is as if the monstrous races persist through a dynamic of their own, overcoming endeavors to suppress them in the name of rationality.

A STORY THAT IS NOT A STORY

The belief that other regions of the world are populated by human beings who deviate in striking ways from the images that one has of oneself is indeed widespread on a massive if not universal scale.[23] Though there was a tendency to locate the monstrous human races in the East (Campbell 1988, 47–86), Columbus's discovery of what he took to be Asia was accompanied by a transplantation of the Plinian races to American soil.[24] Indeed, the Plinian tradition considerably influenced European images of the Amerindian (Mason 1994b).

The ancient Greeks assumed that such monstrous races were harbored primarily in the North and the East. The earliest references to such peoples are in archaic Greek hexameter and lyric poetry (Hesiod, Homer, Alcman, Aristeas of Proconnesus), and they occur in fragments of the earliest prose writers (Skylax, Hecataeus). This literature was familiar to Aeschylus and Herodotus in the fifth century B.C., and the summary way in which some of the monstrous human races are introduced in texts of this period indicates a degree of familiarity with them on the part of their audience.[25]

The number of such monstrous peoples increased dramatically with the expedition of Alexander the Great to the East in the following century. The team of scholars who accompanied him reported on the existence of monstrous peoples and creatures in the countries they reached, and soon after the expedition the list of monstrous human races was expanded even further as a result of the writings of Megasthenes, a Greek envoy to the court of Chandragupta, a powerful Indian ruler.

The monstrous human races became known as the "Plinian" races in modern discussions, after the Roman author who perished during the eruption of Vesuvius in A.D. 79, whose *Historia Naturalis* incorporated much of the previous literature on the subject to arrive at a lengthy though inevitably incomprehensive list (Mason 1990a, 78–79). The popularity of Pliny's work in the sixteenth century, however, was owing above all to the list of monstrous races in book 7, and separate editions of this book were published.[26] The human monstrous races in book 7 are listed in order to show the ingenuity of nature, and Pliny's account is followed by remarkable human individuals, such as exceptional and monstrous births (*HN* 7.2.21–32).

Among the successors of Pliny should be mentioned Pomponius Mela (fl. A.D. 40), Solinus (third century), Macrobius, Martianus Capella, Augustine (fourth and fifth centuries), and Isidore (ca. 570–636), as well as the anonymous *Liber Monstrorum* of uncertain date, provenance, and authorship.[27] The monstrous human races feature in travelers' tales (of Marco Polo, Oderic of Pordenone, "Sir John Mandeville," all from the early fourteenth century, and others), as well as in universal chronicles of history, the immediate predecessors to Münster's *Cosmographei*. There are signs that towards the end of the sixteenth century the viability of the Plinian idiom as an adequate mode of representation was being called into question, and the range of Plinian races appears to have contracted. The relatively free field of fabulation was coming under increasingly heavy constraints. Although Münster explicitly refers to Megasthenes, Pomponius Mela, Pliny and Solinus, it should be borne in mind that Münster, like so many of his contemporaries, need not have consulted all of these authorities firsthand since much of this information, including the references to ancient authors, could be derived from works much closer to him in time.

Besides these textual traditions, we should also mention the pictorial traditions, some of them possibly going back to an early illustrated edition of Solinus. As with the literary tradition, it is pointless to look for a *terminus a quo;* types such as the Wild Man may originate as far back as ancient Mesopotamian representations of the slaying of Humbaba (Burkert 1987). Similarly, certain types that figured in medieval church decoration, of which the most famous are those on the twelfth-century tympanum at Vézélay, may be based on Greek or even Babylonian prototypes (Wittkower 1977, 200 n. 106). At any rate, "there must have been a large stock of classical marvel illustrations" (55). Here too there is no need to suppose that Münster was drawing on particularly ancient sources, since the woodcut depicting a Sciapod and other representatives of the Plinian races (see fig. 7) was common enough in earlier works of the sixteenth century, such as the history of the world known as the *Margarita philosophica* by Gregor Reisch (Freiburg, 1503).[28]

This story of the "Plinian" races, beginning in the vague depths of Mediterranean oral traditions, surfacing in the written word, codified by the Romans, and transmitted throughout the Middle Ages, reaches an apogee in the work of the encyclopedists, world chroniclers, and cartographers before fizzling out towards the end of the sixteenth century. We have already cast doubts on the notion of a clear-cut distinction between a Münster who looks back to a Dark Age and a Belleforest who looks forward to the Age of Reason. As we look at the monstrous human races from the perspective of the *longue durée,* we are bound to consider to what extent the pre-Belleforest tradition can be characterized as a homogeneous Dark Age at all.

Let us begin by considering what people say about what they do. Belleforest, we have seen, called the belief in the Plinian races into question at the same time that he recited their names at length. This contradictory movement of referring to what is taken not to exist is characteristic of many of the earlier accounts as well, although the dividing line between the credible and the incredible is drawn in a different place in each case.[29] Pliny, for example, finds it hard to believe in the people of the one-eyed king, the Agriophagi, the Pamphagi, the Anthropophagi, the Cynamolgi, the Artabatitae, or the locust eaters (*HN* 7.2.21–32). On the other hand, he is prepared to countenance the existence of Hippopodes, Phanesii, and many others races that seem equally fabulous to a modern reader. Before Pliny, Herodotus lists among the wonders to be found west of Libya not only marvelous fauna of various kinds but also dog-headed men (Kynokephaloi), headless men (Akephaloi) with eyes in their breasts, wild men (Agrioi), wild women, "and other beasts in huge numbers, not at all fabulous" (Herodotus *Histories* 4.191).[30] On the other hand, he refuses to believe in the existence of one-eyed or goat-footed men in the far North (3.116, 4.25). Tacitus, writing in the first century A.D., refuses to take up a clear position, concluding his ethnographic treatise *Germania* with the words, "Other stories that are told are completely fabulous: that the Hellusii and Oxiones have human faces and features, but the bodies and limbs of wild beasts: I shall leave this undecided as unproven" (46.4).[31]

In the second century A.D. we find the physician Galen both accepting and denying the existence of centaurs (Veyne 1983, 65–66). In the first half of the following century Philostratus, a Sophist and the author of a *vie romancée* of the sage Apollonius of Tyana, records a discussion between the hero of his book and the leader of the Indian sages, Iarchas, on the wonders of India. Philostratus introduces the conversation with the words, "There is much to be gained by neither believing nor yet disbelieving everything" (*Life of Apollonius* 3.45), and then he launches into a disquisition on the Indian martichoras (a large feline with a human face and impressive teeth),[32] the magnetic pantarbe stone, griffins, Pygmies, and the phoenix. However, he draws the line at the Skiapodes and Makrokephaloi (people with enormous feet and long heads, respectively) reported by Skylax: "They do not live anywhere on the earth, and least of all in India" (3.47). Yet in a comparison of India and Egypt later in the same work Philostratus adduces various pieces of information as evidence of the similarity between the two countries, including the following: "They also produce beasts seen nowhere else, and black men, as no other continents do, and they contain tribes of Pygmies and of humans who bark in various ways, and other amazing things of that kind" (6.1). The latter are the Kynokephaloi, a dog-headed people with a distinguished ancestry.[33] Dog-headed creatures are reported as existing in Asia, China, Java, Siberia, Egypt, America, and Europe (White 1991; Wittkower 1977, 197 n. 29). Yet it remains puzzling why Philostratus could accept the existence of dog-headed creatures but quoted Iarchas's statement of disbelief in Skiapodes and Makrokephaloi without any further comment.

In the prologue to the *Liber monstrorum,* belief in the existence of the monstrous races is mitigated by the assertion that now that the human race has multiplied and filled the world, monsters are less common in the sublunary world (Bologna 1977, 38; cf. Salisbury 1994, 148). Closer in time to Münster we find attempts to limit the number of monstrous races in Joannes Boemus's *Omnium gentium mores, leges et ritus* (1536) and denials of their existence by Maximilianus Transsylvanus (1522) and Joachim Vadianus (1534), to name but a few. There were thus voices before Belleforest who had reservations regarding some, if not all, of the Plinian races, although they could not agree on where the boundary between truth and fable was to be drawn (Céard 1977, 275ff.).

On the other hand, there were still people prepared to believe in their existence after Belleforest. At the end of the sixteenth century Walter Ralegh was prepared to believe the hearsay about Amazons who spent only one month a year with men, though he drew the line at their having only one breast (Ralegh [1596] 1970, 28).[34] He also described "a nation of people, whose heades appeare not aboue their shoulders"; it was reported that they had "their eyes in their shoulders, and their mouths in the middle of their breasts, and that a long train of haire groweth backward between their shoulders" (85). This people, whom he knew by the name Ewaipanoma, were the Plinian Blemmyes. Ralegh believed that such a people existed, though he did not claim to have seen them himself. From the same period, however, we do have a representation by an eyewitness in one of a series of almost two hundred watercolors depicting the flora, fauna, and ethnographica of the Caribbean. The anonymous artist of the Drake Manuscript, who accompanied Drake on his voyage in 1577–80, has depicted one of the Indians with his head shrunk into his shoulders.[35]

Early-seventeenth-century evidence of belief in the Plinian races can be found in the request by Ottho van Heurne, professor of anatomy at the University of Leiden from 1617, to the university board to accept skeletons from the East and West Indies for the university anatomy theater. He had in mind particularly Patagonian giants and skeletons from the Amazon region, where he believed the Plinian Blemmyes could be found (Lunsingh Scheurleer 1975, 241).

One of the most striking cases of persistent belief in this Plinian race, the headless Blemmye, at an even later date—1724!—can be found in the work of Joseph François Lafitau, who spent five years in Canada among the Algonquin, the Huron, and the Iroquois, attached to the Jesuit mission in Sault-Saint-Louis, where he collaborated with Julien Garnier, an expert in Indian languages. Despite his initial skepticism, Lafitau modified his views and attached credibility to a report of an Iroquois who claimed to have come across such a headless human while hunting in 1721 (Fischer 1985, 98–99). Lafitau included an engraving of a such a headless figure to illustrate the appearance of the natives of the Caribbean in his *Moeurs des sauvages amériquains comparées aux moeurs des premiers temps* (1724) (see fig. 12).

Of course, it might be argued that, these exceptions notwithstanding, beginning in the sixteenth century there was a tendency to rationalize the Plinian races out of a mythical existence. The work of the "Pliny of the sixteenth century," Ulisse Aldrovandi, whose *Monstrorum historia* was not published until 1642, is an example of such rationalizing. For instance, he refuses to give credence to the crane-man with an enormous neck and suggests that the Astomoi are simply people with small mouths (Olmi 1992, 47). This type of explanation has persisted into the twentieth century.[36] However, Aldrovandi is prepared to accept the existence of Blemmyes because of the support of St. Augustine (Céard 1977, 457). Although he draws a boundary line, he fails to come down fully either for or against the possibility that some of the monstrous human races did actually exist.

So far we have not examined the pictorial tradition. The makers of visual representations who described what they did not believe in faced an even more acute difficulty than that faced by writers in the same circumstances since the rhetorical device of negation was denied to them (Bucher [1977] 1981, 34–36). It was presumably in an attempt to palliate this dilemma

Fig. 12. American types. From Jean-François Lafitau, *Moeurs des sauvages amériquains comparées aux moeurs des premiers temps* (Paris, 1724). Courtesy of University Library, Amsterdam.

Item ötlich nacket vñ rauch in den flüßen wonend ötlich die an henden vnd füßen sechß finger haben. ötlich in den waſſern wonende halb menſchen vñd halbs pferds geſtalt habende. Item weyber mit per ten bis auff die pzuſt. auff dem haubt öben vnnd on har. Item in ethiopia gegen dem nidergang habenn ötlich vier augē. ſo ſind in Eripia ſchön leüt mit kra nichß helſen vnd ſchnebelen. Doch iſt als Auguſtin ſchreibt nit zů gelauben das ötlich menſchen an dem oit der erdenn gegen vns da die ſunn auffgeet . So ſy wider nider geet die verſen gegen vnſeren füßen keren Doch iſt ein groſſer ſtreyt in der ſchifft wider dē wo ne des gemeinē volcks. das geringßumb allenthalben menſchen auff der erden ſeyen. vnd die füß gegen ein ander kerende darauffſteen. vnd doch alle menſchen jr ſcheytel gem hymel keren in verwunderung war ůmb doch wir oder die die jr ferßen gegen vns wendē nit fallen. Aber das kübt auß der natur. dañ gleicher weiß als der ſtůl des feürs nyndert iſt deñ in dē feüern der waſſer nindert deñ in den waſſern. vñ des geyſts nyndert deñ in dem geyſt . alſo auch der ſtůl der erden nyndert anderßwo deñ in ir ſelbs.

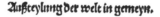

Außteylung der welt in gemeyn.

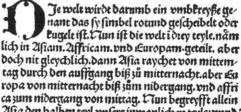

D Ie welt wirdt darumb ein vmbkreyße ge nant das ſy ſimbel rotund geſcheibelt oder kugelt iſt. Nun iſt die welt i drey teyle. näm lich in Aſiam. Affricam. vnd Europam. geteilt. aber doch nit gleychlich. dann Aſia raychet von mittem tag durch den auffgang biß zů mitternacht. aber Eu ropa von mitternacht biß zům nidergang. vnd affri ca zum nidergang von mittag. Nun begreyfft allein Aſia den halben teyl vnſers inwonlichen teyls vnnd Affrica vnd Euro pa den anderen halben teyl. zwiſchen dyſen teylen rynnen von dem ge meinen meer ein groß meer vnnd vnderſcheydet die ſelbē . So du nun die welt in zwey teyl. als des auffgangs vñ nidergangs taylſt. So iſt in dem einen teyl Aſia. vñ in dem anderē Affrica vñ Europa. alſo habet ſy die ſün Noe nach der ſüntfluß außgeteylt. vñ Sem mit ſeinen nach komen Aſiam. Japhet Europam. vñ Cham Affricam beſeſſen. als die ſchifft auch Criſo ſtomus. yſidozus vnd plinius ſagen.

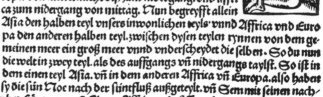
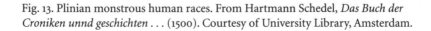

Fig. 13. Plinian monstrous human races. From Hartmann Schedel, *Das Buch der Croniken unnd geschichten . . .* (1500). Courtesy of University Library, Amsterdam.

to (a certain conception of) history: "All of history has shown that each time an *event* has been produced . . . it took the form of the unacceptable, or even of the intolerable, of the incomprehensible, that is, of a certain monstrosity" (Derrida 1995, 387).

OUT OF BOUNDS

As already mentioned, what exceeds the bounds of the historian was a matter to which Wittgenstein devoted some attention in his "Remarks on Frazer's *Golden Bough.*" His emphasis on affinities, or "family resemblances," suggests a different way of approaching the monstrous human races, even though this approaching, as we have seen, will be likely to take the form of an *Entfernung.* Instead of trying to insert the monstrous human races within a unilinear story, we could look for chains of morphological affinity and pay close attention to their points of intersection.

Take the Blemmyes, for instance, the Plinian race of headless beings with their faces on their chests. We have already identified headless beings (Akephaloi) in Herodotus and noted Ralegh's belief in headless Ewaipanoma two millennia later. Moreover, they also occupy a well-established place in the pictorial tradition, probably going back at least to Solinus. The same iconography lies behind the illustration of a *monstrum acephalon* in Aldrovandi's *Monstrorum Historia.* As Wittkower (1977, 66) notes, however, the traditional shape of the monstrous races is here being put to a different use, for the text refers to the birth of a monster with its eyes and nose in its back at Villefranche in 1562. The image of a representative of a race has been transferred to a different category: a freak of nature, deformed at birth. Treatment of individual monstrous births in connection with monstrous human races was already a feature of the earlier discussions, for example, in Augustine and Isidore.[39] The familiar monsters of the world chronicles thus find their way into the collections of individual monsters as portents that were so popular in the sixteenth century (Park and Daston 1981),[40] such as Lycosthenes' *Prodigiorum ac ostentorum chronicon* . . . or Ambroise Paré's *Des monstres et prodiges.*[41] In particular we can single out Boaistuau's *Histoires prodigieuses,* for one of the contributors to this work was none other than François Belleforest (Simonin 1992, 131; Wilson 1993, 53–54). Belleforest's interest in both cosmography and teratology stood him in good stead to switch from one genre to the other,[42] and the images of the monstrous could be taken to represent monstrous births as well as monstrous races.

Hence, although Belleforest's reworking of Münster eliminates the wood-cut illustrations of the monstrous races, it retains a monstrous portrait of a freak born in Krakow in 1547 despite its incredible appearance (Belleforest 1575, 1814). This to-and-fro movement between monstrous individuals and monstrous races was facilitated by the practices of publishers at the time: a publisher like Petri, who issued both Münster's cosmography and Lycosthenes' work on prodigies, might easily be tempted to recycle woodcuts from one work to another.

Whereas Belleforest thus straddles both ethnographical and medico-teratological concerns, a seventeenth-century treatise by John Bulwer is situated somewhere in between. Bulwer (who pioneered the deaf-and-dumb alphabet) was the author of *Anthropometamorphosis,*[43] in which he presented a vast survey of techniques by which peoples throughout the world manipulated different parts of the human body to produce a particular effect: long-headed, dog-headed, or headless people (the Makrokephaloi, Kynokephaloi, and Akephaloi of the Greeks) were simply the product of a wrongheaded desire to modify the shape of the head by artificial means.[44] Although what he regards as monstrosities are thus produced by human beings themselves, he links them with the freaks of nature by suggesting that in time nature begins to conspire with custom. In other words, after a while the contingent products of human folly are reproduced by nature itself. Although his theory on the origins of such types as the headless Blemmyes is relatively novel,[45] the illustration of a headless man that accompanies it is taken directly from the pictorial tradition of the monstrous races.[46]

Yet another use to which the same image could be put can be seen in a pamphlet published in 1645 entitled *A Declaration of a Strange and Wonderfull Monster: born in Kirkham Parish in Lancashire (the childe of Mrs. Haughton, a Popish Gentlewoman) the face of it upon the breast, and without a head.* . . . The pamphlet contains a crude woodcut of a headless creature based on the headless Blemmyes. Part of the pulp press propaganda war conducted during the English Revolution, the pamphlet was intended to show the divine retribution that fell upon a young woman reported to have said during pregnancy, "I pray God that rather than I shall be a Roundhead or bear a Roundhead, I may bring forth a child without a head."[47] The pamphlet is one of many: about 10 percent of newspaper stories during the interregnum were about monsters and portents (Friedman 1993, 273 n. 1). Whether they were born to Anglicans or Puritans depended on the political and religious persuasions of the pamphleteers. Either way, they were always a sign that the times were out of joint;[48] they could therefore be cited as evidence that God was displeased with the present state of affairs.

Besides in the two-dimensional world of the printed image, the interest in monstrous individuals and races found expression in collections of curiosities.[49] In the early eighteenth-century *Kunstkammer* of Peter I in Russia a peasant boy with only two digits on each hand and foot was included among the live exhibits; after his death he was stuffed and exhibited beside the skeleton of a giant (Neverov 1985).[50] Another Plinian type, the siren (half-woman, half-fish), was discovered off the coast of Brazil by Dutch merchants early in the seventeenth century (Bartholinus 1654, 171). It was taken to the Dutch university town of Leiden, where it was dissected by the professor of anatomy Pieter Pauw[51] under the eyes of Johan de Laet (director of the West India company, amateur naturalist, and author of an authoritative work on the New World) and the Danish physician Thomas Bartholinus, and the skeletal remains of a hand and a rib found their way to Bartholinus's private collection of *naturalia* (see fig. 15).

At the beginning of the eighteenth century, as noted above, Lafitau was still using the image of the Blemmyes to illustrate the peoples of the Caribbean. At the end of the same century, and still in the Caribbean, John Gabriel Stedman, a Scotsman serving in the Dutch army in Surinam, was bemused by what he referred to as a "hetoregeneus [*sic*] tribe being so much deformed on hands and Feet, that while some have but 3, or 4 fingers, and toes, on each, the Greatest number have Absolutely but 2 fingers and 2 Toes on each hand and foot" (Stedman 1988, 515). In fact, according to the modern editors of Stedman's manuscript, they were a group of eight to ten tropical forest Indians with varying degree of genetic deformity who had come to live with the Saramaka around 1760. That belief in the monstrous races had not completely died out by this time is also illustrated by a remark by Anders Sparrman, a Swedish pupil of Linnaeus, who was sent to southern Africa in 1772, one year before Stedman was sent to Surinam. In the preface to his *Voyage to the Cape of Good Hope* Sparrman stated that "men with one foot, indeed, Cyclopes, Syrens, Troglodytes, and such like imaginary beings have *almost entirely* disappeared in this enlightened age" (1785, xv–xvi, emphasis added).

The idiom of monstrosity thus continued to haunt the mentality of a later period, and with it one of the theories of the origin of such abnormalities. The fifth cause of monstrous births, according to Ambroise Paré ([1585] 1971, 4 and 35–38), was located in the imagination; this belief was

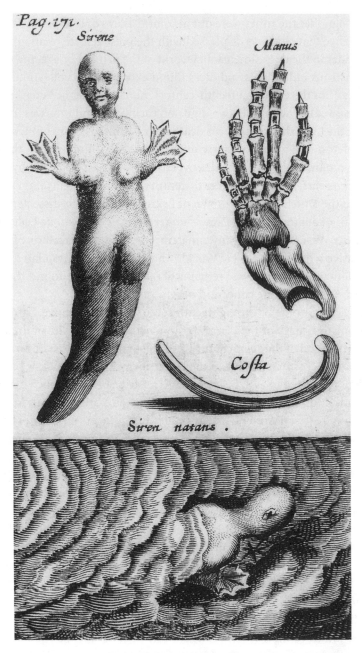

Fig. 15. "Siren" discovered off the coast of Brazil. From Thomas Bartholinus, *Historiarum anatomicarum rariorum, Centuria I et II* (Amsterdam, 1654). Courtesy of University Library, Amsterdam.

based on the assumption that the image in a parent's mind at the moment of conception or after could leave its imprint on the child.[52] There is evidence from later centuries too of the belief that experience during pregnancy could affect the form of the foetus. In the eighteenth century Sir Hans Sloane's collection of anatomical, pathological, and curious human specimens included "a foetus of seven months old resembling a monkey w[h] a cloak which the woman saw playing tricks at Rochester" (Day 1994, 72). Things were not very different in the following century. A short story by Thomas Hardy published in the collection *Life's Little Ironies* (1894) is about a woman who falls so much under the spell of a minor poet that she gives birth to a son whose features resemble those of the poet rather than those of her husband: "the dreamy and peculiar expression of the poet's face sat, as the transmitted idea, upon the child's, and the hair was of the same hue" (Hardy 1979, 330).

SENT ON TO CREWE

The trajectory we have followed has been marked by a good many deviations from the straight line. At times the digression seems to have been the thing itself.[53] The perspective on the *longue durée* opened up the fear that it might be interminable; and the introduction of the concept of *Entfernung* made it seem equally doubtful that the end would ever be in sight. Yet these Sternean loops and swerves have their attractions. In the introduction to part III we noted Grafton's use of the railway metaphor to counter rectilinear and teleological accounts. Let us cite him again: "Paradox, contradiction and confusion hold illimitable dominion over all; we wanted the humanists to give us a ticket for Birmingham but they have sent us on to Crewe. The only consolation is to sit back, relax, and enjoy the leather upholstery and gaslights that made old-fashioned journeys so much more pleasant than modern ones" (1991, 103).

The present ride has been less comfortable. The reader may well have the sensation that, rather than being sent on to Crewe, he or she has been endlessly shunted back and forth in an international goods wagon, with a derailment or two somewhere near Paris. In trying to define the difference between the approaches of two sixteenth-century cosmographers to the monstrous human races, we ended up bringing them closer together and further apart at the same time; and in trying to approach the monstrous human races within the perspective of a much longer *durée*, we ended up losing sight of them altogether as they dissolved within a plurality of different chains and contexts. In other words, each time the attempt to reduce the distance between us and the subject in hand resulted (results) in a further distancing of that subject. The present text, then, is itself marked by the processes it sets out to describe: it *shows* what it is unable to *say*. And the name of the game?—*Entfernung*.

6

THE *LONGUE DURÉE* OF RITUAL PUNISHMENT

A BIZARRE RITUAL

LONG AFTER IT HAD VANISHED A PARTICULARLY HORRIFIC FORM OF capital punishment managed to hold the attention of a scholarly public. It was imposed for the murder of a parent or another close relative. The murderer was put into a leather sack together with four animals—a cock, a dog, a serpent, and a monkey—and thrown into a sea, river, or lake to be drowned.[1] One might expect such a punishment to belong to the realm of fiction or the customs of "primitive" tribes in foreign countries; however, like the burning of witches and other baroque forms of capital punishment, the *poena cullei,* or *Säcken,* as it was called, had its heyday during the fifteenth, sixteenth, and early seventeenth centuries. Between about 1200 and the mid-eighteenth century it was known in various parts of the German-speaking countries and in the Netherlands, France, Spain, and Italy. Furthermore, Roman origins, reaching back at least to late imperial days and possibly even to early Roman times, have been claimed for this punishment.[2]

In spite of its important role in a discussion about forms of capital punishment that spanned most of the nineteenth century and the first half of this century, the *poena cullei* is now forgotten except by a handful of scholars.[3] Yet there are good reasons to resume the debate and to concentrate on this punishment again. In recent years discussion among social historians about various types of punishment has circled around issues of control, repression, discipline, civilization, and state formation, clearly revealing the influence of Michel Foucault and Norbert Elias.[4] The concomitant focus on repressive systems and on long-term changes in types of punishment—which have often been studied as indicators of degrees of civilization or modernization—has to a considerable extent deflected attention from the forms of punishment themselves.[5] The formal aspect was of central importance in the discussions conducted from 1820 to about 1950, which have remained largely unknown outside the German-speaking world of (legal) historians and folklorists.[6] A new look at the nineteenth-century "German" debate might help to broaden the modern discussion and reintroduce these formal aspects.

Another look at old questions seems all the more worthwhile since several of the problems discussed by nineteenth-century German scholars such as Jakob Grimm and Karl von Amira have returned in different guises to become important issues in cultural history and historical anthropology. This is especially true of sacrifice, ritual, and, to use an anachronistic term, the *longue durée* and transmission of cultural forms. Present-day historical research only rarely refers to these German forerunners, however, but it frequently mentions French scholars such as Emile Durkheim, Marcel Mauss, and Louis Gernet or the historians of the Annales school.[7] The turn away from the German research tradition has also entailed a shift away from legal and judicial subjects in the study of ritual to a focus on, for instance, carnival (Le Roy Ladurie 1979; Muir 1981), popular protest and punishment (Davis 1975; Le Goff and Schmitt 1981), or the investiture of medieval kings (Le Goff 1977, 349–420). At the same time a considerable section of legal history has been moving away from general history towards a fundamentally ahistorical approach to law and justice in past times: law and legal categories are (often implicitly) regarded as both unchanging and self-evident. As a result, scholarly interest in the study of legal and judicial ritual from a broader historical perspective has been inconsiderable for several decades.[8]

There are many ways in which the study of crime and criminal justice opens windows on the past (Muir and Ruggiero 1994). Judicial ceremonial offers particularly valuable openings for research on ritual. This is not least because in the legal domain written documentation (whether of the laws and procedures themselves or of evidence, verdicts, and punishments) was always considered important, even when major aspects of judicial procedure were conducted through gesture and speech and when writing itself was uncommon. Public punishment can be understood as one such relatively well-documented judicial ritual, a ceremonial event in which at least four parties participated: the convict, the authorities, the executioner, and the public. Although the history of all forms of public punishment pertains to such issues as the interpretation of ritual and the *longue durée* of cultural forms, the peculiar punishment of *Säcken* bears a special historical and historiographical gravity: it stands at the point of intersection between ideas about criminal justice and religious sacrifice, relations between types of crime and forms of punishment, and attitudes towards "ultimate" crimes (including both the murder of a parent and lese majesty or lese dieu).

Another look at the old debates centering upon the *poena cullei,* or *Säcken,* may also be helpful in making us reconsider some of the current topics in the anthropological study of ritual. In spite of rapprochements between anthropology and history, the synchronic study of ritual predominates in anthropology, where the debate centers mainly on meaning, function, and, if change is discussed at all, the internal or external causes of change.[9] Could rituals be meaningless? Should we throw overboard the reservations voiced in chapter 4 and distinguish between an indigenous (surface) explanation and a hidden (deep) meaning that was perhaps unknown even to the participants? Do rituals serve to emphasize or even create (a sense of) community? Can changes in certain rituals be attributed to deliberate personal intervention or to internal dynamics, or do they reflect long-term social developments? The general lack of historical depth and the concomitant absence of attention to time and change in all but a very few anthropological studies have induced a strong emphasis on the (supposedly) unchanging character of ritual. Even in those studies that concentrate on a period of more than just a few decades there seems to be little debate about what it is that is supposed to show continuity or change—form, meaning, function, or all three?[10]

The *poena cullei* was known for many centuries in diverse societies. In such a case it is useless to start looking for a single meaning or function. Only fragments of a few "indigenous" interpretations can still be traced, which severely restricts any modern attempt at reconstructing its various meanings in the past. As we shall see, this very scarcity of evidence has invited much speculation. Insofar as function is concerned, we do not gain much by applying various anthropological interpretations of ritual to the *poena cullei:* should we interpret it as a *rite de passage* or as a ritual conducive to either "communitas" or the demarcation of social boundaries; was the victim a scapegoat?[11] All of these interpretations could be true alternately or even at the same time, but as much could be said of any form of capital punishment: none of them tells us much about this specific punishment. Besides, we simply do not have the evidence to either prove or disprove such hypotheses. Apart from a small number of extremely brief descriptions of actual verdicts, the whole body of our evidence comprises some legal decrees, a number of juridical treatises, and only a handful of contemporary interpretations.

This evidence does, however, include some fairly detailed information about the long-term morphology of this ritual. We shall therefore concentrate on the tangible, external aspect of form. We shall go back in time, not in order to trace "the origins" of the *poena cullei,* but to see whether formal aspects can throw light upon continuity and change in a particular ritual over a period of almost two thousand years.[12] By a careful examination of its formal aspects and of the fragmentary evidence on its contemporary interpretations, we shall try to establish whether its *longue durée* should be sought in its form, its meaning, or elsewhere.

Because the *poena cullei* must of necessity be studied through the writings of scholars from the nineteenth and early twentieth century who were involved in debates having a strong ideological component, we cannot trace its history without at the same time considering its historiography. Among the central issues in these debates were two closely related questions: (1) whether the origins of punishment and criminal justice in the parts of Europe where (High and Low) German was spoken and in Scandinavia were "indigenous" (Germanic) or "foreign" (Roman);[13] and (2) whether the various forms of death penalty current in Germanic and early modern German history should be understood as forms of criminal punishment or as remnants of ritual sacrifice. The former question should be understood as part of a larger debate in the world of German legal history that revolved around the conflicting claims of "Romanists" and "Germanists" regarding the history of criminal justice and punishment in Germany. Obviously, in this quest for origins the issue of German identity was not far off.[14]

The latter problem touched upon the central tenets of evolutionary historical doctrine. At the same time as, for instance, Durkheim in France, these German historians were trying to clarify patterns in the evolution of societies. It was no coincidence that on the first page of his *Die germanischen Todesstrafen* (1922), which has become a much disputed classic in this field, Karl von Amira quoted Theodor Mommsen: "The progress from private defense and vengeance to collective protection and punishment by the state is the history of mankind" (Von Amira 1922, 1). It was generally assumed that all societies progressed from private forms of vengeance or feuding to public (i.e., state-regulated) forms of criminal justice and punishment.[15] In the prestate phase particularly heinous offenses and crimes that affected the common good or the gods were not subject to private vengeance. In such cases ritual sacrifice in public of the person who had committed such a monstrous act was required.

In itself the classification of societies according to their ways of dealing with crime and public order might make sense, depending on the type of questions to be dealt with. However, their arrangement in a progressive series caused enormous problems, especially in combination with the assumption that public punishment must be linked to a state in order to be regarded as legal and real. What was one to think of the public punishments imposed by the Germanic tribes claimed as ancestors by these scholars? If they were tribes, they could not be states and their punishments could not be genuine punishments. Dozens of scholarly treatises tried to determine whether the early Germanic punishments described by Tacitus and the late Germanic punishments reported in the famous *Sachsenspiegel* and the so-called *Landrechten* (compilations of legal regulations) of other German-speaking territories could perhaps be sacrificial acts. Should the miscreant therefore be envisaged as an offering and not as a criminal? In other words, were these killings acts of punishment within a rational, state-organized system of criminal justice or sacrificial manifestations in stateless societies characterized by prerational, prelogical, or even irrational thought?[16]

Put this way, the problem may sound dated and slightly ludicrous. Nevertheless, very similar evolutionary assumptions continue to play a considerable part in postwar publications on criminal justice and public punishment.[17] As Yan Thomas put it,

> From private to public, from family to city, that is the primary axis of an exploration in which jurists in particular, but not only they, operate using categories that, because they are absolute, can only be articulated in sequence. This model has remained remarkably stable in the historiography of punishment since the beginning of this century. . . . In the Roman field, apart from a few exceptions, the history of punishment tends either to reconstitute the rise of the penal function, albeit by means of the very modalities of punishment themselves, or to demonstrate the various purposes punishment successively assumed as an isolate whose position changed in history. (Thomas 1984, 5–6)[18]

THE GERMANS DID IT

Even if the German scholars exploring the history of capital punishment were as interested in the discovery of their own cultural roots as in the origins of forms of punishment, they nonetheless attempted to document and establish the historical continuity of various ritual forms. What did this continuity look like in the case of the *poena cullei?*

Bukowska Gorgoni's (1979) survey of the history of the *poena cullei* as a legal notion—which, as we shall see, is by no means the same as a judicial practice—shows that it originated as a Roman capital punishment that could be imposed for the murder of a close relative (generally a parent) or for high treason, lese majesty, and its religious counterpart, lese dieu. In the most comprehensive form of the Roman ritual the *parricida* was transported to the place of execution on a cart drawn by black oxen and flogged with special rods, the *virgae sanguineae*. Then the miscreant's head was covered with a cap made of wolf's skin (the *folliculus lupinus*) and wooden soles were tied to his or her feet. The *parricida* was then put into a leather sack together with four live animals—a cock, a dog, a serpent, and a monkey—and drowned. The *poena cullei* eventually disappeared along with many other Roman legal notions, customs, and institutions. It made its reappearance in learned legal treatises in the course of the twelfth century and figured in the *Landrechten* of several German territories north of the Alps and in Spanish (and Neapolitan) law during the late fifteenth and sixteenth centuries. In its revived form the punishment no longer included the flogging with special rods, the ritual procession with the cart drawn by black oxen, the wooden soles, or the cap of wolf's skin. Only the drowning in the leather sack together with the four animals remained. Changes were not restricted to its formal appearance: "During this reincarnation the use, purpose, and execution of the poena cullei changed" (Bukowska Gorgoni 1979, 145). If this is true, are we still talking about one and the same phenomenon?

If we continue to draw on the excellent survey by Bukowska Gorgoni and take a closer look at the manifestations of the *poena cullei* as a legal notion in the areas to the north and west of the Alps, we find that the punishment made its comeback during the twelfth century. It appears in the commentaries of jurists glossing the *Codex Justiniani,* the *Digesta,* and other sixth-century compilations of Roman law. From the twelfth century to about 1750 the *poena cullei* surfaces now and then in the growing number of learned juridical treatises explaining "received" Roman law and glossing previous commentaries and glosses.[19] This new lease on life of the *poena cullei* proved to be tenuous. For one thing, jurists did not agree about its use. Did the punishment apply only to parricides or also to persons who had committed high treason? How exactly should *parricide* be defined? Could it include infanticide as well as the murder of a parent, and to which degrees of kinship did the concept of parricide extend? Could the murderer of a stepparent be called a parricide and be "sacked"? Moreover, almost from the moment the *poena cullei* reemerged in juridical treatises during the twelfth century jurists began to declare that it had been abolished in practice and was no longer applied; parricides, whatever the exact meaning of the term, were punished in different ways.[20] To say that it was no longer applied was, of course, an understatement, for there was no indication that it had ever been applied since Roman times.

Considering its feeble claims to existence at the time of its reemergence in the twelfth century, it is astonishing that the *poena cullei* managed to continue in use for another six hundred years. Few things might seem less consequential than the treatises of jurists who piled comment upon comment discussing an ephemeral punishment that might or might not be imposed for an indeterminate range of extremely serious crimes. All the same, their writings contributed to its eventual (re)instatement in judicial practice. From the twelfth century to the mid-fourteenth century the *poena cullei* figured only in these treatises, remaining a "paper" punishment, but in 1335 a gloss by the Bologna-trained jurist Johann von Buch on the extremely influential *Sachsenspiegel* (ca. 1230) helped to propel the *poena cullei* into actual criminal law: "Those who murder their parents should first be dragged, and then sewn in a skin together with a dog and with a monkey and with a serpent and with a cock" (Grimm [1828] 1899, 2:279).[21] Although jurists continued to emphasize that it was "no longer" applied, the *poena cullei* subsequently found a place in the *Landrechten* of various German territories.[22]

The *Säcken* was not included in the great codification by Charles V, the *Constitutio Criminalis Carolina* of 1532, but it does figure in the southern German *Schwabenspiegel* and in the ordinances of Württemberg, Magdeburg, and Dresden.[23] First and foremost, however, it is documented in Saxony, where it was formally introduced by statutes issued in 1572 by Duke August, who followed the example of a Leipzig tribunal that strongly stimulated the propagation of Roman law (Bukowska Gorgoni 1979, 154–55). The fact that the *poena cullei* appears in various German ordinances does not necessarily mean that it was applied in practice, however. Its description in the influential sixteenth-century *Practijcke ende hant-boeck in criminele saacken* by Joos(t) de Damhouder van Brugge (1507–81), of which an illustrated edition was published in 1555, is illuminating in this respect:

> And these [i.e., parricides] as well as their accomplices are terribly punished *according to the law,* for they are flogged with rods and afterwards sewn in the hide of a cow or in some other piece of

leather or skin together with four live animals, that is, a dog, a capon
or cock, a monkey, and a small snake called vipera, and thus thrown
into the sea or the river, or otherwise they are thrown to the dogs,
lions, bears, wolves, and other ferocious and hungry animals to
be torn to pieces and devoured. But *according to custom* parricides
are dragged to the scaffold, decapitated, whereupon their bodies
are exposed on the wheel and their possessions confiscated. (Damhouder [1555] 1616, 109–11, emphasis added)

Damhouder (and his predecessor Philips Wielant) distinguish clearly between punishment prescribed by (Roman) law and punishment according
to custom.[24] It is hardly surprising to find that at a time when large parts of
northwestern Europe were only slowly adapting to a combination of customary and Roman law judges often preferred to follow custom. Nor should
we forget that in many parts of Europe the *poena cullei* had never been (re)in-
troduced at all.[25] The presence of the *poena cullei* in legal ordinances should
not lead us to assume that it was actually imposed, let alone carried out, but
only that it *could* be imposed, depending on the judges' wishes and on practical circumstances. After all, monkeys were rare and expensive, and not
every town had a nearby river, lake, or sea.

A survey of the relevant literature indicates that the *poena cullei* was even
more of a phantom punishment than we have suggested. Examples from judicial practice are extremely rare, and most authors quote the same handful of cases over and over again. In 1576 a man was condemned by the court
of Kassel to be put in a leather sack together with a dog, a cock, a monkey,
and a snake for the murder of his mother; the punishment was not carried
out, however, because he was mentally deficient (Berkenhoff 1937, 111–14;
Grimm [1828] 1899, 2:279). Another instance can be found in Brandenburg:
in May 1594 a woman named Else Koch was actually drowned in a sack together with a snake, a dog, a cock, and a *cat,* but the court allowed her body
to be recovered from the water and buried (Berkenhoff 1937, 111–14; Fischer
1936, 22). Three more examples pertain to an even later period. In 1697 a
German executioner was paid to have images made of a dog, a cat, a cock,
and a snake, which apparently were destined to accompany a convict in the
sack.[26] In 1715 someone was "sacked" in Dresden accompanied by a dog, a
cat, a cock, and a painting or drawing of a snake. Several authors mention
as a last example the punishment of a woman for infanticide in Saxony in
1734: she was drowned in a sack together with a dog, cat, and snake (Berken-

hoff 1937, 111–14; Grimm [1828] 1899, 2:279–80; Von Hentig [1932] 1954–55, 1:304–5).

To this handful of examples we may add those described by Benedictus Carpzovius, the learned jurist and counselor of the Elector of Saxony, in his *Practica nova imperialis saxonica rerum criminalium*, which first appeared in 1625. He not only states that Saxon law allowed the replacement of the expensive monkey by a cat but also mentions examples from 1571, 1583, 1588, 1592, 1598, 1602, 1614, and 1617 in which the *poena cullei* was imposed (though not always carried out) by courts in Saxony.[27] Jacobus Doeplerus mentions two more cases in his *Theatrum poenarum* (1693–97, 2:291–92): one from 1583, in which a Leipzig court condemned a woman for triple infanticide to *Säcken* with a dog, a cock, a snake, and a cat but had to resort to breaking on the wheel because of the lack of a suitable river or lake; and another from 1624, in which the court at Magdeburg condemned to *Säcken* a man who had murdered his first wife and his children.[28]

Even if another dozen or so examples were eventually to turn up, the result remains meager: this famous punishment, decreed for the most horrible crimes imaginable, was imposed and carried out so rarely in these parts of Europe that it might have escaped notice completely if not for its extensive discussion by jurists. It is also striking that none of the known cases in which it was imposed dates from before the late sixteenth century.[29] Clearly a mere reappearance in legal treatises from the twelfth century onwards by itself had not been enough to trigger its introduction in judicial practice. Even its ensuing insertion in various German ordinances had not been immediately followed by its application. The time-lag between ordinance and application varied considerably from one German region to another.[30]

The implications are significant. First, the history of the *poena cullei* so far has turned out to be very much an affair of the elite, or more precisely, of that small part of the European elite trained in Roman law. Neither its form nor its brutal character can therefore be linked to popular custom. This finding was certainly contrary to the hopes and expectations of the German scholars who studied the punishment during the late nineteenth and early twentieth centuries. The "Germanists," after all, were tracing the history of various forms of capital punishment partly in order to find their roots in indigenous (non-Roman), popular (in the sense of *völkisch*) Germanic origins. Grimm's disappointment is evident when he declares, "But the whole punishment looks virtually un-German" ([1828] 1899, 2:279).[31] The elite background of the *poena cullei* also contradicts the implicit link between "ritual" and "popular" in many modern historical and anthropological studies. This particular punishment belonged completely to learned tradition.

Second, anyone searching for an explanation of why the *poena cullei* was mainly imposed during the late sixteenth and early seventeenth centuries even though it had been known since at least the twelfth century should not turn to its legal chronology for an answer. This is not the place to go into the complex history of public punishment in Europe. All the same, it can hardly be a coincidence that the heyday of the *poena cullei* coincided with a phase of more general intensification and aggravation of public punishment, as exemplified by the burning of witches, heretics, and Jews. This phase saw not only the unfolding of various painful and baroque forms of punishment but also a growing concern (at least on the part of the authorities) with sexual and religious transgressions and an increasing prominence of torture as a means to obtain proof. In a legal context these developments have been discussed as the consequences of the transition from accusatorial to inquisitorial procedure in continental Europe. In historical terms, they have been linked mainly with the formation of nation-states and in particular with the growth of state bureaucracies. Whatever perspective is adopted on these long-term changes, it seems obvious that any attempt at an explanation of the "revival" of the *poena cullei* in practice should also address the larger issue of the changes in the organization and forms of criminal justice during the early modern period.[32]

Finally, if the main link between the *Säcken* of late medieval and early modern times and its Roman forerunner was not its continued practice but merely its continued existence as a learned tradition in a mainly juridical written discourse, there is no need to go into the difficult question of the perception and interpretation of the ritual by the public at large. What we do need to ask, however, is what the jurists thought they were continuing. From the writings of Carpzovius and Doeplerus, as well as from the survey of late medieval and early modern juridical authors by Bukowska Gorgoni (1979), it is clear that they regarded themselves as following directly in the footsteps of their Roman predecessors. This is exactly what we should expect them to say. In an age when antiquity meant respectability and old did not mean passé, scholars generally did their best to emphasize the directness of their connections with the past. As has been stated in a very different context, "one should be cautious in taking the humanists at face value by believing the justifications put out under the guise of antique culture by these professional propagandists" (Muir 1993, 71).[33]

It is one thing to recognize these references to tradition and antiquity; it is something else to accept implicitly what these scholars wanted to believe or state about themselves. To point to the "reception of Roman Law" as the explanation for the (re)appearance of any legal form in late medieval Europe does just that. It takes origins for explanations (cf. Bloch [1949] 1953, 29–35). It neither does justice to the vital differences between Roman and early modern criminal justice nor acknowledges why so many Roman legal rituals were not "rediscovered" or why parts of Roman law were "received" precisely at this time and in precisely these areas. More specifically, it does not make clear why it was the *poena cullei* that was selected for reintroduction and not, for instance, crucifixion, which was, after all, a far better known Roman punishment. If only to preclude further attempts to explain such etiologies, it might be useful to abolish the hackneyed phrase *reception of Roman law.* Instead of a passive reception or an indiscriminate rediscovery, a far more active process of selection, omission, appropriation, or iteration was going on at the time, as in many other fields in which knowledge was transmitted.[34]

THE ROMANS HAD A WORD FOR IT

If only because of the interval of at least six centuries, the directness of a connection with classical Roman law should not be taken literally. In fact the twelfth-century jurists might not even have noticed the classical *poena cullei* if it had not been publicized and promoted after Roman times by the Visigothic *Breviarium Alarici,* by the writings of the famous bishop Isidore of Seville, and by a Carolingian legal source in which the *culleus parricidialis* is described in connection with Jews who had committed crimes against Christian law (Bukowska Gorgoni 1979, 149–50; cf. Grimm [1828] 1899, 2:280). Nor should the idea of a reintroduction, which presupposes an interval and a resumption of continuity, be taken at face value. As we have already seen, the form of the ritual fluctuated in western Europe. By no means did it correspond exactly to the most comprehensive Roman version. German jurists freely borrowed and combined elements of what they obviously regarded as a Roman punishment. But how much of a Roman punishment was it?

Information is easier to find than might be expected considering the outlandish character of the *poena cullei.* During the late nineteenth and early twentieth century it came to be regarded as one of the "most interesting problems of Roman criminal law" (Düll 1935, 363). Brunnenmeister devoted a monograph to *Das Tötungsverbrechen im altrömischen Recht* (1887) in which *parricidium* and the *poena cullei* are of vital importance. In Mommsen's famous *Römisches Strafrecht* (1899) a lengthy paragraph deals with the *poena*. Düll discussed its meaning in a treatise nearly fifty pages long (1935), and in a 1984 volume on punishment in Roman and Greek antiquity the *poena cullei* and the interpretation of *parricidas* once more occupy a prominent place.[35]

The main reason for this prominence is etymological. Nineteenth-century philological research showed that the term *parricidium* did not derive from its supposed ancestor, *patricidium*. *Parricidas* thus did not originally mean the murderer of a parent, a child, or another close relative but in all likelihood referred to any murderer of a free Roman.[36] In this way the *poena cullei* suddenly became linked to an offense of far more general importance, and its history was presumed to be of use in tracing the various stages in the development of Roman thought about murder. That topic in turn was regarded as crucial to the study of Roman ideas about criminal procedure and forms of punishment in general and to the study of the links between offenses and punishment in Roman society.[37] From an extraordinary ritual the *poena cullei* had turned into a key issue.

Etymological problems concerning the meaning of *parricidas* are hardly the only complication in the study of the *poena cullei*. Even to establish a basic chronology for the Roman period poses serious problems. Most of the following five scholars take it to be one of the oldest punishments known in Roman history, but they disagree on almost every other point. Grimm ([1828] 1899, 2:279) quotes a passage from the Law of the Twelve Tables (ca. 450 B.C.): "Who kills a parent, let his face be covered and let him be sewn into a sack and submerged in running water." Düll (1935, 365) traces the punishment back to the era of the kings of Rome and connects it both with the murder of a parent and with crimes against state and religion, whereas Bukowska Gorgoni (1979, 146) merely states that it was believed to have its origins in pre-Republican times. It may have been applied for the first time during the reign of the last king, Tarquinius Superbus: the *duumvir* Marcus Atilius was apparently drowned in a sack for treason, though no animals were involved (Valerius Maximus 1.1.13). Mommsen (1899, 922) suggests that the *poena cullei* was originally connected with the murder of any free person and only later became specifically linked to the murder of a close relative. Magdelain (1984, 548–50), in contrast, follows Brunnenmeister (1887, 186–89) in claiming that the *poena cullei* was never imposed for any other crime than the murder of a parent. He argues that the *poena cullei* was probably first laid down in some sacerdotal text but eventually became a real law during the late Republic. In this controversy much, if not all, depends on the way the various authors define the punishment. They all agree, however, that at first the *poena cullei*—for whatever offense it was imposed—consisted simply in drowning in a sack *without* any animals or any of the other ritual elements mentioned above.

Disagreement diminishes only momentarily with respect to the further chronology of the *poena cullei*. It is undisputed that during the Gracchian troubles (ca. 133 B.C.) a certain Gaius Villius was condemned for *perduellio*, or lese majesty, and was to be drowned in a sack together with some serpents (Bukowska Gorgoni 1979, 146; Düll 1935, 367). After the second Punic War some form of the *poena cullei* was applied to Lucius Hostius, who had murdered his father; and in 101 B.C. Publicius Malleolus was punished in a similar way for the murder of his mother (Bukowska Gorgoni 1979, 146). New problems crop up with regard to the Sullan *Lex Cornelia de sicariis et veneficiis* (ca. 80 B.C.) and the subsequent *Lex Pompeia* (ca. 55 B.C.) because of three apparently contradictory remarks in the great juridical compilations of Justinian's time—that is, of almost 600 years later—which form our principal source for classical Roman law.

The *Institutiones*, which dates from 533, is a legal textbook largely based on the writings of the jurist Gaius, who lived around the middle of the second century A.D. It states (4.18.6) that the *Lex Pompeia* introduced a new punishment that consisted in drowning in a leather sack together with a dog, a cock, a monkey, and a snake.[38] In the *Digesta* (48.9.1), however, a collection of statements and interpretations by classical jurists that also dates from 533 and includes some of their sources, the third-century jurist Marcian declares that this same *Lex Pompeia* extended the punishments prescribed by the preceding *Lex Cornelia* to parricides.[39] Some interpret this as a confirmation of the longstanding use of the *poena cullei* in cases of parricide. Mommsen disagrees. According to him, the *Lex Cornelia* dictated only one regular punishment—deportation—for all sorts of offenses; if the *Lex Pompeia* extended the prescribed punishment of the *Lex Cornelia* to parricide, it therefore effectively abolished the death penalty for this crime.[40] Levy (1963, 343) also disagrees but argues that the *Lex Pompeia* merely expanded the already considerable discretionary powers of Roman magistrates (who directed the execution of punishments) but did not abolish the *poena cullei*. Finally, another statement in the same *Digesta* (48.9.9) causes further complications. The third-century jurist Modestin refers to the four animals as well as the *virgae sanguineae*, adding, however, that according to Hadrian's instructions the malefactor might be thrown to the wild beasts if there was no water nearby. According to Modestin, the *poena cullei* originated in the so-called *mos maiorum*. In other words, it was a punishment belonging to ancient, undated custom rather than to law. Since it seems that no new evidence has been forthcoming that might support one or another of these interpretations, recent literature leaves open the question whether the *Lex Pompeia* merely perpetuated the *poena cullei* for parricide (while possibly presenting a new list of the relevant degrees of kinship), reintroduced it after it had been abolished, or abolished it.

The *poena cullei* certainly seems to have figured in Roman criminal justice by the first century B.C. It was mentioned by Seneca the Elder (who refers to a snake) and by Cicero. The latter's famous oration *Pro Sexto Roscio Amerino* (80 B.C.) is one of the most influential Roman sources for the crime of parricide and the *poena cullei*.[41] In this speech Cicero defended Sextus Roscius, who had been accused of having his father murdered, during a political trial. Cicero discusses the *poena cullei* at some length both in this speech (25–26/71–72) and in his *De Inventione* (2.50.149) but makes no mention of any animals. Even more significantly, he refers in a letter to his brother Quintus (*QFr.* 1.2.5) to the actual execution by means of the *poena cullei* ("insuisses in culleum") of two Mysians in Smyrna on the orders of this same brother. The subsequent history of the punishment is not particularly clear. According to Mommsen and those who follow him, it was formally reintroduced during Augustus's reign,[42] but still no mention is made of the four animals. For the first few centuries A.D. the evidence increases: several authors, such as Suetonius, Seneca the Younger, Quintilian, and Juvenal, mention the *poena cullei* and occasionally refer to the wooden soles and the cap of wolf's skin.

Only by Hadrian's time (76–138 A.D.) was the ritual known in its most elaborate form, that is, including all four animals, the wooden soles, the cart and black oxen, the flogging with the *virgae sanguineae*, and the cap of wolf's skin. Even during this period, however, the punishment was by no means always applied in cases of parricide—a parricide might also be thrown to the wild animals—while the *poena* may also have been imposed for crimes against the state or religion.[43] After Hadrian the *poena cullei* disappeared from sight once more, to be "revived" during the reign of Constantine (306–37). All of the animals except the snakes had vanished again by then, and the punishment was restricted to the murder of close relatives and perhaps to some cases of infidelity.[44]

If something can be gathered from this complicated and perplexing history, it is that the *poena cullei* seems to have been forgotten as many times as it was (re)introduced during Roman times. Its application was uncertain, and it may have been carried out only in some extremely rare cases. In its simplest form of drowning in a sack the *poena cullei* was undoubtedly a very old Roman punishment, but the use of none of the animals can be traced back earlier than the era of the Gracchi (ca. 133 B.C.). The snake was clearly first, as it should be; the monkey came second.[45] The dog and the cock only materialized after Hadrian's time, during the early third century A.D.[46] The whole series of four in the order snake-dog-cock-monkey only occurs in the compilations of the sixth century.[47] Nor do we hear of any of the other ritual elements before the first century B.C. Cicero mentions the wooden soles and the wolf's cap. The flogging with the *virgae sanguineae* occurs for the first time in the *Digesta* (which tells us nothing about its age), and the cart and black oxen are not found before the third century A.D. (Düll 1935, 369–70).

What sort of historical continuity is this? If we survey the whole diachronic series, the standing of this punishment appears to have suffered some severe damage. In both Roman and early modern times the gaps are enormous, the evidence is scarce, and the number of times the punishment was actually carried out must have been extremely small indeed. Even based on the most optimistic view of its history we are left with gaps of more than three or four centuries. In the worst case we might well doubt whether the *poena cullei* has any history at all except during Justinian's reign (sixth century) and in late sixteenth-century Saxony. If we concentrate instead on the history of *the idea* of this punishment, the gaps still remain, but some striking parallels emerge between Roman times and the period from the twelfth to the early eighteenth century. In both societies the punishment was repeatedly forgotten or declared abolished and subsequently revived by legal specialists. In the Roman case as in the German we are dealing with a learned tradition that existed mainly on paper, not with a popular ritual. And in both societies legal specialists tended to locate the origins of the punishment in an almost forgotten past: the *Lex Pompeia*, the times of the last Etruscan kings, or even age-old *mos maiorum* according to the jurists of Justinian's time; Roman antiquity according to late medieval and early modern German jurists.

All of these characteristics together indicate not the longevity of ritual tradition but a similar interest in tradition, a similar appreciation of antiquity as a source of validity and authority, and consequently similar ways of inventing tradition. "Invented tradition" has been defined by Eric Hobsbawm as "a set of practices, normally governed by overtly or tacitly accepted rules and of a ritual or symbolic nature, which seek to inculcate certain values and norms of behavior by repetition, which automatically implies continuity with the past" (1983, 1). What we have found looks more like the *longue durée* of the (re)invention of tradition than the historical continuity of a particular ritual punishment.[48]

VARIABLE MEANINGS

Several Roman texts proclaim that the murder of a parent is an act against nature that deserves exceptional punishment. Cicero, for instance, calls the parricide a *prodigium,* a *portentum,* and a *monstrum* (*Rosc. Am.* 25–26).[49] He stresses the atrocious character of the offense, which takes away the life of the person who had given life to the perpetrator, and says that thereby the culprit placed himself beyond the boundaries of the community of all living beings, including the wild animals (22/63; 23/64). Cicero goes on to declare that the early Romans had rightly devised an exceptional punishment for such an outrageous offense. The convict's body was denied the sky, the sun, water, and earth for ever. A person who had murdered someone to whom he owed his existence was thus denied access to those elements that formed the basis of natural life on earth.[50] Similar references to the act of isolating and removing a perverse, unnatural phenomenon, a monster, from any further contact with the elements can be found in the above-mentioned text in the *Institutiones:* "Or let him be cast into the nearby sea or river so that he may begin to lack all use of the elements while still alive and may be denied the sky while alive and the earth when dead" (4.18.6).[51]

The Roman stress on the expulsion of a malignant being—on the removal of a polluting element from human society (including both the living and the respectable dead)[52]—left its traces in several early modern descriptions of the *poena.* Stepping briefly outside the legal domain, we find, for instance, an account of the punishment by the sixteenth-century French cosmographer André Thevet. As pointed out by the modern authority on Thevet, Frank Lestringant, Thevet's *Cosmographie de Levant* (1554) is not simply a travel journal. The author's own observations during a journey to the Near East are interpolated with remarks, stories, and reports concerning the history and customs of the areas he visited, which he had borrowed from compilations of earlier writers.[53] Thevet's account of the *poena cullei* adds a Christian God, but the rest of his description clearly echoes Roman sources. The emphasis is on depriving the culprit of all elements, and it is stated that the miscreant could not be thrown to the wild animals because the animals might be degraded and made more cruel by eating his flesh: "The Romans sewed parricides into a leather sack, and with them a dog, a cock, and a serpent, so that they would be deprived of all elements, the use of which they were not worthy of, since they had violated the image of God, that is, he who has created us. The body of a parricide was not thrown to the wild animals, so that they would not become more cruel after having eaten or touched such a great and prodigious evil-doer" (Thevet [1554] 1985, 122).

Seventeenth-century juridical treatises likewise refer to the expulsion of a monstrous, unnatural phenomenon but pay far more attention to the four animals. Doeplerus, for instance, devotes only a few lines to Cicero's remarks on isolating the culprit and concludes that the sack served to prevent the water from being polluted by the miscreant's body.[54] He soon goes on to an explanation of the presence of the animals: "There are grave reasons why these four animals are put into the sack. The dog because it is blind for nine days after it is born and does not see or recognize its parents; just as a parricide has proved by his evil act that he does not recognize or honor either his father or his mother. Or because the dog is a nasty, unclean, shameful, and snappy creature, just like the parricide. . . . Or that the hungry dog will attack, bite, and perhaps even eat such a parricide in the sack" (Doeplerus 1693–97, 2:279). About the cock he declares: "The cock because it is a proud animal, which does not suffer its own father in its vicinity, but bites him and chases him away, yes even kills him, just as this parricide had done. Or perhaps because the cock and the snake have a great enmity for each other and would fight in the sack" (280). Doeplerus then remarks that according to some scholars, the cock would not let the sinner sleep in his sack but kept him awake by his crowing. From under water it thus warned passing ships that something extraordinary was to be found there, though Doeplerus finds the latter opinion rather far-fetched: "The cock would not crow much under such conditions" (280).

As pointed out above, Doeplerus's *Theatrum poenarum* was a compilation of legal regulations as well as of interpretations. It is not surprising, then, to see that large sections of Doeplerus's explanation of the animals paraphrase Carpzovius's interpretations from the early seventeenth century, which in their turn combined various older views: "The dog no doubt to indicate the criminal and impure man who kills a parent; or to show infidelity, because the dog is the most faithful animal to man; or because the dog is aroused by raving hunger and feeds on the body and corpse of the parricide." Carpzovius also mentions the cock's crowing under the water: "The cock because it is belligerent and hostile to the serpent which is sewn inside [the sack] with it; or because the wakeful cock with his crowing prevents the parricide from alleviating his torture by sleep; or because passing vessels hearing its crowing from within are invited to reflect on the awful punishment of the criminal parricide" (Carpzovius [1625] 1652, 1.8.9). It is impossible to regard Doeplerus's or Carpzovius's explanations concerning the four animals as uncomplicated examples of "indigenous" seventeenth-century thinking about animal symbolism and ritual punishment. They echo, reflect, and reiterate earlier views and beliefs, which may incorporate older popular as well as learned ideas about animals, death, punishment, and the hereafter.

The examples of interpretation presented here are fragments from a period of almost two thousand years that can neither be regarded as representative of contemporary opinion (for lack of further evidence), be welded together into a consistent whole, or fixed in a progressive sequence.[55] Although each piece of interpretation belongs to a larger treatise—Cicero's, Thevet's, Doeplerus's—none of these authors offers any more comprehensive interpretation. There appears to be a qualitative difference, however, between the Roman fragments, on the one hand, and the late medieval and early modern ones, on the other. The Roman references leave the impression that the *poena cullei* was regarded at the time as a conceivable, perhaps veritable, though archaic ritual. They do not demonstrate that the ritual had one generally accepted meaning within the Roman era, which in any case seems unlikely. By 1200 the situation had changed. For the jurists of the twelfth to the fourteenth century who mention the *poena,* it was already an antiquated punishment that was "no longer" applied. By the early modern period the punishment had turned into a collector's item. It figured as a curiosity in larger seventeenth-century collections of intriguing forms of punishment, outlandish customs, and their various interpretations.[56] Because it was Roman it was (still) respectable, but as for its meaning, one (learned) person's speculation was as good as another's.

The opacity of the *poena cullei* invited not only the speculative interpretations collected and proposed by Doeplerus and Carpzovius. As we have seen, the curious form of the punishment began to present even more of a challenge as soon as modern scholars came to regard the *poena* as a clue to ways of thinking about questions they regarded as crucial: relations between offense and punishment in Roman history; the indigenous or foreign roots of certain forms of punishment; and possibly even the development of whole societies from prerational to rational stages, from sacrifice to punishment. It was a modern, philological discovery—disconnecting the *poena* from parricide and linking it to murder in general—that helped to give this punishment one more lease on life. Even now, however, "old" interpretations continued to structure this modern debate about its form and meaning.

Whereas the emphasis in the Roman texts had been on isolation—on the removal of a monstrous and polluting creature—the early modern jurists paid more attention to the four animals. Carpzovius and Doeplerus tried to explain the choice of these particular animals by pointing to the similarities between the animals' nature and that of the parricide. In other words, the animals resembled and represented the miscreant.[57] By way of further explanation, the seventeenth-century jurists referred to the aggravating effects of putting these venomous and aggressive animals into the sack: their presence added to the severity of the punishment. The two, complementary explanations proposed by the early modern jurists contain in a nutshell the principal themes underlying the controversies in nineteenth- and twentieth-century scholarly interpretation of this punishment.

"Modern" scholarly debate translated the two forms of interpretation into the twin themes of the symbolic/magical and the functional/rational role of the animals: the animals either accompanied the parricide as symbolic representations of his nature or they served as a pragmatic means to aggravate the punishment. What is more, in an age when development and evolution were key terms in scholarly discourse, these two roles were gradually split into successive stages and linked with the (presumed) development from sacrifice to punishment.[58] The "Germanist" branch of legal history in particular showed a tendency to search for a shift from a magical act, with a predominantly symbolic role for the animals, to a rational punishment, in which the role of the animals was largely functional. This approach is epitomized by Karl von Amira's extremely influential *Die germanischen Todesstrafen* (1922), in which he characterizes all forms of capital punishment as sacrificial in origin.

Compared with the speculations of some of Von Amira's successors, Doeplerus's story about the cock crowing under the water looks decidedly orthodox. In his *Tierstrafe, Tierbannung und rechtsrituelle Tiertötung im Mittelalter* (1937) Berkenhoff quotes "the charming ideas" of Doeplerus and goes on to suggest that the *poena cullei* might have originated as a form of burial that then turned into a punishment. The animals might originally have been meant as the servants of the expelled person in the realm of the dead.[59] In several respects Berkenhoff came close to Fischer, who suggests that the animals might be negative burial gifts ("negative Grabbeigaben"), which would torment and persecute the sacked person after his death. Fischer designates the *poena* during its later development as a postmortal defamatory ritual and tends to follow Von Hentig in his opinion that it served to expel the parricide from human society and include him among the wild animals (Fischer 1936, 23–24).[60] Von Hentig himself had been only slightly more cautious in *Die Strafe* (1932), where he repeats the description of the *poena* as a *procuratio prodigii*, the ritual disposal of an inauspicious phenomenon, in Roman times and suggests that the drowning itself may have originated as a human sacrifice to the water gods (Von Hentig [1932] 1954–55, 1:297–98, 304–6).[61] None of these legal historians paid any particular attention to an earlier essay by Storfer (1911), in which he analyzed the crime of parricide and its punishment in various societies from a psychological (Freudian) as well as a legal historical perspective. Drawing on Bachofen's publications on "das Mutterrecht," he pointed out the link between the murder of a father and incest with the mother, emphasized the sexual symbolism of all four animals, and suggested that the drowning in a sack should be interpreted as a way of preventing the murderer of a father from uniting with mother earth (26–34).

The "Romanists" were far less interested in the search for such a shift from a ritual sacrifice to an "ordinary" punishment. Mommsen (1899, 613–15, 643–46, 911–42) and Levy (1963) did not attempt to interpret the ritual but placed the *poena cullei* in a broader context of changing Roman criminal procedure and capital punishment. Others, such as Brunnenmeister (1887) and Düll (1935), concentrated instead on its connections with religious ritual and its symbolic meaning and development, starting from the notion of the *poena* as a *procuratio prodigii*. Present-day French research continues this tradition of putting the punishment into a broader context rather than placing it in a line of development. Magdelain (1984), for instance, attempts to clarify the complicated etymology of *par(r)icidas* by studying it against the background of Roman legal history, and Briquel (1984) discusses the Roman *poena cullei* in the context of Indo-European ritual forms of punishment and their relations with types of crimes.

Nonetheless, the Roman evidence can be used to test the hypothesis of a shift from ritual sacrifice to rational punishment. After all, from the chronology established above we know that the four animals appeared only very late in Roman history. Therefore, either the stage of "sacrifice"—which is closely linked with the notion of the four animals as symbolic companions of the parricide—must have followed upon that of "punishment" in Roman history, instead of vice versa, or the whole idea of a succession of stages does not make sense in the Roman context. Both cases raise doubts about the value and suitability of similar models for western Europe from the early Middle Ages on. The chronology of the *poena cullei* from about 1200 on reinforces such doubts. After all, the animals did not figure in old Germanic law but only found a place in early modern German criminal law with the introduction of fragments of recovered, (re)invented, and modified Roman law. What is more, this happened not at a time when a larger political unit was disintegrating into tribal segments but during a period of unmistakable centralization and bureaucratic growth. We cannot but infer that the whole theory of a development from sacrifice to punishment is deficient. Under these circumstances a central tenet of the development from tribal (stateless) societies to state societies loses much of its plausibility.[62] And if that is the case with forms of punishment, similar revisions may be needed with respect to other criteria of "modernization" and "development."

"Romanist" research has important implications for the postclassical period in other respects as well. Like the "Germanists," "Romanist" scholars were intrigued by the four animals and offered various, sometimes contradictory interpretations. In what is still the most comprehensive commentary on Cicero's *Pro Sexto Roscio Amerino,* Gustav Landgraf suggests that the dog and the cock may have been symbolic representatives of good fighting the forces of evil, as exemplified by the snake and the monkey: "Since in the enumeration of these animals dog and cock are immediately connected with one another, but on the other hand, if they are lacking, monkey and snake appear in combination (e.g. Iuven. 8. 214), it may be concluded that the former are the symbolic representatives of Good and the latter of Evil, and the combination of these two pairs in a sack represents the struggle between Good and Evil" ([1882–84] 1914, 151). Düll reaches a rather different conclusion in his long essay "Zur Bedeutung der poena cullei im römischen Strafrecht," which may be regarded as the most consistent and detailed effort to trace the symbolic meaning of the animals. In a careful exploration of religious thought, punishment, and animal symbolism he demonstrates the unlikelihood of *any* intrinsic connection in Roman thought between the nature of the animals and the nature of the culprit. Instead, he argues the more plausible association of all four animals with the gods of the underworld to whom the parricide was dispatched (1935, 389–90). If, indeed, no intrinsic connection existed in Roman thought between the animals and the murderer, hardly anything remains of continuity in the domain of meaning or interpretation. The attempts in the seventeenth century to specify the association between the four animals and the parricide are revealed as a strictly early modern approach to the ritual, and their claims to a close connection with their Roman predecessors are invalidated.[63]

What we find in the domain of meaning, then, is layer upon layer of interpretation, reflecting and reiterating each other and making an opaque ritual more and more impenetrable. For all we know, this could be typical of the interpretive history of many other rituals as well. This might make us reluctant to add more layers ourselves, and it certainly should warn us not to look for a single authentic meaning or to equate original with authentic. It also helps to discredit the facile belief that equates formal continuity with continuity of meaning (or, inversely, change of ritual forms with change of meaning). Ritual need be neither unchanging nor meaningless, and it is open to many interpretations, whether by participants, "indigenous" interpreters, or modern scholars. If this makes things more complicated for those who study ritual, that should merely add to its attraction.

In several respects our conclusions on the interpretation of the *poena cullei* are beginning to resemble those on its long-term chronology. Earlier we found that the *longue durée* of the punishment turned into the *longue durée* of the idea of a ritual form and the *longue durée* of inventing tradition. In this section we discover that no continuity of meaning can be established but that the successive patterns in the process of inventing, constructing, or fabricating meaning resemble each other, whether they originated with modern legal historians, classical Roman jurists, sixteenth-century French travel writers, or early modern German jurists. If we look closely, the divisive nineteenth-century debate on sacrifice versus punishment clothed old interpretations in "new" evolutionary theories. That process can be traced right up to the present, to the split along the same lines between "symbolic" and "functionalist" interpretations in anthropology and the problems entailed by what has been called the dual nature of ritual as both statement and action.[64]

SACKING SANS SACK?

In returning to the German debates of the last hundred or more years we have come full circle, but it may seem that we have lost the *poena cullei,* or *Säcken,* somewhere along the way. As a practical punishment its continuity has been shown to be at least problematic during the Roman era and almost nonexistent after Roman times. As an idea—as a cultural form—it belonged both to a category of legal punishments and to a larger body of purifying rituals in classical antiquity. Although the idea of the *poena cullei* continued to be given new leases on life from the later Middle Ages to the seventeenth and eighteenth centuries, even its existence on paper remained precarious. After Roman times the *poena* was largely confined to the studies of legal scholars, judges, and a handful of legislators. Their main interest in discussing it was related not to any intrinsic quality of the punishment but merely to the opportunity it presented to demonstrate their knowledge of Roman legal matters, their closeness to tradition and to classical antiquity, and their expertise in the interpretation of legal curiosities—all of which proclaimed and underscored their respectability and status as professional jurists and the legitimacy of their measures. It seems ironical, to put it mildly, that such high-brow exercises in scholarly proficiency resulted in the introduction of the *poena* in Saxon criminal law and its imposition on a few non-elite convicts. Almost as incongruous was the search by some nineteenth-century German legal historians for indigenous (i.e., non-Roman) popular elements in this punishment.

Incongruities likewise characterize the interpretive history of the *poena cullei*, in which the learned speculations of seventeenth-century legal scholars vie in subtlety and resourcefulness with those of their nineteenth-century counterparts. Nearly every possible interpretation has been suggested for the four animals: servants in the netherworld, symbolic representations of the parricide, representatives of the gods of darkness, negative burial gifts, torturous companions, warning signs to passing ships, and so on. Finally, even the formal continuity of the *poena cullei* turned out to be doubtful. Its appearances ranged from a simple drowning in a sack to a full-fledged ritual performance including the *virgae sanguineae*, a cart drawn by black oxen, a cap of wolf's skin, shoes with wooden soles, and, of course, the four animals. But the monkey might be replaced by a cat, the serpent could disappear together with the oxen and the whipping, and the animals might even be represented by their paper or wooden images.

Do these formal variations actually make a difference? To start raising problems about the presence of a cat or monkey alive or on paper might seem fastidious. It is. Details are crucial in such cases because of their considerable practical as well as theoretical implications. For if even the simplest form of drowning in a sack without any animals might still be called *poena cullei* or *Säcken*, we should perhaps include simple drowning *without* a sack as well. After all, if one cat, dog, serpent, or monkey more or less does not make a difference, should we bother about one sack more or less? That question is all the more important since the punishment of drowning without a sack did in fact exist. It was fairly regularly imposed in several western European countries during the late Middle Ages and the early modern period, and in some regions and ages it even involved a sack, although it was never denoted as *Säcken*.[65] Germanic origins also have been claimed for this "simple" form of drowning. Should we be surprised that some of the "Germanists" tried to connect this punishment with *Säcken* in their attempts to claim indigenous, Germanic origins for the *poena cullei*?[66]

Put in more abstract terms, we may ask whether such considerable formal variety can still be regarded as one and the same phenomenon and described by one term. If not, we have virtually abolished the *poena cullei*. If it can be regarded as such, this means rejecting an essentialist definition that presupposes one or more fixed characteristics. Considering the evidence presented above, it is easy to see that the historical continuity of the *concept* of the *poena cullei* cannot be located in any one aspect of the ritual, not even in the act of drowning or in the crime for which it was imposed, but should be found in the family resemblances linking its diverse manifestations and interpretations over more than two thousand years.

7

IMAGES OF THE BARBARIAN

CONTEMPORARY ANCESTORS

Among the sixteen pictures described in *A Descriptive Catalogue of Pictures, Poetical and Historical Inventions, painted by William Blake in water colors...*, printed in 1809, is a large composition of a battle between Romans and Britons entitled *The Ancient Britons.* Although five of these sixteen pictures, including *The Ancient Britons,* are no longer extant, we know from the catalog description that the human figures were painted in such a way that "the blood is seen to circulate in their limbs," displaying "the flush of health in flesh exposed to the open air, nourished by the spirits of forests and floods in that ancient happy period" (Blake 1966, 580–81). In addition to this source, we know from the testimony of a contemporary, Crabb Robinson, that Blake's ancient Britons were almost crimson and that the observer regarded their color as being very like that of the Indians of North America (Erdman 1954, 40 n. 39). For Blake the conflation of ancient Britons and Amerindians was understandable: just as the former were claimed by opponents of the court of George III as illustrious predecessors in the traditions of resistance to tyranny, so the native peoples of North America were viewed as natural allies in the resistance to empire. But although Blake's political stance certainly facilitated this conflation between rebels of the past and of the present, it did not bring it about. The archaeological course of the present chapter, like that of the two preceding ones, will be to place the instance under discussion within a broader history of representations. We are not concerned here with Blake's direct literary or other sources, in the traditional sense of the word, itself a hotly contested issue, but with what E. P. Thompson refers to as "sources external to Blake—sources which, very often, he may not have been aware of himself" (1993, xxiii). The question addressed in this chapter is thus, Which morphological chains can we identify that concur in William Blake's *Ancient Britons?*

The assumption of a "family resemblance" between the native peoples of the New World and the ancestors of the inhabitants of the Old World was already being made within less than a century of the discovery of the Americas in the work of another English artist, John White. Little is known about the man himself; it is likely that he accompanied Martin Frobisher on his second voyage, and he may well have accompanied Philip Amadas and Arthur Barlowe on their reconnaissance of the North American coast in 1584 (Hulton 1978). Most of the sixty or so drawings that have survived, however, were made during the following year, when he spent around twelve months in Ralegh's Virginia, based on the fort on Roanoke Island.[1] Collaborating with the mathematician and astronomer of the expedition, Thomas Harriot, whose *Briefe and true Report of the new found Land of Virginia* was published in London in 1588, White illustrated Harriot's observations of life among the Pomeiooc, the Aquascogoc, and the Secoton with sketch maps and ethnographical and natural historical portraits. When the engraver Theodor de Bry visited the geographer Richard Hakluyt in England in 1587, he received information about White (and about the work of the French artist Jacques Le Moyne de Morgues, who had carried out a job similar to White's in Florida), which prompted him to publish Harriot's account together with engravings based on White's drawings in the first volume of the *Great Voyages,* a monumental collection published between 1590 and 1634 in thirteen volumes by the De Bry family.

Besides the engravings of Algonquian scenes, volume 1 of the *Great Voyages* includes five figures of Picts and ancient Britons (see fig. 16). The title page by De Bry introduces them as:

> Som Picture of the Pictes which in the olde tyme dyd habite one part of the great Bretainne.
>
> The painter of whom I have had the first of the Inhabitans of Virginia, give my allso thees 5. Figures fallowinge, fownd as hy did assured my in a oolld English cronicle, the which I wold well sett to the ende of thees first Figures, for to show how that the Inhabitants of the great Bretannie have bin in times past as savage as those of Virginia. (Reproduced in Hulton 1984, fig. 28)[2]

Although De Bry's reference to the artist who drew the Indians must be to White, there are considerable discrepancies between the series of drawings of "Picts" that White made in the 1580s and the versions in De Bry's publi-

The trvve picture of one
Pićte I.

IN tymes paſt the Picts, habitans of one part of great Bretanne, which is nowe nammed England, wear ſauuages, and did paint all their bodye after the maner followinge, the did lett their haire gro we as fare as their Shoulders, ſauinge thoſe which hange vppon their forehead, the which the did cutt. They ſhaue all their berde except the muſtaches, vppon their breaſt weat painted the head of ſom birde, and about the pappes as yt waere beames of the ſune, vppon the bellye ſum feete full and monſtreus face, ſpreedinge the beames very fare vppon the thighes. Vppon the tow knees ſom faces of lion, and vppon their legges as y chath been ſhelles of fiſh, Vppon their Shoulders griffones heades, and then they hath ſerpents about their armes: They caried about their necks one ayerne rimge, and another about the midds of their bodye, about the bellye, and the ſaids liange on a chaine, a cimeterre or turkiſ ſoorde, the did carye in one arme a target made of wode, and in the other hande a picke, of which the ayerne was after the maner of a Lick, which taſſels on, and the other ende with a Rounde boule. And when they hath ouercomme ſome of their ennemis, they did neuer felle to carye a wei their heads with them,

Fig. 16. Pict. From Thomas Harriot, *A briefe and true Report of the new found Land of Virginia*, with engravings after John White. Published as volume 1 of *Great Voyages* by Theodor de Bry (Frankfurt, 1590). Courtesy of University Library, Amsterdam.

cation. Since Le Moyne also appears to have made paintings of Picts, this may be another case of De Bry's confusing the work of the younger artist with that of his senior (Hulton 1984, 17–18, and 1985, 25).[3] At any rate, these drawings and engravings are among the earliest evidence for a convergence of the iconography of the ancient inhabitants of northern Europe with representations of the New World (Piggott 1976, 9).

In pointing out this convergence we have by no means exhausted the list of different iconographical threads, or morphological chains, that intersect in these representations. For instance, these images also have their counterparts in another iconographical tradition that colored the representation of America during the sixteenth century, that of the alleged homology between European demonology and Amerindian religion (MacCormack 1993; Mason 1987; Pagden 1982, 174ff.; Silverblatt 1987, 160ff.). In this connection, some of the tattoos on the bodies of the Picts recall medieval representations of the devil (Van de Waal 1952, 1:92).

De Bry was not alone in assuming that the Amerindians resembled the ancient peoples of northern Europe; that they could be "read off" from one another.[4] In his *New English Canaan*, published in 1632, Thomas Morton put forward the claim that the natives of New England were descended from the Trojans. In making the shipwreck Brutus the founding father of both the Amerindians and the ancient Britons (the latter legend was to be found in Geoffrey of Monmouth's history of the kings of Britain) Morton thus provided a genealogy to support those who assimilated the ancient peoples of the Anglo-Saxon world to the newly discovered peoples of the Americas (Kadir 1992, 183–86). William Camden, Robert Burton, and Samuel Purchas were among those in the early seventeenth century who felt that the ancient Britons must have been as "brutish" as the Virginians (Burke 1995, 42). At the same time, the lawyer Marc Lescarbot was citing Tacitus on the ancient Germans to throw light on the exact limits and prerogatives of American "sovereigns" in Virginia, Florida, and Brazil (Lestringant 1987, 45). Before considering a number of other examples of this convergence of "Anglo-Saxon" or "Germanic" iconography with representations of the peoples of the New World, however, it is first necessary to look in more detail at who the "Germans" that the Amerindians were supposed to resemble were.

TACITUS AND THE FORTY-FIVE TRIBES OF GERMANY

Although Lucius Annaeus Seneca is credited with a monograph entitled *De situ et sacris Aegyptiorum*, the only complete ethnographic monograph that has come down to us from the Greco-Roman world is *De origine et situ Germanorum liber*, which Publius Cornelius Tacitus wrote towards the end of the first century A.D. (Lund 1988, 17, and 1990b, 19). For more than a century scholars have been aware that aside from the (disputed) value of the *Germania* as a source for German antiquity,[5] it is also important to consider the place of the work within ancient ethnographic literature.[6] In other words, apart from the information that can be gleaned from Tacitus's text about the ancient Germans, it should also be scrutinized in order to discover how it conforms to certain formal patterns that can be defined in generic terms. In the last analysis, these two fields of investigation interlock, for the presentation of ethnographic material always leaves its imprint on that very material itself.

It is in conformity with the ethnographic genre that the *Germania* can be divided into two parts: a description of the peoples of Germania as a whole (chapters 1–27) and a description of some of the various peoples and of the ways they deviate from the general pattern (chapters 28–46). Commentators have generally been aware that Tacitus's account is solidly Italocentric in that his entire text inevitably contrasts the Germani with the people of Rome (or rather, with an implicit representation of the people of Rome).[7] Indeed, the term *interpretatio romana,* a technical term used to describe the interpretation of other peoples and their practices and customs through Roman eyes, is itself taken from the *Germania* (43.3). Thus, the absence of temples or anthropomorphic deities among the Germani contrasts with the situation in Rome (9); their lack of cities contrasts with the urban culture of Rome (16); their lack of separate military techniques for fighting at close quarters and for fighting at a distance contrasts with Roman military specialization (5). One of the clearest and most elaborate examples of this opposition is the account of a day in the life of an ancient German—the earliest ethnography of everyday life to have come down to us (22). According to Tacitus, the Germani slept until late in the day, washed immediately after waking, usually with warm water, and then had a meal. Much of their time was spent in the company of others, and they drank night and day. They discussed their affairs while they were in their cups and reconsidered their opinions the next day. The Romans, in contrast, rose early, did not wash in the morning, and disapproved of continual drinking. Other details of Tacitus's account confirm the impression that the world of the Germani is here being presented as an inverted Rome.

The rhetorical force of inversion is derived from the lack of contamination between two clearly opposed entities, a logic that applies to the narrative of the *Germania* as well. To substantiate his case, Tacitus adduces the argument that the Germani are an indigenous people who have retained their purity through their geographical isolation. Since migrations in the past generally took place by sea, he argues (2.1), the relatively inaccessible position of Germania with regard to the sea routes was responsible for preserving it intact from foreign influences and thus from the degeneration that such contacts were always supposed to bring about. Since there was no intermarriage with other peoples, the Germani have all remained physically alike (4).

The isolation and purity of the Germani thus contribute to the rhetorical effectiveness of a contrast between Germania and Roma. Furthermore, the theme of inversion also finds support in the contrast between the warm, dry climate of Italy and the cold, damp climate of the north. No doubt drawing on the climatological theories of Poseidonios and his predecessors, Tacitus attributes a number of characteristics of the Germani to the effects of the climate. Hence, their hot temper is a natural reaction to their cold environment; and since their temperament leads to irascibility and conflict, they devote more time and energy to fighting than to agriculture, which in turn has its effects on their social organization and economic activities.

It is therefore ecological factors, in the wide sense of the term, that make the Germani what they are: non-Romans. One consequence of this theory is that the barbarians of the north are more or less interchangeable with one another, since they are all subject to the same climate (see Lund 1988, 113). A second consequence is that the Germani are presented as unchanging. On the one hand, Syme (1979, 1:127) notes that there are anachronisms in the *Germania* and concludes that it reflects the conditions that prevailed before the Flavian emperors had moved the frontiers of Upper Germany and of Raetia beyond the Rhine and beyond the Danube. On the other hand, Tacitus seems to have incorporated up-to-date information about the course of the sun in the far north from his father-in-law, Agricola. His climatological theory justified him in a certain indifference to the problem of anachronism.

However, the clear-cut opposition between Germania and Roma is disrupted at a few points in the text. For instance, Tacitus claims that the Germani in the interior are more simple and old-fashioned in their use of barter ("interiores simplicius et antiquius permutatione mercium utuntur" [5.3]) but that those living closer to the Roman frontier have become accustomed to the use of coined money. A similar distinction is introduced with regard to the wearing of animal skins, which accords with the Roman ethnographic cliché that the barbarians of the north wore animal skins instead of woven textiles (Lund 1988, 160). Whereas the Germani living close to the Rhine frontier wear simple animal skins, those who live further away adorn themselves more elaborately with variegated (marine) animal skins. Tacitus describes this as being more luxurious ("exquisitius"), but it is a form of luxury appropriate to those who have not been corrupted by the taste for luxury induced by trade contact with the Romans ("ut quibus nullus per commercia cultus" [17.1]).[8] In explaining the introduction of these forms of differentiation among the Germani in terms of their proximity to the Roman frontier, Tacitus assumes that the further one lives from the Roman frontier, the more primitive is one's mode of life. In this respect he conforms to the rule of ethnographic method that goes back at least to Herodotus (see Mason 1994b) and survives today in the use of terms like *Third World:* geographical distance from ego (Rome in the present case, Athens for the Greek ethnographers) can be mapped in cultural terms, in which geographical distance and cultural distance are homologous. Contact at the frontier therefore introduces the very contamination that threatens to disrupt the symmetry of the Germania-Roma opposition in its duality. Buttressed as it was on the geographical isolation of the Germani, Tacitus's argument was bound to run into difficulties once this isolation itself was called into question.

We can detect two responses to the difficulty, both of which address the problem of internal differentiation among the Germani without abandoning the dual Germania-Roma opposition. The first is a simple denial of differentiation at all. Hence, Tacitus ignores differences between the sexes despite the archaeological evidence to the contrary. In spite of the size of the German population, with the scope for variation that that might seem to imply, Tacitus claims that all of the Germani have threatening blue eyes and sandy-colored hair, are large in stature, and lack endurance (4). Similarly, he claims that the men and women dress in the same way (17.2). The Germania-Roma opposition is thus reinforced in two ways: stressing the homogeneity of the Germani makes it easier to contrast them as a whole with the Romani; and the (incorrect) statement that the men and women there dress alike points up the (implicit) contrast with Rome, where this was not the case.

The alternative strategy for dealing with internal differentiation is to acknowledge its existence *on both sides of the opposition.* Schematically, we could represent this as follows:

Germania *a* (*b, c,* . . .) / Roma *a* (*b, c,* . . .)

As long as the distinctions made on either side of the divide correspond, the dual opposition remains intact. For example, Tacitus's account of Germanic social structure certainly implies the presence of different categories arranged in a hierarchical order, namely, in descending order of rank, *rex/princeps, proceres/nobiles, ingenui/plebs, liberti/libertini,* and *servi* (see Lund 1988, 36). This is patently a case of *interpretatio romana,* but it is precisely this *interpretatio romana* that is required to preserve the symmetry of the Germania-Roma opposition. It is only because the two terms in each case share the same set of underlying features that they can be compared and contrasted at all. The same logic applies to the effects of this attitude to social structure at other points in the text of the *Germania*. For instance, in describing the clothing worn by different categories of Germani according to rank—the use of the *spina* or the *fibula*, the difference between *omnes* and *locupletissimi*—or the existence of different funeral practices for different statuses (27.1) it is the assumption that the Germani differentiate status in the same way as the Romans that renders this differentiation harmless to the integrity of the Germania-Roma opposition.

No account of the articulations of the Germania-Roma opposition would be complete without mention of its articulation with a different opposition, that between ancient Rome and imperial Rome. For the *simplicitas* attributed to the German contemporaries of Tacitus is the same *simplicitas* that Roman tradition attributed to a bygone era in the history of Rome itself. The identity of male and female clothing was not only attributed to the Germani; it was assumed to have been a characteristic of ancient Rome as well (see Lund 1988, 161). Tacitus is here following another general rule of ethnographic practice: geographico-cultural distance is homologous to temporal distance, so that contemporary "primitive" peoples present us with a picture of how our ancestors lived.[9]

The existence of a rival opposition (ancient Rome–imperial Rome), the signs of internal differentiation among the Germani, the intrusion of historical events into a timeless picture—these aspects are all articulated with and pose a threat to the clear-cut, dual opposition that Tacitus implicitly maintains between Germania and Roma. The turning point comes in the middle of chapter 27, where the transition is made from the origin and customs of the Germani as a whole to the specific institutions and rites of individual groups, of whom Tacitus mentions 45 separate tribes and 7 groups of tribes (Lund 1988, 31). What happens to the dual opposition between Germania and Roma now that the former is so fragmented?

Let us take Tacitus's portrait of the Chatti (30–32). The first point he makes is an ecological one: the region of the Chatti differs from the regions in which the other Germani live in being more rugged and drier. The effect of this environment on the Chatti themselves is to make them tougher and more capable of endurance than the other Germani, who lack sustaining power. Another difference from the other Germani is the Chatti's knowledge of iron (30.3). These distinctive traits of the Chatti have a double function: not only do they set them off from the other Germani but they bring them closer to the Romani. The language and description of their rites of adulthood (31.1) are a case of *interpretatio romana,* in which the difference between Chatti and Romani is reduced to a minimum. What particularly brings them close to the Romans is their attitude towards warfare. Although they are no more lacking in military spirit than the other Germani are, they engage in hostilities in a more concerted and rational way. Hence, whereas the rest go to battle, the Chatti go to war ("alios ad proelium ire videas, Chattos ad bellum" [30.3]). Tacitus's list of their military techniques, with its stress on strategy and sustained attack rather than on skirmishes, could almost be a portrait of a Roman army at war.

All the same, distinctions have to be maintained, and if the Chatti possess Roman-like qualities, it must not be forgotten that they possess them to a lesser extent. This is the meaning of "ut inter Germanos" (30.2): they possess considerable skill *considering that they are Germans*. The restrictive force of the expression cannot be ignored, for it is the basis of the fundamental distinction between near-Roman and Roman. The Chatti may come close to the Romans in some respects, but they are still Germani for all that. Tacitus emphasizes the gap in a number of ways. For example, while the wearing of an iron ring was shameful to the Chatti, this was not the case in Rome. Moreover, if Tacitus is indirectly poking fun at the *dura virtus* of the Stoics in his portrait of the unkempt appearance and lack of agriculture of the Chatti, as has been suggested, the effect of the irony is to suggest an association between these barbarians and a philosophical sect and to distance them both from Roman values.[10]

The picture of the Chatti thus disrupts the rigid Germania-Roma opposition of the first part of Tacitus's monograph. The possibility is now introduced of degrees of barbarism, measured in terms of distance from Rome. Thus the Chatti are less barbarian than the other Germani (as a result of ecological factors); they are surprisingly Roman-like given the fact that they are not Romans but Germani.

The lion's share of the second half of *Germania* is devoted to the various tribes that together form the Suebi. They are distinguished from the other Germani by the way they wear their hair, which is swept to one side and knotted or bound up at the back of the head. The latter style, which is particularly a feature of the *principes,* corresponds to a style that was followed by Roman women. In this respect the Suebian practices are already an inversion of Roman practices. Among the Suebi the Semnones consider themselves to be the foremost tribe, basing their claim on their antiquity. It is in line with this that they are credited with the most atavistic rites, including human sacrifice (39.1), a practice that was prohibited in Rome at this time. The Nahanarvali, another Suebian tribe (43.3–4), are also distinctly archaic in their religious practices. They make their fearsome appearance even more so by painting their bodies black and engaging in battle at night,[11] a strange procedure in the eyes of the Romans, for whom *dies atri* (literally, "black days") were not suitable for fighting. They assume the terrifying appearance of an army of the dead. Both the Semnones and the Nahanarvali represent a degree of barbarity that is considerably removed from the near-Roman qualities of the Chatti. The primitive character of the religious practices of the Semnones implies that they are wilder than the other Germani, and the infernal character of the Nahanarvali projects them into an imaginary space bordering on the division between the living and the dead.[12]

However, we are not yet on the border of humanity. This extreme position is occupied by the Fenni, who are described in the concluding chapter of the monograph (46.3). The Fenni are presented in terms of what they lack: they lack weapons, horses, and homes; socially they lack a sexual division of labor ("idemque venatus viros pariter ac feminas alit"); they live on wild plants, wear animal skins, and sleep on the ground, and their only weapon is the arrow.

As Lund points out (1988, 50), the Fenni represent wildness par excellence. Wildness was not foreign to the rest of the Germani, of course. The preference of the Germani for acquiring what they needed by shedding blood rather than by the sweat of their brow (14.3) could be seen as a sign of their wildness. The reference to their use of underground caves also bore primitive connotations, suggesting an association with the belief that the first human beings were troglodytes (16.3). This primitivism could have both negative and positive aspects. For instance, the absence of legislation could be interpreted as evidence of high moral standards (19.2). Some Germani carried this wildness shared by them all to greater lengths. Thus the Nahanarvali were only carrying to excess a wildness inherent in all Germani in proceeding like an infernal army ("insitae feritati arte ac tempore lenocinantur" [43.4]). It is the Fenni who take this wildness to the limit—one step further and they would have overstepped the divide separating humanity from the animal world.

This is precisely the point made by Tacitus himself in the concluding sentence (46.4): the half-human, half-animal hybrids that we came across in chapter 5 are beyond his ken because they are beyond the borders of humanity (Lund 1990b, 18) and therefore beyond the scope of ethnography and anthropology. The Germani, it is true, had certain animal-like features, but the half-human hybrids have exchanged metaphor for metonymy: no longer content with *resembling* animals through their *feritas,* they actually partake in animality.

The hybrids close a chain of decreasing degrees of humanity, extending from the Romani to the Fenni. As the model of a civilized nation, Rome sees itself not only as a geographical center but as the cultural point of reference. The more removed one is from the center, the less one shares in the Roman definition of culture. There are thus degrees of barbarism and civility, which we could schematically represent as follows:

civility >>>>>>>>>>>>>>>>>> barbarism
Rome >>>> Chatti >>>> Suebi >>>> Fenni

The movement from left to right can also be represented as a temporal regression, since the barbarian Fenni hold up to Rome a mirror of what the Romans' own primitive ancestors must have been like.

At this point we should note a striking result of the mechanism of comparison at work here: although it is arranged in terms of more than and less than, the sliding scale of civility and barbarism itself contains two opposite poles—the Romani and the Fenni. The sequence of negatives used to describe the Fenni ("non arma, non equi, non penates" [46.3]) is contrastive, and the implied contrast is with the *arma, equi,* and *penates* of the Romans. The dual opposition between Germania and Roma that brooked no internal differentiation among the Germani is reinstated at the culmination of a differentiated scale of wildness (see Mason 1994b). Furthermore, as we have seen, it is articulated at this point with the opposition between humanity and animality.

Two types of mechanism for representing the other interlock in the *Germania:* a rigid, dual opposition between self (the Romani) and other (the Germani) as its negative inversion; and a system of gradations of civility and barbarism centered on self (the Romani) and moving outwards from the center in ever-decreasing levels of civility.

Finally, we should take note of the nature of the indicators of barbarism and civility. As we saw, physique was one. For Tacitus, physiognomy, measured above all in terms of the eyes and hair, is itself an effect of climate and ecology, so that one can "read off" the physical nature of a people from a description of its natural surroundings. The existence and degree of social and sexual differentiation is another indicator of the level of civility. In the field of material culture the presence or absence of weapons, clothing, buildings, agriculture, technology, and minerals are significant markers. As for intellectual or spiritual ability, religious practices and military techniques can both serve as markers of development. Food and dietary practices can also indicate degrees of refinement.

Most Greco-Roman ethnographies (including imaginary ethnographies, such as accounts of the monstrous human races) are structured along similar lines (Friedman 1981, 26–36; Müller 1972, 57). They also often record the possession of articulate language, a point that is ignored in the *Germania*, but apart from this omission Tacitus's ethnography largely conforms to such records of eating habits, civic institutions, religion, technology, and physical attributes. These are the areas that are combined to produce variegated pictures of degrees of civility and wildness.

CLÜVER AND THE BATAVIANS

In the Netherlands, interest in the Germanic peoples naturally focused on the Batavi, who first entered Dutch humanist studies around 1510, soon after the rediscovery of manuscripts of Tacitus's works and the first printed editions. The early years were dominated by a dispute over where the Batavi were to be situated. Although this debate extended into the eighteenth century, the view that soon won widespread acceptance placed them in the province of Holland, as argued by Cornelius Aurelius in his *Defensio gloriae Bataviae* (1516) and particularly in the same author's *Die Cronycke van Hollandt, Zeelandt and Vrieslandt*, which went through numerous reprints and revised editions after the Leiden first edition in 1517.[13] In the second half of the century Tacitus was valued not only as a model of style and thought but also because "he cast a special illumination on the chiaroscuro world of revolt and repression in which late-sixteenth-century scholars lived" (Grafton 1991, 39).

This is the background to the voluminous *De Germania Antiqua* by Philipp Clüver (1580–1622), "one of the most critical historians in the Leiden of his day" (Schöffer 1975, 91 n. 31). Clüver, who has gone down in history as Cluverius, made the acquaintance of the famous classical scholar Joseph Scaliger in Leiden and resolved to dedicate himself to a critical appraisal of classical geography as a pendant to the lexicological and chronological compilations being produced there. In some respects the result, the three volumes of *De Germania Antiqua,* first published in Leiden in 1616, could be read as an extended commentary on Tacitus, including as they did both the *editio Lipsiana* and a new *editio Cluveriana.* However, much of the text is taken up with illustrative examples that have no direct bearing on the Germanic peoples at all but betray a lively interest in the exotic peoples in recently discovered parts of the world, including the Americas. In addition to this mass of comparative data, Clüver included a number of visual illustrations by various artists as additional information to the text.[14] In turn, these illustrations are related to earlier models, in particular the etchings after Pieter van der Borcht in Abraham Ortelius's *Aurei Saeculi Imago* and the etchings by Pieter Kaerius for the atlas *Germania Inferior* (Van de Waal 1952, 1:176–77).

The scope for interpreting Clüver's work is thus very wide, since besides the question of intertextuality arising from the combination of the two Tacitean texts with his own remarks and the question of the relation between his illustrations and their predecessors, there is also the question of the fit between text and image. Just how tight this fit was and thus the degree of control Clüver exercised over his artists can be gauged from the following example. In describing the sacrifices of the Germani, Clüver followed classical and biblical sources to conclude that in offering an animal the priest would grasp the beast with his left hand and pour a libation with his right (295).[15] In an etching made to illustrate this by Simon Frisius the roles of the left and right hand are reversed.[16] The version that finally found its way into the pages of *De Germania Antiqua* (fig. 17) was a copy of this etching, but printed in reverse in order to restore the conformity between text and image (see Van de Waal 1952, 1:190 and 202). We shall therefore assume that Clüver closely supervised the fit between text and illustration, justifying their treatment in combination with one another.[17]

For our present purposes we need only consider the illustrations contained in book 1 of *De Germania Antiqua,* since this was the book that dealt with the ethnography of the Germani, books 2 and 3 being reserved for geographical description. The purpose of this analysis is twofold: to ascertain whether the degrees of civility that we have traced in the text of Tacitus's *Germania* have left their mark on the visual record and to examine the uses to which Clüver puts his exotic material.

One important index of both social rank and civility, as we have seen, is clothing.[18] Nudity, bodily decoration (like the tattoos on the bodies of the Picts drawn by John White), and simple or elaborate clothing could all be

Fig. 17. German sacrifice. From Philipp Clüver, *De Germania Antiqua* (Leiden, 1616). Courtesy of University Library, Amsterdam.

used by artists to indicate how far those concerned had progressed from barbarism to civility. The twelve prints connected with the chapter on clothing (inserted between pages 148 and 149 in the 1616 edition) might therefore be supposed to present sufficient material to determine whether Clüver also adhered to such a vestimentary code.

We can begin with an illustration of a man, woman, and child returning from the hunt (fig. 18). The man carries a hare dangling from his bow, while the woman carries a child on her back and grasps a bundle of four arrows in her right hand. Both are clad in short tunics made of animal skins.

Fig. 18. Fenni returning from the hunt. From Philipp Clüver, *De Germania Antiqua* (Leiden, 1616). Courtesy of University Library, Amsterdam.

Fig. 19. Germans in animal skins. From Philipp Clüver,
De Germania Antiqua (Leiden, 1616). Courtesy of University
Library, Amsterdam.

This description matches that of the Fenni, the most primitive of the peoples
described in Tacitus's *Germania,* among whom both sexes hunted together
and whose only weapon was the arrow (*Germania* 46.3). For ethnographic
parallels for the bows, Clüver refers to the contemporary Britons and to "ex-
teri orbis populi omnes" (361).[19] The same cultural level seems to be represented in figure 19. Here the short tunic has been replaced by a rude animal

Fig. 20. German dress: the *sagum ingenuorum*. From Philipp
Clüver, *De Germania Antiqua* (Leiden, 1616). Courtesy of
University Library, Amsterdam.

skin knotted on the chest. Clüver himself stresses the antiquity and primitiveness of this item of clothing by tracing it back to the Garden of Eden.[20]

The presence of a ram and a sheep in figure 20 serves not only to indicate
the sources of the woolen items of clothing but also to connote the higher cultural level attained by these pastoralists as compared with the more primitive
hunters and gatherers. A more elaborately decorated tunic can be seen in fig-

Fig. 21. Dress of the German aristocracy: the *sagum no-bilis*. From Philipp Clüver, *De Germania Antiqua* (Leiden, 1616). Courtesy of University Library, Amsterdam.

ure 21, marking its bearer as a member of the nobility, here shown engaged in hunting ducks for sport instead of hunting as an economic necessity.

In figure 22 we see the baggy costume of the Gauls, which Clüver takes to be so universal that it must go back to the time of the Tower of Babel (141). He contrasts it with the tight-fitting garments worn by the German nobility (fig. 23). It is remarkable that the evidence adduced by Clüver for the assertion that this was an authentic ancient mode of dress is drawn from sixteenth-century German paintings (143).[21] What was only one century old

Fig. 22. Baggy costume of the Gauls. From Philipp Clüver, *De Germania Antiqua* (Leiden, 1616). Courtesy of University Library, Amsterdam.

Fig. 23. Tight-fitting dress of the German nobility. From Philipp Clüver, *De Germania Antiqua* (Leiden, 1616). Courtesy of University Library, Amsterdam.

Fig. 24. Infantrymen. From Philipp Clüver, *De Germania Antiqua* (Leiden, 1616). Courtesy of University Library, Amsterdam.

was thus sufficiently distant in time in his eyes to justify labeling it "antiquius" and assuming that it must be an accurate representation of fashions dating back more than a millennium![22]

Weapons also illustrate gradations of primitiveness and marks of social distinction. The most primitive weapon, the club, is carried by one of two infantrymen who have no protective clothing (fig. 24). Some members of the nobility are also shown with clubs, but they are dressed in animal skins, and the head of the beast is used as a helmet (fig. 25). The model for these

Fig. 25. Warriors in animal skins armed with clubs. From
Philipp Clüver, *De Germania Antiqua* (Leiden, 1616). Courtesy of University Library, Amsterdam.

figures, as Clüver explicitly states (341), is Hercules, though in view of the
absence of lions in Germany the artist has seen fit to replace the lion's head
with more suitable animal heads. Just as the nobility were dressed more
elaborately, they were also equipped more elaborately for fighting, their
shields bearing heraldic devices (fig. 26).

Whereas Kampinga (1917, 200) tried to attribute the gradations contained
in these illustrations to different historical periods, Van de Waal (1952, 1:181ff.,
esp. 183 n. 3) stressed their importance as markers of social differentiation.

Fig. 26. Heraldic devices and swords. From Philipp Clüver,
De Germania Antiqua (Leiden, 1616). Courtesy of University Library, Amsterdam.

It is certainly the case that the panorama presented in the illustrations is as
static as that of Tacitus's *Germania* itself, lending support to Van de Waal's
position. However, the difference of opinion between the two scholars may
be less important than they supposed, since refinement in terms of social
rank is here treated as homologous to refinement in terms of social progress.

Be that as it may, with the exception of the Fenni in figure 18, the illustrations in Clüver's *De Germania Antiqua* indicate little interest in depict-

ing the differentiation of the Germani in accordance with the tribal divisions of Tacitus's *Germania*. Apart from the presence of the Suebian knot, no other signs enable the reader to narrow the people portrayed down to one particular tribe or group of tribes. As we have seen, however, the articulations of Tacitus's *Germania* contained both the ethnic divisions among the Germani and the social hierarchy among the Germani as a whole, the latter corresponding closely to Roman norms. The very existence of these ranks is a sign that some groups have reached a higher level of civility than others. The vestimentary and military codes embodied in the illustrations therefore suggest a development from barbarism to civility, but this time it is a development that has been achieved by certain ranks rather than by certain ethnic groups within the Germani as a whole. Hence, despite the refraction in terms of social rank, the framework of degrees of wildness and civility that we detected in the *Germania* can also be shown to inform the illustrations in Clüver's work. A further point corroborating this homology between divisions along ethnic lines and divisions according to social rank is that when we compare the significant elements of these illustrations with the distinctive features that formed the basic parameters of most Greco-Roman ethnographies (see above), we note the recurrence of food and dietary practices and the degree of development of weaponry, armor and clothing, buildings, agriculture, and religion[23]—all signposts along the road from barbarism to civility.

It is therefore difficult to accept Schöffer's claim that "Cluverius accepted the general view of looking at the Teutons as decent 'burgher-citizens'" (1975, 91 n. 31),[24] for some of them were more "decent" than others. It is rather the case that Clüver views them from his perspective as a burgher-citizen himself. While Tacitus's egocentric account had its center in the civilization of Rome, the cultural levels of the various peoples of the Germania being arranged in terms of a greater or lesser proximity to Roman norms and standards, the center of the Cluverian scheme is in bourgeois Dutch society, in terms of which the cultural levels of the ancestors of the Dutch could be arranged by social rank. The resulting degrees of cultural attainment are homologous: they are distributed geographically among different tribes in Tacitus, and they are distributed socially among different strata in Clüver.

The relative order of importance has been reversed: whereas in the *Germania* ethnic differences play a greater role and social distinctions play a lesser role, Clüver devotes more attention to social distinctions than to ethnography. Nevertheless, the *De Germania Antiqua* does contain an ethnographic component, albeit a less accentuated one, to which we now turn.

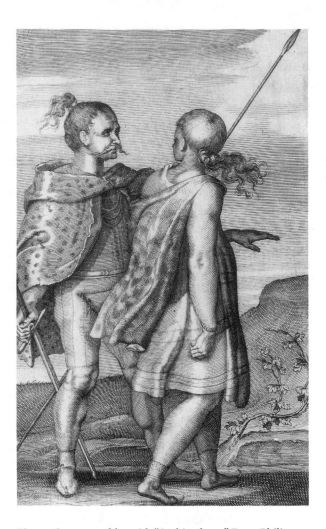

Fig. 27. German nobles with "Suebian knot." From Philipp
Clüver, *De Germania Antiqua* (Leiden, 1616). Courtesy of
University Library, Amsterdam.

As his treatment of the baggy clothing of the Gauls illustrates, Clüver as
sumes that the universal distribution of this style of dress indicates that this
was the state of things in the era of the Tower of Babel. In this he expresses
adherence to a monogenetic, diffusionist theory, whereas Tacitus's description of the development of the Germani in isolation bears witness to a belief in a polygenetic theory on the part of the Roman author (Lund 1988,
20). In adducing ethnographic parallels to illustrate Germanic practices,

Fig. 28. German nobles with "Suebian knot." From Philipp Clüver, *De Germania Antiqua* (Leiden, 1616). Courtesy of University Library, Amsterdam.

Clüver was assuming, on the basis of the postulate of diffusion, an organic link between phenomena drawn from far-flung peoples. He was certainly not alone in doing so; indeed, the clearest precedent is probably Lipsius, who included references to exotic peoples in his annotated editions of the works of Tacitus published in the 1580s (Nippel 1990, 60 and n. 22).

Figure 27 depicts two Germanic nobles, indicated as such by the decoration of their clothing and by their hair style. After quoting Tacitus on the Suebian knot, Clüver describes it as "a fashion observed by certain American tribes today and by certain island peoples in the East Indies" (131). In a comment on another illustration featuring the same hair style (fig. 28) he is more precise in attributing the Suebian knot to the Americans who live in Florida (340). Clüver sees another parallel between the Germani and the Amerindians in the use of heraldic devices (fig. 29).[25] The descriptions of similar practices among the Amerindians led him to wonder how they had been disseminated: did the Americans derive the practice from the Romans,

Fig. 29. Insignia of the nobility. From Philipp Clüver, *De Germania Antiqua* (Leiden, 1616). Courtesy of University Library, Amsterdam.

from the Greeks, or from the Egyptians (340–41)? Finally, in commenting on the illustration of a widow who follows her dead husband beyond this life by voluntary hanging (fig. 30) Clüver notes the distribution of suttee-like practices among the contemporary Indians and Americans (396). Clüver concludes that there is such a close degree of correspondence between peoples who are so remote from one another that the practice must have a common origin in Asia,[26] resulting from the scattering of peoples after the fall of Babylon (398).

This theory of an Asiatic origin helped to explain why Germans wearing their hair in a "Suebian knot," for example, could be mistaken for Chinese or Japanese (Van de Waal 1952, 1:56). In fact Van de Waal claimed that "for artists in the sixteenth, seventeenth, and eighteenth centuries the Ger-

Fig. 30. German "suttee." From Philipp Clüver, *De Germania Antiqua* (Leiden, 1616). Courtesy of University Library, Amsterdam.

man is like the Moor, the Turk, the Chinese, or the Indian, and as his iconography was in part derived from that of the Turk in the sixteenth century, it passed into Chinoiserie in the eighteenth century" (1:92). This homology between various exotic peoples as well as with Europe's own ancestors, the homology between those who were distant in space or remote in time, takes on a life of its own in the pictorial tradition.[27] This is because of the difference between the constraints that bind the visual artist and those that bind the writer of texts. Since the graphic image lacks the equivalent of the syntax for comparing two separate items, the act of comparison turns into an act of substitution. As Bucher points out ([1977] 1981, 36), De Bry was able to explain why he utilized John White's drawings of Picts to illustrate a book on the Indians of Virginia by means of a textual commentary. Once the textual commentary was missing, however, the similarities between peoples was bound to give way to the conflation of peoples: the portraits of the Picts became a means of portraying Indians.

A second constraint to which Bucher draws attention is what she refers to as "loss of negation as a rhetorical device" (36). As we saw in the case of Tacitus, classical ethnography resorted to the use of a boundary category—in the *Germania* it is constituted by the Fenni—which presents self with an inverted representation of itself. This mechanism of "negative self-definition," as Vandenbroeck (1987) calls it, presents the Indians as what the Europeans are not; their culture is defined by its lack of European cultural elements. In its extreme form, the definition of a people "sans foi, sans loi, sans religion, sans civilité aucune," as Thevet described the Brazilians, implies the existence of a culture as a tabula rasa, waiting to receive (European) inscription (Greenblatt 1990, 17; Whatley 1986, 321).

Although it is capable of being inscribed in a text, absence cannot be depicted visually. Indian nudity, for instance, could not be portrayed by the absence of clothing; the only alternatives open to the engravers were to depict the Indians in accordance with Greco-Roman canons of the nude or to resort to the world of medieval imaginary, peopled with the dwarfs, giants, and monstrous beings we encountered in chapter 5.

Let us now turn to a set of illustrations of Brazilian Indians for which there exists no textual commentary. Although the possibility of negation was ruled out as a representational device (the Indians as the reverse of the Europeans), the system of degrees of barbarism and civility was still applicable in theory. Moreover, the possibility of (implicit) comparison by (explicit) conflation could provide an idiom by which to translate the unfamiliar into familiar terms. Both possibilities interlock in the work of the northern Netherlandish painter Albert Eckhout.

ALBERT ECKHOUT'S PAINTINGS OF BRAZILIAN INDIANS

Among the 803 oil, crayon, and pencil sketches of animals, plants, and people by the northern Netherlandish artist Albert Eckhout (ca. 1607–65) discovered in the Jagiellon Library in Cracow in 1977 are five depicting Brazilian Indians.[28] These and five pencil drawings now in the Print Room of the Staatsbibliothek Preussischer Kulturbesitz in West Berlin make up the record of the artist's face-to-face confrontation with his subject. Eckhout formed part of the artistic and scientific retinue that accompanied Count Johan Maurits von Nassau Siegen to the Dutch colony in northeastern Brazil between 1637 and 1644. Besides these natural-history sketches, Eckhout's work includes a series of oil paintings of human figures that now hang in the Ethnographic Department of the National Museum in Copenhagen.[29] Eight of the paintings are more or less the same size, measuring approximately 265 cm by approximately 160 cm; they comprise four pairs: two pairs of Brazilian Indians, one black African pair, and two half-bloods. A ninth painting, a horizontal composition measuring 168 cm by 294 cm, depicts an Indian dance.[30] Most of these paintings are signed by the artist and dated between 1641 and 1643.

Eckhout's paintings have always attracted interest and admiration for their ethnographical accuracy rather than for any intrinsic artistic worth; however, none of them were used in Caspar Barlaeus's historical account of the expedition. Alexander Von Humboldt admired their descriptive quality, and William Sturtevant has called them "the first convincing European paintings of Indian physiognomy and body build" (1976, 419), a view that has been received favorably by other scholars in the field of American iconography (see Honour 1975, 83, and 1979, 295; Joppien 1979, 303; Whitehead 1987, 155; and Whitehead and Boeseman 1989, 203). After all, Eckhout did go to Brazil, and he had the opportunity to observe the various Indian peoples whom he came across there.[31]

Despite this ethnographical verisimilitude, however, it should be remembered that Eckhout was painting at a time when naturalistic effects did not rule out the possibility of symbolic interpretation (De Jongh 1995). Hence, if the realism of Eckhout is more than dispassionately observed and secularized naturalism, we may be justified in asking about the possible moral connotations of his paintings. Do Eckhout's paintings of Brazilian Indians betray a concern with degrees of civility? Such ideas were certainly in the air among Eckhout's close associates at the time. Johannes de Laet, whose *Beschrijvinghe van West-Indien* was published in 1625, recognized degrees of savagery and civility, measured in terms of religion, technology, habitat, and moral character (Van den Boogaart 1990, 393). It is therefore admissible to inquire whether Eckhout's paintings of the peoples of Brazil are similarly couched within a framework that implies a differentiation between greater or lesser degrees of wildness.

Let us compare the portrait of a "Tapuya" woman (fig. 31) with that of a Tupi woman (fig. 32).[32] The Tupi woman is clad in a short white cotton skirt; the "Tapuya" woman is naked except for an arrangement of leaves covering her pubic area. The Tupi woman carries a child on one arm, from which there also hangs a gourd; the other arm supports an ornamental basket on

Fig. 31. "Tapuya" woman, by Albert Eckhout, 1641. Oil on canvas, 264 cm × 159 cm. Reproduced by kind permission of The National Museum of Denmark, Department of Ethnography.

her head. The "Tapuya" woman carries a different load: a basket on her back suspended from a band over her head contains a severed human foot, and in her right hand she holds a severed hand by the wrist. The contrast between the two figures is further accentuated by the landscapes in the background. Whereas the Tupi woman stands in front of an orderly plantation, the "Tapuya" woman is in a wild, uncultivated landscape. Furthermore, the armed Indians on the skyline behind her seem intended to be related to war-

Fig. 32. Tupi woman, by Albert Eckhout, 1641. Oil on canvas, 265 cm × 157 cm. Reproduced by kind permission of The National Museum of Denmark, Department of Ethnography.

fare and the dismembered limbs she bears, contrasting with the scene of agricultural prosperity and peace in the Tupi background. The allegorical use of landscape as a form of *paysage moralisé* points up the opposition: the relatively civilized, that is, Westernized, Tupi versus the wild and savage "Tapuya."

A similar opposition emerges between the male counterparts. The "Tapuya" man (fig. 33) is naked, whereas the Tupi man (fig. 34) wears wide-legged cotton shorts. The "Tapuya" man is armed with four spears, a spear-thrower,

Fig. 33. "Tapuya" man, by Albert Eckhout, 1643. Oil on canvas, 266 cm × 159 cm. Reproduced by kind permission of The National Museum of Denmark, Department of Ethnography.

and a club. The Tupi man has a bow and five arrows; moreover, he has a wooden-handled metal European knife tucked into his waistband. The "Tapuya" man is adorned with facial ornaments, a feather headdress, and sandals, which give him a more primitive appearance than that of the unadorned Tupi man with his European-looking body. As for the natural settings in which the two men are placed, the "Tapuya" man is depicted in proximity

Fig. 34. Tupi man, by Albert Eckhout, 1643. Oil on canvas, 267 cm × 159 cm. Reproduced by kind permission of The National Museum of Denmark, Department of Ethnography.

to the dangers of the wilderness—a boa constrictor with blood issuing from its eye and mouth and a bird spider—whereas the human figures who are sailing and swimming in the river to the rear of the Tupi man seem to enjoy a relatively untroubled existence.

The opposition is not just a binary one between civilized and uncivilized, for the other paintings in the series introduce the possibility of gradations of

Fig. 35. Mamluk woman, by Albert Eckhout, 1641. Oil on canvas, 267 cm × 160 cm. Reproduced by kind permission of The National Museum of Denmark, Department of Ethnography.

civility. Thus the Mameluca, a woman of mixed parentage, is presented as a "dusky Brazilian Flora" (Whitehead 1985, 140).[33] Standing under a fruiting cashew tree, she is wearing a long white robe and carrying a basket of flowers in her right hand (fig. 35). At her feet are a pair of harmless guinea pigs. The existence of this half-blood creates a triad of relations: the "Tapuya" are wilder than the Tupi, who in turn are less civilized than the mestizos.[34] And the criterion for measuring this wildness is precisely their distance from the

European ego that perceives them. As Van den Boogaart puts it: "The absence of whites in the series is puzzling. Still, it can be said that they are indirectly present. In the portraits he painted of the non-whites Eckhout presented the white colonial enterprise as a civilizing force" (1990, 403).

A comparison of Eckhout's portraits of Tupi Indians with those depicting "Tapuya" shows that the humanity of the latter is stunted or incomplete. The contrast is between wildness and savagery on the one hand and a relatively cultivated habitat and elementary civility on the other. The series of Eckhout's paintings can thus be seen as showing the different grades of civility. The measure of these degrees of civility is the degree of resistance or acceptance of Dutch intrusion on native territory. It therefore becomes possible to compare the "message" of the paintings with the actual problems faced by the employees of the Dutch West India Company in their dealings with the Brazilian Indians, as Van den Boogaart (1979) has shown in detail.

A painting that has been brought into this context by Vandenbroeck (1987, 205) is a portrait of a wild man with his prey by Jacob van Oost the Elder (fig. 36). Van Oost (1601–71) was a close contemporary of Albert Eckhout, and both the dimensions of his canvas (180 cm by 105 cm) and the naturalistic style of painting recall Eckhout's Brazilian paintings. Vandenbroeck suggests that this was one of a series depicting figures from different historical eras and that the wild man in question is intended to represent one of the primitive inhabitants of the Netherlands. Could Eckhout too have been influenced by a "Batavian" iconography?

The period from the 1580s onwards saw the appearance of a spate of publications in the Netherlands relating to the Batavi (Schöffer 1975).[35] Of course the underlying message of most of these works was a patriotic one, intended to revive the Batavi's love of liberty now that the Dutch Republic was at war with Spain. It was here that American and European fates intertwined, with the publication of the first Dutch translation of Bartolomé de Las Casas's *Brevíssima relación de la destruyción de las Indias* in 1578 marking the beginning of a northern Black Legend modeled on the *leyenda negra* of Spanish cruelties in America (Schama 1987, 83ff.; Schmidt 1994; Swart 1975).[36] Another work related to political developments in this period, the *Liber de antiquitate reipublicae Batavicae* (1610), by Hugo Grotius, argued that what Grotius regarded at the time as the best possible form of government had been present in Holland from the beginning.[37] Grotius, however, also advocated the theory that the Americans were derived from Teutonic stock, basing his argument on alleged philological parallels (cf. Droixhe 1978, 72;

Fig. 36. Wild man with prey, by Jacob van Oost. Oil on canvas, 180 cm ×
105 cm. Reproduced by kind permission of V. Laloux.

and Keen 1971, 208f.), so that his Batavian arguments were not irrelevant to the American continent.[38] The point was driven home forcefully in 1620 with the publication of a companion volume to that containing the Spanish atrocities. The new volume, *De Spiegel der Spaensche Tyrannye geschiet in Nederlandt*, contained text and illustrations describing the most sensational Spanish war crimes in the Netherlands (Swart 1975, 54).

Besides the new works published in this period, the Batavian debate also created a demand for reprints of older works. Wilhelmus Heda's history of the bishops of Utrecht, written around 1520, was printed in 1612; the contemporary *De Rebus Batavicis Libri XIII*, by Renerus Snoyus, was printed in 1620. Nor was the debate a purely antiquarian one: although Pieter Corneliszoon Hooft's tragedy *Baeto* (written in 1617 and published in 1626) was only staged on a few occasions in the seventeenth century apparently without success, it was succeeded by popular histories in which the legend of Baeto, the eponymous hero of the Batavi, was retold.

Finally, mention should be made of the picture series commissioned from Dutch artists by Christian IV of Denmark (1588–1648) in 1637 to display the heroic achievements of his ancestors in Kronborg Castle after the fire of 1629.[39] The forty-five drawings that survive, which are mainly the work of the so-called Utrecht school, are based on various Dutch works of cultural history, ethnography, topography, and geography (Schepelern and Houkjær 1988). Not only was the project more or less synchronous with the plan of Johan Maurits to commission the Eckhout paintings for the great hall in Vrijburg, the residence he had built to the east of Mauritsstad in Brazil, which was completed in 1642, but that the paintings are now in Copenhagen is itself a reflection of the close ties between Johan Maurits and his cousin Frederick III, Christian IV's successor, to whom the Eckhout paintings were given in 1654 (Gundestrup 1985).

During the preliminary debates that took place in Amsterdam before the Dutch West India Company decided to embark on the Brazilian adventure led by Johan Maurits von Nassau, information was obtained through the interrogation of Indian informants about the various communities of Indians in Brazil (Van den Boogaart 1979, 522). Before the departure of the expedition, therefore, there was a lively interest not only in the Batavian question but also in the nature of the Brazilian Indians. As for a *terminus ante quem*, the chronicler of the expedition of Maurits in Brazil from 1637 to 1644, Caspar Barlaeus, published his *Rerum per octennium in Brasilia*, a historical account and justification of the seven years spent in Brazil, in 1647. In his

defense of Dutch imperialism Barlaeus did not fail to draw parallels between the Brazilian Indians, the Homeric Greeks, and the Teutonic ancestors of the Dutch (Mason 1994b, 135).

There was keen interest both in the Batavian question and in the nature
of the Brazilian Indians in the 1620s; Barlaeus was still suggesting parallels
between the Batavi and the Indians in 1647. The intervening period must
have formed the cultural ambience in which Albert Eckhout painted his
portraits of some of the peoples of Brazil. It is hard to resist the conclusion
that the "Batavian" iconography can hardly have been absent from his mind
when he set himself the task of portraying the native peoples of Brazil. And
like his literary (Tacitus) and visual (Clüver) predecessors, he described the
native peoples of Brazil in terms of degrees of civility.

CONCLUSIONS

It would be all the more convincing if the morphological affinities between Tacitus, Clüver, and Eckhout detailed in the preceding sections could
be backed up by the establishment of a historically founded sequence and
a reasonably secure chronology. Material of both a textual and an iconographical nature lends support to such an assumption.

We have seen how Clüver found parallels between his Germani and the
Indians of America, particularly those of Florida. Florida, it will be recalled,
was the object of French attentions after the failure of the French expedition to Brazil in which Jean de Léry had participated. France diverted its
gaze to North America, sending an expedition to Florida in 1562. Two years
later a second group of colonists, led by René de Laudonnière, arrived there,
only to be virtually wiped out by the Spanish in 1565.[40] After 1591, when the
second volume of De Bry's *Great Voyages,* containing a narrative of Laudonnière's expedition, was published, the general public had access to visual im-
pressions of the Indians in Florida in the forty-two engravings made by De
Bry based on drawings brought back from Florida by Jacques Le Moyne de
Morgues,[41] with captions probably added by Hakluyt (Bucher [1977] 1981,
7–8; Duviols 1982; Hulton 1978; Mason 1991a).

Apparently independent of the Le Moyne–De Bry connection, however,
is a portrait of a Floridan king in André Thevet's *Les vrais pourtraits et vies
des hommes illustres* (1584, 663) (fig. 37). Since Le Moyne had taken his drawings to London with him and De Bry's volumes had not yet been published,
it is unlikely that Thevet's portrait of the Timucuan king is based on a first-

Fig. 37. Portrait of Paraousti Satouriona, Roy de la Floride. From
André Thevet, *Les vrais pourtraits et vies des hommes illustres* (Paris,
1584), fol. 663. Courtesy of University Library, Amsterdam.

hand visual source. As cosmographer to the king and curator of the Cabinet
royal des curiosités, Thevet must have been in a position to obtain information from Laudonnière himself after the return of the expedition, but
this would not have provided him with a visual source for the portrait. The
figure dressed in an animal skin with a lynx helmet and in particular the
characteristic knot formed by the paws of the feline have their closest parallels in the Germanic warriors clad in animal skins, including animal heads
as helmets, that are by now familiar to the reader from the discussion of the

illustrations in Clüver. Obviously, Thevet could not have seen Clüver's *De Germania Antiqua* in 1584. But the common source of Thevet's king of Florida and Clüver's Germanic warriors lies in the Greco-Roman iconography of Herakles/Hercules.[42] If we add to this the conflation of Germanic and exotic peoples that was visible in the works of Lipsius in the 1580s, as well as the evidence for the assimilation between northern European ancestors and North American Indians in John White's portraits of the Picts from the same decade, it becomes hard to resist the conclusion that the emergence of a "Germanic" iconography of America can be placed in the last two decades of the sixteenth century—precisely the period in which this iconographic theme was being reinforced textually in the resurgence of the "Batavian myth."[43]

Although it is beyond the scope of the present chapter to examine the decline of this convergence between "Germanic" and Amerindian iconography, we feel bound to reproduce one of the clearest pictorial illustrations of the convergence from a work published as late as 1724 (fig. 38). The "Germanic" figure on the left, bearing obvious reminiscences of the Cluverian iconography, has as his pendant a Virginian on the right, deriving from De Bry and John White. As for the convergence between Britons and Amerindians with which we began, its persistence can be seen from the pamphlets associated with the failed attempt of the Company of Scotland to found a port in the southern part of what is now Panama at the beginning of the eighteenth century: the patriotic pamphleteers felt that, in defending the natives of the place (the Dariens) they were defending a culture that in many ways resembled that of the Scots (McPhail 1994).

Those for whom the historical conjectures made above are convincing may well wonder why so much attention has been devoted to the question of degrees of civility and barbarism. If the filiation from Tacitus via Clüver to Eckhout can be sustained in both textual and iconographical terms, why need one make so much fuss about what appear to be underlying structures?

First, the structure of differing degrees of civility and barbarism is not an underlying one. There is nothing "unconscious" or mysterious about its existence; like the markers of Jewishness discussed in chapter 4, it is produced by, and underscores, the texts and visual representations that are its vehicle.

Second, the objects of comparison are *systems* of degrees of civility and barbarism. This systematic aspect of the comparison is all-important, for it

Fig. 38. Batavians and Amerindians. From Jean-François Lafitau,
*Moeurs des sauvages amériquains comparées aux moeurs des premiers
temps* (Paris, 1724). Courtesy of University Library, Amsterdam.

would have been both possible and pointless to compare isolated elements
across the centuries. The system of degrees of civility can accommodate a
variety of idioms. Thus, Tacitus could operate with a predominantly ethnic
classification, relegating questions of social hierarchy to a relatively minor
role. Clüver reversed this code, assigning prime importance to markers of
social rank and only minor importance to ethnic distinctions. As for Eckhout,
we can note the introduction of a racial component into the comparison

through the inclusion of half-bloods and Negroes. Despite the transition from ethnic to sociological to racial codes, however, the overarching (rather than underlying) system of differentiation remains intact, since however one chooses to look at them, accounts of other peoples and cultures cannot be contained within a simple distinction between self and other because gradations exist within the other. It is because some others are more other than others that such graded systems are called into existence. Moreover, it should not be assumed that the comparison of fixed, isolated elements is here simply being replaced by the comparison of fixed, isolated systems. The notion of a system of degrees of barbarism and civility should not be taken to imply that such a system can be applied in all contexts in an instrumental or mechanical way, since the configuration of such a system itself is, of course, subject to change over time. In particular, notions like civility or civilization have their own peculiarities of historical semantics (Benveniste 1966, 336–45; Golubtsova 1969; Starobinski 1989).

Finally, and most importantly, the aim of this analysis of Tacitus's *Germania,* the illustrations in Clüver's *De Germania Antiqua,* and Eckhout's Brazilian paintings in terms of differing degrees of civility and barbarism was to provide an answer to the question, What are the *modalities* by which a chain of historico-genealogical filiation is generated? In language usage, the act of translation depends on the presence of comparable structures between one language and another, permitting the transference of terms. Similarly, if the "message" of Tacitus's *Germania* regarding the classification of other peoples is to be conveyed, it must be capable of being "translated" from one structure to another *that is capable of sustaining it.* The demonstration of the existence of a common structure over a span of some sixteen centuries is necessary to show the foundation on which a genealogical filiation could be established at all. It is thus specifically aimed at that point at which analysis of formal constraints interlocks with the history of cultural borrowings—the point at which history and morphology interlock.

POSTSCRIPT:
MORPHOLOGY AND HISTORY

And this time it vanished quite slowly, beginning
with the end of the tail, and ending with the grin, which
remained some time after the rest of it had gone.

Lewis Carroll, *Alice in Wonderland*

STRUCTURALISM AND THE "NEW HISTORICISM"

TWO RECURRENT FEATURES OF MANY OF THE CHAPTERS CONTAINED
in this book are reminiscent of the structuralist theory associated with
Claude Lévi-Strauss. One is the size of the strides that are made through
space and time. The other is the use of terms like *dual opposition*.

However, though obviously indebted to structuralism, the theoretical
framework adopted here differs from that of structuralism in a number of
ways. First, the geographical and temporal strides, inordinate though they
may seem to some readers, are not on the same scale as the comparisons
made by Lévi-Strauss. In comparing myths and masks from the Amazon region with those from the natives of the northwest coast of North America,
or in going even farther afield to China or Greece for his comparisons, Lévi-
Strauss was engaging in appreciably more daring procedures than those followed here. The circle from which the material for our comparisons is drawn
is considerably more homogeneous and restricted than that on which the
volumes of *Mythologiques* rest.

Second, in one of the pioneering works of structuralism, *Le totemisme
aujourd'hui*, Lévi-Strauss explicitly formulated the rule that *"it is not the resemblances, but the differences, which resemble each other. . . .* The resemblance presupposed by so-called totemic representations is *between these
two systems of differences"* ([1962] 1969, 149, emphasis in the original). As
pointed out in the introduction to part II, however, a focus on the allomorphic makes it impossible to trace the isomorphic series that interest us. Nat-

urally, we have pointed out differences *between* the entities *within* each system, for classification and discrimination are what systems are all about, but at the level of comparison it is the resemblances, not the differences, that resemble each other.

Third, Lévi-Straussian structuralism was always proud to assert that what it was uncovering was underlying structures, like the "deep structures" addressed by Chomskian linguistics. We have voiced our distrust of the value of "deep structures" in particular in chapter 2. Topologically, the series of long-term phenomena analyzed in this book, especially in part III, belong neither to the depths nor to the surface. If one had to situate them anywhere at all, it would have to be to a sphere "situated between the abstract depth of structure and the superficial concreteness of the event" (Ginzburg [1989] 1990a, 22). Yet perhaps the quest for a topological explanation is misguided; what is most salient is not the point at which the phenomena under discussion are situated but the processes linking long-term phenomena to their short-term eruptions. In this respect, Edward Muir's *Mad Blood Stirring* (1993) is a good example of what analysis of this kind can achieve. In his monograph on the Cruel Carnival of 1511 in Udine Muir relates the uprising and its bloody suppression to the narrative of the events by a local historian, Gregorio Amaseo. A wider time perspective is opened up by including within the analysis the portents that appeared before 1511 and the signs of divine wrath that appeared after 1511. And an even broader framework is required to accommodate those aspects of the Cruel Carnival that relate specifically to practices associated with carnival and the human body (see Ferrari 1987), such as dismemberment, the disposal of corpses, and so on, which derive from a much longer timespan (Muir 1993, 191–214). At one point Muir's analysis even rejoins one of the long-term themes to which Ginzburg (1983) has devoted a lot of attention, that of the Wild Horde, for in Amaseo's account of the assassination of Antonio Savorgan in 1512 the diabolic horde rushes to capture the sinner's soul (Muir 1993, 229). These various strands, each with its own temporality, are hard to fit into a simple model of the surface versus the depths, and they certainly do not imply the superiority of deep structures over surface structures that is implied in much structuralist writing.

Besides engaging in a dialogue with structuralism, our remarks are related to the cultural criticism associated with labels like "New Historicism," and in particular the work of Stephen Greenblatt (1980, 1990, 1991). Some of the themes under discussion make their appearance in, for instance, his

"Murdering Peasants: Status, Genre, and the Representation of Rebellion" (Greenblatt 1990, 99–130). In this article the author discusses the text and illustration of Dürer's proposed "Monument to Commemorate a Victory over the Rebellious Peasants," the slaughter of peasants in Sidney's *Arcadia*, the victory over popular rebellion in book 5 of Spenser's *Faerie Queen*, and the representation of Jack Cade's rebellion in Shakespeare's *The Second Part of King Henry the Sixth*. Greenblatt draws conclusions from this comparison that point towards a transition from status relations to property relations, from heroic commemoration to the new genre of the history play (1990, 125–26).

However, there is a difference between our treatment of morphological series and a "New Historical" approach. Tied as it is to certain conventions of literary criticism, the latter compares works whose only reason for being considered together is that they belong to the same century—the sixteenth—and that they belong to the canon of the leading figures in "European culture." Incidentally, this predilection for the canon marks a number of Ginzburg's articles since *Ecstasies*, in which the voices of members of the subaltern classes tend to be dwarfed by discussion of the "giants" of Western literature, such as Diderot and Montaigne. In this respect, a shift appears to have taken place from the "prosopography from below" of the programmatic "The Name and the Game" by Carlo Ginzburg and Carlo Poni (1991) to a mainstream program strongly reminiscent of Erich Auerbach's *Mimesis*.

Many of the more or less obscure names that appear in the chapters of this book—part of a "prosopography from below"—can hardly lay claim to such importance. Moreover, at issue is not just the question of which tradition is the most relevant but the related one of how eccentrically or eclectically various individuals made use of it. In this respect the approach to tradition in our work is closer to that of, say, E. P. Thompson in his recent discussion of William Blake's sources (1993) than to what he calls the "polite" tradition, represented in Blake studies by scholars like Kathleen Raine.

DIFFUSION, HISTORY, MORPHOLOGY

By water the sentiment might easily have come down the
Ganges into the Sinus Gangeticus, or Bay of Bengal, and so into
the Indian Sea; and following the course of trade, (the way
from India by the Cape of Good Hope being then unknown)
might be carried with other drugs and spices up the Red Sea to

> Joddah, the port of Mekka, or else to Tor or Sues, towns at the
> bottom of the gulf; and from thence by karrawans to Coptos,
> but three days' journey distant, so down the Nile directly to
> Alexandria, where the sentiment would be landed at the very
> foot of the great stair-case of the Alexandrian library, —and
> from that store-house it would be fetched. —Bless me! what a
> trade was driven by the learned in those days!
>
> Sterne, *The Life and Opinions of Tristram Shandy*

Thus did Laurence Sterne delight in mocking contemporary theories of the transfer of ideas via the trade routes. But if the occurrence of similar phenomena at different points in time or space is not explicable in terms of diffusion, how are we to explain it? Despite convergences on certain points with the literary and anthropological approaches outlined above, the ways in which our analysis differs from these approaches may serve to indicate some of the distinctive characteristics of the morphological approach to history. It is therefore appropriate to conclude by reconsidering the interaction between history, morphology, and diffusion in Ginzburg's research on the sabbath. Ginzburg had recognized in the stereotype a "compromise cultural formation," the hybrid result of a conflict between folk culture and learned culture (1984; cf. [1989] 1990a, 11). A number of the elements contained in this stereotype can be detected in the alleged plot by lepers and Jews in France of 1321, the Lake Geneva pogrom of 1348, the sect of witches dated to the last quarter of the fourteenth century attested by Johannes Nider, the new sects of Jews and Christians in the Dauphiné referred to in a papal bull of 1409, and the witches to whom Nider referred in 1435–37. Thus, by the mid-fifteenth century there was a fairly well established tradition on the witches' sabbath in western Europe (63–86; cf. Moore 1987).

As Ginzburg points out ([1989] 1990a, 80), however, two components of the witches' sabbath do not appear until the Valais trials of 1428: the witches' ability to transform themselves into animals and their ability to fly to their nocturnal meetings. Where did these two elements come from? The strictly historical study of the origins of the stereotype in the fourteenth and fifteenth centuries could not account for these two elements. However, the belief that certain individuals had the power to transform themselves into animals or to journey into the beyond on animals, associated with trances, fertility rites, and processions of the dead, existed over a long period of time and over a large area, perhaps encompassing the whole of central Europe.

In his earlier examination of these beliefs and practices, focusing on the *benandanti* of Friuli, Ginzburg had already pointed out the striking parallels with the beliefs of the Baltic or Slavic world and more particularly with the phenomenon of shamanism. Refusing to fall back on a pseudoexplanation in terms of archetypes, Ginzburg suggested that the connection between shamans and the *benandanti* of Friuli, who engaged in night battles against witches and warlocks, was a real one, not just one based on an analogy ([1966] 1983, 32), but he was unable at this stage to make the connection in terms that would satisfy the community of historians.

Similar considerations also played a part in his study of the cosmos of a sixteenth-century miller, Menocchio. A remarkable analogy between Menocchio's idiosyncratic theories about the substances of the world, on the one hand, and an Indian myth in the Vedas, on the other, suggested the existence of "a millenarian cosmological tradition that, beyond the difference of languages, combined myth with science" ([1976] 1980, 58). Such a cosmogony and the diffusion of a "cult with shamanistic undercurrents such as that of the *benandanti*" are taken to belong to a deep-rooted cultural stratum, an irreducible residue of oral culture. The intellectual turmoil brought about by the Reformation gave these subterranean beliefs and practices the opportunity to surface (21).

The time of the publication of the original Italian editions of these studies, in the 1960s and 1970s, coincided with the debate on how to reconcile structuralism with history that had been unleashed by Lévi-Strauss and Sartre (cf. Ginzburg 1981). Ginzburg's work has to be set against this background, for the encounter with structural anthropology put his allegiance to the historical camp (associated with the work of Marc Bloch) under pressure. In the choice between typology and history, however, it was the latter that triumphed, albeit uneasily (Ginzburg [1986] 1990b, vii–ix).

The publication of *Ecstasies* marked the provisional closure of this cycle of work. Making giant strides through time and space, Ginzburg draws out connections that are made on the basis of morphological affinity. The central section of the work "frequently drops the narrative thread, and even ignores chronological succession and spatial contiguities, in an attempt to reconstruct through affinities certain mythical and ritual configurations, documented over millennia, sometimes at a distance of many thousands of kilometres" (Ginzburg [1989] 1990a, 12). Behind the mass of material presented in this work is the nucleus of the sabbath situated in the theme of the journey to the world of the dead. It is this deep layer of beliefs that underlies the marking of certain figures in a particular way as a sign of their ability to communicate with the dead, such as the Friulian *benandanti* (born with a caul), the Hungarian *táltos* (born with teeth), the Dalmatian *kersniki*, the Corsican *mazzeri*, or the werewolves of central Europe (Ginzburg 1984, [1986] 1990a).

In trying to come to grips with the sabbath, Ginzburg asks, "Could the reappearance of analogous symbolic forms at a distance of millennia, in utterly heterogeneous spatial and cultural environments, be analyzed in purely historical terms?" ([1989] 1990a, 16). He does indeed present such an analysis by translating the alignments formulated on purely morphological bases into a conjectural historical sequence in which the folkloric roots of the witches' sabbath are traced from the nomads of the steppes of Central Asia via the Scythians and the Thracians to the Celts (207–25). His first conclusion is that "the series we have constructed on purely morphological grounds is compatible with a documented web of historical relationships" (215). However, as Ginzburg himself is fully aware, compatibility is not necessarily the same as connection. Such external connections between peoples can explain transmission, but only internal connections can account for the persistence of certain traits over extremely long periods and in extremely heterogeneous contexts (217 and esp. n. 54).

It is obvious that the analysis of typological connections as practiced by Ginzburg in *Ecstasies* takes place in a field that is, as he admits, out of bounds for the historian ([1986] 1990b, ix). Hence, he sees the results of his morphological analysis as provisional and preliminary because they were arrived at prior to being set within a historical context. However, one of the lessons to be drawn from the previous chapters, and one by which they are themselves bound, is that the context itself is provisional. It is regulated by rules of protocol that can suddenly change without notice. If analysis of the rituals of the *benandanti* leads both to the shamans of central Europe and to Freud's Wolf Man (Ginzburg [1986] 1990b, 155), then it is our task to rethink the categories of the act of interpretation and the role of the reader in the production of knowledge. It is the very productivity of the text that is at issue.

The claims being made here go beyond a provisional reliance on "family resemblances" as a first step towards serious analysis. Instead, we consider morphological analysis not just as a useful practical tool but as a theoretical stance. Without relinquishing the degree of conceptual rigor the morphological approach entails, we reverse the hegemony of history over morphology. In doing so, we open up a plurality of contexts that otherwise would be excluded a priori by the imposition of the protocols of the historians. This theoretical stance does not entail blindness to historical contexts; it entails only an awareness of the fact that such contexts, by virtue of their provisional nature, are not given but are themselves constituted within a field of contestation. If any conclusion imposes itself at this point, if anyone is to be allowed the last word, then let it be Wittgenstein (1993, 153):

> The correct and interesting thing to say is not: this has arisen from that, but: it could have arisen this way.

NOTES

CHAPTER 1: EXCURSIONS

1. Jefferson initially thought the remains were those of a large lion, but soon afterwards he realized that the Virginian bones were similar to those of the huge beast reconstructed in Madrid by Juan Bautista Bru (1740–99), which Cuvier (1769–1832) had called the "megatherium" (Rudwick 1992, 32; cf. Peale 1988, 203 n.14).

2. The name *mastodon,* referring to the peculiar shape of the creature's teeth, came to be used to distinguish this North American variety from the mammoth of Siberia. Later taxonomies did much to confuse the issue (see Cohen 1994).

3. "Et se ben non vorrei negare in modo alcuno la verità in genere della traditione di giganti, nulladimeno, io dubitarei facilmente, che siano ossa di giganti tutte quelle che si scoprono in diversi luoghi" (Peiresc 1989, 198). Peiresc expressed himself in similar terms two months later: "As for my conception of giants, whose existence I would in no way wish to deny, I fear that the majority of the bones which have been found are of various cetaceans and perhaps some are of elephants like that of Utica" [intorno al concetto mio delli giganti, la cui essistenza io non vorrei negare in maniera alcuna, ma temo che la maggior parte dell' ossatura che se ne son trovate, siano di animali cetacej molto diversi, et forzi alcuni d'elephanti, como quello d'Utica] (207, our translation; unless otherwise indicated, translations are ours). On Peiresc's attitude towards giants, see also Schnapper 1988, 100.

4. Rembrandt Peale published three essays on the mastodon: a broadside in 1802, a forty-six-page essay to accompany the London exhibition in the same year, and the *Disquisition* (see Peale 1988, 543–79).

5. Peale was an eminently practical man. At a time when the American Philosophical Society had been a research center for stove and fireplace innovation for half a century, Peale took a great interest in stove design, as well as in bridges, fan chairs, and the perfection of a polygraph (Peale 1988, 139).

6. For the important part played by Banks's academic correspondence at this time, see Crosland 1994. In 1802 Rembrandt Peale painted a portrait of Banks, which is now in the Academy of Natural Sciences of Philadelphia.

7. For instance, Peale suspected Barton of diverting a shipment of birds destined for the museum to his own ends, noting that Barton "never scrupled to take the feathers of others to enrich his own plumage" (Peale 1988, 156 n.2; cf. 202 n.9).

8. Peale's idea was copied from the Eidophusikon of Philip James de Loutherbourg (1740–1812). This German painter, who came to London in 1771, was an expert in stage illusion and mechanics. After a dispute over his salary, Loutherbourg left the theater and started up his own scenic exhibition in London, which reproduced natural phenomena using Argand lamps, various materials, color, and sound effects.

9. Peale painted *Noah and His Ark* after Charles Catton Jr. in 1819.

10. On the fascination with albinism in the eighteenth century, see Stafford 1991, 319ff.

11. Peale 1983, 620 (Negro); Peale 1988, 8 (cow), 763 (snake), 287 (petrified man), 763 (man aged 104 and lock of hair). Peale later painted a portrait of the albino woman (Peale 1988, 588).

12. Peale had first named this son Aldrovandi, after the Italian naturalist Ulisse Aldrovandi (1522–1605), to whom Peale often compared himself (Peale 1988, 177 n. 4).

13. The theme of harmony between Indians and whites was visually represented in Peale's waxwork of the explorer Captain Meriwether Lewis in Shoshone dress, which was added to the museum in 1807 (Peale 1988, 1055–6).

14. On these debates, see Cohen 1994, 113–34; the classic study of the so-called Dispute of the New World is by Gerbi (1973). On the notion of American exceptionalism, whose roots can be traced back to the sixteenth century, see Greene 1993.

15. More specifically on the sexual politics involved, see Rigal 1993.

16. The *Federal Gazette and Baltimore Daily Advertiser* published a "Dialogue between the Skeletons of the Mouse & of the Mammoth" in 1804; this anonymous poem was probably the work of one of Peale's sons (Peale 1988, 712–14).

17. Of Charles Willson Peale's seventeen children by three wives six died in infancy and only nine outlived their father. See the Peale family genealogy in Peale 1983, xlv–xlviii.

18. The information in this paragraph is taken from Rudwick 1992, 141ff.

19. The correct position of fossil tusks continued to stir up controversy. Albert Koch, a scientist and showman who exhibited a skeleton much larger than that of Peale's mastodon in London in 1841, mounted the tusks upside down on top of its head like horns. This dramatic effect no doubt matched the name the beast had acquired, "Missouri Leviathan," but as Owen was quick to point out, Koch had assembled it from the bones of several distinct animals, and once it had been reassembled on more scientific lines it reverted to a mastodon (see Altick 1978, 289).

20. Schama (1995, 188) reproduces an albumen print by Charles C. Curtis of a quadrille on a redwood stump.

21. According to the program of the "concert vocal et instrumental, qui sera executé dans le corps de la balaine" in Antwerp on 19 March 1829. Information on the blue whale of 1827 is derived from Moens 1977.

22. Like Peale, Kessel had a large family; four of his nineteen children embarked on a military career.

23. After years of circumnavigation, the whale skeleton eventually ended up in the Royal Academy of Sciences in St. Petersburg.

24. For the text of this song, see Braekman 1990.

25. Six members of the Osage tribe arrived at Le Havre on board the *New England* on 27 July 1827. By the end of the summer the public had lost interest in them. After they had been displayed in the Netherlands, Germany, and Italy, a public collection had to be organized to repatriate them (Honour 1976, cat. no. 292). Three of them were presented to the nobility and royal family of Italy in 1828 (Clerici 1987, 418).

26. The manuscript sources for the life and work of Adriaen Coenen are "Een visboock" (Fish book), Koninklijke Bibliotheek, The Hague, no. 78 E 54 (1577–79); "(Wal)visboock" (Whale book), Koninklijke Maatschappij voor Dierkunde, Antwerp, no. 30.021 (1584–85); and "Haringkoningboek" (Herring book), Cologne Municipal Archive, W. f 296. We are presently preparing a facsimile edition of the "(Wal)visboock" in Antwerp. All citations and illustrations in this chapter are from the manuscript in The Hague.

27. Coenen exchanged information on unusual fish with the renowned botanist and zoologist Rembert Dodoens (Dodonaeus). For example, Dodoens passed on to Coenen an illustration he had received of an extraordinary fish that had been washed up on the coast of Zealand in August 1584. Coenen then used the illustration as the basis for a new drawing in his Antwerp manuscript.

28. On Americana in Coenen's texts, see Egmond and Mason 1994; on Coenen and the barnacle goose, see Egmond and Mason 1995b; on Coenen's reading and his influence on his son, the landscape painter Coenraet van Schilperoort, see Egmond and Mason 1995a.

29. On the role of Charles de St. Omer, seigneur de Moerkercke, Dranoutre, etc., as patron and friend of Charles de l'Ecluse and Rembert Dodoens, see Hunger 1927, 85–88.

30. Municipal Archive Leiden, City Archive, inventory no. 44: Gerechtsdagboek Leiden, pt. A, fol. 234.

31. Cf. Céard's introductory remarks to Ambroise Paré's *Des monstres et prodiges* (Paré [1585] 1971, xlv); some parts of Paré's book resemble his cabinet of curiosities.

32. The name has been connected with Anvers, the French name for Antwerp, which may have been one of the centers of production. Coenen was an old hand at the construction of these monsters, which hung in the homes of many well-to-do compatriots.

33. In England, one of the principal courtyards of Whitehall Palace, designated Whalebone Court because of the display of whalebones there, was one of the sights of London. Bearbaiting was organized within its confines (MacGregor 1989, 413).

34. The negative connotations of the whale go back to medieval sources, in which it was associated with the devil (see Ziolkowski 1984, 113).

35. One could compare the combination of an analytic interest in detail with an allegorical framework in the work of Ulisse Aldrovandi (Olmi 1992, 110), whom Peale regarded as a spiritual ancestor.

36. For another case of boldness and originality in elaborating the materials from "high" culture—that of the proponent of "spagyrical" medicine Costantino Saccardino, who was hanged in the market square in Bologna in 1622 as an example to all nonconformists—see Ginzburg and Ferrari 1991; and Eamon 1994, 248–50.

37. In this respect Coenen stands apart from a movement of his time that can be regarded as a sort of "philologization" of knowledge (see Copenhaver 1991).

38. On the politico-military background to these events, see Parker 1977, 165–66.

39. The verdict on the museum in the 1820s was that it had degenerated from a distinguished museum to a Barnum-like showcase (Miller 1966, 134). The argument advanced here is that it was a combination of both types from the first.

40. The connections between Enlightenment "mathematical recreations" and "philosophical entertainments," on the one hand, and the rise of the electronic media, on the other, are discussed in Stafford 1994.

CHAPTER 2: POINTS OF HONOR: THE LIMITS OF COMPARISON

1. For a recent survey see Israel 1995.

2. Unless otherwise stated, all of the following information about the Haarlem court case comes from the records of the Great Council of Mechelen, dossier 725 of the appeal cases from the province of Holland. The original records of the Great Council can be found in the Royal Archives at Brussels.

3. The last document in the dossier is dated 3 March 1572. The Sea Beggars entered the town of Den Briel on 1 April and captured a number of other towns in Holland in the course of May and June. In June, Alkmaar, Gouda, Leiden, Dordrecht, and various smaller towns switched their allegiance to the rebels. Haarlem followed in July, but only after considerable military pressure. For a contemporary account detailing what happened in Haarlem from 1572 to 1581, during and after the Spanish siege, see Verwer 1973, 3–8; and for a further account of events in Haarlem, see Spaans 1989.

4. Like many of the dossiers of the Great Council, this one contains documents pertaining almost exclusively to one side (Cornelis's) of the case.

5. See esp. Davis 1988; Ginzburg [1976] 1980, [1986] 1990b, 1992; Hsia 1992; Muir and Ruggiero 1994; and Ruggiero 1993.

6. Obviously, this does not mean that court cases inform us only about legal categories, as some legal historians have suggested. For the importance of literary forms for the presentation of cases see, e.g., Davis 1988.

7. Haarlem was one of the largest towns in Holland at the time. The others were Amsterdam, Delft, Leiden, and Gouda.

8. A good example is Adriaen van Berckenrode (1543–1605), who was burgomaster seventeen times between 1577 and 1603. Ampzing's early-seventeenth-century history of Haarlem (Ampzing 1628) also mentions many of Geertruyd's kinfolk.

9. His parents were Gerrit Thomas Pieterszoon and Ermgard Jan Louwendochter. Cornelis died before 1580 (Thierry de Bye Dolleman 1958).

10. This seems to have applied more often to the women in the Van Berckenrode family than to the men.

11. Hadrianus Junius (1511–75) lived and worked for decades in Haarlem as a physician and governor of the "Latin school" (Ampzing 1628, 117–19; Veldman 1974).

12. Berkhout had been appointed sheriff in December 1558; the search for a successor had already begun by 1560 (Verwer 1973, 23).

13. Adriaen Claesz died during this controversy, but not before August 1570.

14. It should be emphasized again that the dossier primarily presents Cornelis's side of the controversy.

15. The document from which this quotation is taken is probably not in Cornelis's own handwriting, but it is written in the first person. The phrasing likewise seems to indicate that it was composed by Cornelis himself, not by his counsel. This is all the more likely since it does not present a particularly favorable image of Cornelis.

16. Cornelis's mother and sisters were preparing to take Geertruyd to court for "iniurien," or injuries, in the sense of both insults and damages.

17. This is by no means the only case in the records of the Great Council in which female initiative (whether or not the women were represented by men) started and largely controlled court cases in family affairs.

18. Not only were public fights and boisterous behavior deemed inappropriate for a man of honor but they constituted a threat to public order.

19. See, e.g., Stone 1990 and esp. Schama 1987. The latter remarkable study of Dutch seventeenth-century culture reveals a constant preoccupation with the modernity of Dutch society.

20. Examples of publications in these categories are Künzel 1983; Van Buuren 1988; Van Oostrom 1987; Vanderjagt 1981; and Van Nierop 1993. Exceptions are a special issue of the *Volkskundig Bulletin* (1992) dealing with insults and a few publications on prostitution and on women and honor, such as Koorn 1986 and Van de Pol 1992.

21. Cf. Stone 1990: "For in *such* societies honor in a man is defined by sexual potency and shame by cuckoldry; honor in a woman is defined by sexual purity and shame by adultery" (280, emphasis added).

22. For some influential anthropological studies, see Blok 1981; Campbell 1964; Gilmore 1987; and Peristiany 1965.

23. See the literature mentioned in the preceding note, and compare historical studies of the Mediterranean, which seem to point to the *longue durée* of a typically Mediterranean concept of honor. See, e.g., Ruggiero 1993, 57–87, though Ruggiero does pay considerable attention to divergences between male and female notions of female honor in Renaissance Italy; and Muir 1993.

24. The term meaning "virtue" *(deugd)* did exist at the time, but its range of meanings in sixteenth-century Dutch usage has not yet been explored.

25. A reverse situation obtained in the early-fifteenth-century Burgundian court circles described in Van Oostrom 1987, which show up even worse anomalies. What is one to think of a court society characterized by Van Oostrom as a classic shame culture and yet marked by new professional administrators and types of bureaucratic organization?

26. Other cases dealt with by the Great Council show that a woman's sexual conduct *could* be of great importance in conflicts about honor. However, in most of those cases too control of family capital and property played a considerable part.

27. See Schama 1987, 398ff., on the situation in the seventeenth century.

28. This conception of honor radically undermines statements linking money to "new" or "modern" value systems, such as Stone's statement that "some of the changes involved a prolonged tug of war over several centuries between old values and new ones, for example between honor and money" (1990, 277).

29. On violence and honor in late medieval German towns see Groebner 1995a and 1995b.

30. Cf. Frevert 1995 and Nye 1993, among others. Stone remarks that "the two moral codes ran side by side in the early years of the nineteenth century" (1990, 282), which could have had implications for the rest of his argument. For an analogous argument with respect to (changing) attitudes towards children, see Egmond 1993a.

CHAPTER 3: POINTS OF COMPARISON: SAINTS, SORCERERS, AND SHAMANS

1. In a later article in which Klaniczay discusses traces of a shamanistic background in the historical data on Hungarian witch beliefs, however, he notes that the shamanistic background is only found in a small minority of the trials (1990, 249).

2. The impetus Ginzburg's work gave to folklore studies can be gauged from the plethora of references to *Ecstasies* in a collection of studies and documents on fantastic beings in the Alps (Abry and Joisten 1992).

3. As pointed out in the introduction to part I, Wittgenstein introduced the notion of "family resemblances" in his "Remarks on Frazer's *Golden Bough*" and in *Philosophical Investigations* (1958). The former text was first published in German in 1967, and an English translation followed in 1971. For the genesis and further discussion of this very influential text, see Cioffi 1981; Needham 1985, 149–77; Rhees 1982; and Tambiah 1990. We have used the translation by John Beversluis (Wittgenstein 1993, 119–55). For G. E. Moore's notes on Wittgenstein's lectures on *The Golden Bough*, see Wittgenstein 1993, 106f.

4. For instance, Ruggiero points out that while it is possible that certain elements of lore were passed on from generation to generation, it is equally possible that in some cases such parallels are the result of discoveries made independently numerous times in different cultures (1993, 169).

5. As pointed out by both Severi (1992, 170) and Grottanelli (1991, 105–8), Ginzburg's uncritical adherence to the work of Luc de Heusch at this point in his argument ([1989] 1990a, 285 n. 150, 287 n. 185) is curiously at odds with the highly critical treatment of sources in the rest of his magnum opus.

6. Grottanelli (1991, 108), on the other hand, draws attention to a complex of phenomena that are typologically more distant from one another but closer in time and space.

7. It is quite possible for two incommensurable cultures to operate for long periods based on an ultimately false but in practice workable presumption that the concepts used by the other culture are analogous to its own. Examples of this can be seen in the interaction between the Nahuas of Mexico and the Spaniards (Lockhart 1994) and in the history of Kongo accommodation to a European presence (MacGaffey 1994).

8. In this connection, there are some useful remarks on incommensurable lexical structures, phrased within a critique of the Kuhnian notion of paradigm, in Biagioli 1993, 211–44.

9. Perrin explicitly acknowledges his debt to structuralism and French sociology (1992, 104 n. 2).

10. For a more detailed treatment of two visions—the Vision of Thurkill and the Vision of Godeschalk—see Gurevich 1992, 50–64.

11. Le Goff distinguishes between learned and popular dimensions in reports of journeys to the underworld (1985, 103–19).

12. Le Goff's dating in the twelfth century (1981) is considerably later than that advanced by other scholars; see Carozzi 1983; Gurevich 1988, 148; and McGuire 1989.

13. On the articulation of bi- and tripartite organizations, see in particular the essay "Les organisations dualistes existent-elles?" in Lévi-Strauss 1958.

14. For the growth of livestock breeding among the Guajiro and its role in Guajiro symbolic thought, see Perrin 1987.

15. This decline in the status and the power of the shaman has been accompanied by a feminization of the profession. Today some 80 percent of Guajiro shamans are women (Perrin 1992, 13, 234).

16. This essay by Ginzburg appeared after the original Italian edition of this collection of essays in 1986.

17. For an interesting case of the *failure* of the Inquisition and the Church to impose a diabolization of popular idea complexes, see Henningsen's discussion of the Sicilian *donni di fuora* (1990).

18. On Michel Perrin's "hybridity," see the amusing anecdote about his alleged connections with the dancer Joséphine Baker (Perrin 1992, 20). Is it a coincidence that Clifford (1988, 198) singles Baker out as a source of modernist inspiration?

19. Is this taste so postmodern after all? Alpers points out the resemblance between Clifford's alternative museum displays and the work of Rauschenberg or Kienholz and concludes, "Our way of seeing can open itself to different things, but it remains inescapably ours" (1991, 30). For criticisms of the "grotesque amorality" and "political irresponsibil-

ity" of Clifford's "global-shopping-mall approach," see Faris 1992, 261 n. 23. Coombes tries to break down what she refers to as the monolithic repetition (despite postmodernist pretensions) of hybridity as an encounter between the West and its "Other" by stressing the hybridity of *all* cultures (1994, 217–25).

CHAPTER 4: POINTS OF IDENTITY:
SKETCHING A JEWISH PROFILE

1. Pamphlet no. Pfl.Q.n.27, University Library, Amsterdam. Other archival sources used in this chapter are Gemeente Archief Amsterdam, Rechterlijk Archief (RA) 438 (August 1773); Algemeen Rijksarchief, Hof van Holland 5496/3 (1769); Streekarchief Hoorn, RA Hem and Venhuizen 4817 (1743); Gemeente Archief Hertogenbosch, RA 44 (1783); Gemeente Archief Haarlem, RA 55/8 (1740); and Gemeente Archief Alkmaar, RA 48, 48BII and 48BIII (1768). On the organization of Dutch criminal justice and the archival records, see also Egmond 1993b.

2. For the role of German Jews in organized crime in the Dutch Republic see Egmond 1990, 1993b. On Jewish immigration, poverty, and occupations in the Netherlands, see Bloom 1937, 24–32; Israel 1985, 104–5, 145 55; and Shulvass 1971, 73. Bloom gives the numbers of Ashkenazim living in Amsterdam as follows: in 1674, 5,000; in 1720, 9,000; in 1748, 10,000; in 1780, 19,000; in 1795, 21,000; and in 1805, 24,000. These numbers should be seen in the context of a more or less stable total population of about 200,000. About 19,000 of the 24,000 Ashkenazim living in Amsterdam in 1805 were poor.

3. For a critical and wide-ranging discussion of theories of personality and its social formation see Burkitt 1991. The first sentence of his first chapter provides an apt illustration: "The view of human beings as self-contained unitary individuals who carry their uniqueness deep inside themselves, like pearls hidden in their shells, is one that is ingrained in the Western tradition of thought."

4. For an anthropological approach to individual (rather than group) identity in the Mediterranean, see St. Cassia 1991, which emphasizes the importance of role-playing: "The true self is not a pure self without role nor a pure role without self as certain readings of [Marcel] Mauss seem to have suggested, the former for highly developed Northern European societies and the latter for clan-based ones such as the Zuni" (12). St. Cassia has not adjusted his metaphors, however, for he continues to speak of the need to "move to a much deeper level of analysis" (8).

5. A similar shift from (metaphorical as well as literal) inner core to outer boundaries can also be discerned in some discussions of honor and truth among literary historians; see Greenberg 1990; Hanson 1991; and Maus 1991.

6. Gemeente Archief Amsterdam, Rechterlijk Archief (RA) 438 (August 1773).

7. The same type of description can be found in criminal prosecutions of Gypsies, who were designated as "Heathen" (Egmond 1993b, 87ff.).

8. The increase in the frequency of the use of the word *smous* during the second half of the seventeenth century has been connected with the arrival of a growing number of poor German Jews (Van Cleeff-Hiegentlich 1987, 56–57).

9. See ibid., 60–61. On the virtual absence of Jews from the rest of Dutch literature see Weijtens 1971, 18–21.

10. Algemeen Rijksarchief, Hof van Holland 5496/3 (1769).

11. This list comprises short biographies and criminal careers as well as descriptions of 650 predominantly Jewish thieves.

12. Gemeente Archief Amsterdam, RA 438 (August 1773)

13. On occupational activities see Bloom 1937; Endelman 1979; Katz 1973; Löwenstein 1985; Schama 1987, 587–95; and Wischnitzer 1965.

14. Streekarchief Hoorn, RA Hem and Venhuizen 4817 (1743).

15. The Provincial Estates of Holland explicitly prohibited the institution of ghettos in 1619. This rule did not apply in other parts of the Netherlands, where local regulations determined where and how long Jews were allowed to stay. Until the late eighteenth century the city of Utrecht, for instance, did not admit any Jews for more than twenty-four hours (Huussen 1989, 116; Reijnders 1969).

16. On the Great Dutch Band and the role of the Jacob family, see Becker [1804] 1972; and Egmond 1986 and 1993b, 146–51.

17. Guild regulations generally did not apply to Jewish butchers, who were allowed to live and work in most rural parts of the country, although their customers did include Christians.

18. For a discussion of the predominantly Protestant emphasis on the distinction between true, inner religion as epitomized by prayer, on the one hand, and spurious, "superficial" religious ceremonial (mainly identified with Roman Catholicism and with "primitive" religious observance), on the other, in Picard's influential *Cérémonies et coutumes religieuses de tous les peuples du monde* (Amsterdam 1723), see Pregardien 1985.

CHAPTER 5: THE RESISTANCE TO HISTORY

1. In discussion with the anthropologist Michael Taussig in the 1970s a Sibundoy shaman from southwestern Colombia referred to the inhabitants of the lowland forest as Huitoto people "who have no soul, but just a spirit of air. They don't eat. What they eat is wind, or flowers, nothing more than the fragrance of flowers" (Taussig 1984, 100).

2. On Flaubert's sources for this episode, see Lestringant 1991a, 335–41; and Seznec 1949, 59–85. On Odilon Redon's illustrations to Flaubert, see Eisenman (1992).

3. For instance, during his stay in France from 1561 to 1563 Thomas Cecil (1542–1623), the only son of Queen Elizabeth's minister of state William Cecil by his first wife, had to read Münster for an hour each morning, in addition to study of Josephus's *De bello Judaico*, legal study, French conversation, and dancing lessons (Guilleminot 1987).

4. On the Alexander tradition, see especially Cary 1956; Pfister 1976; and Ross 1963.

5. On Thevet's criticisms of Belleforest's revision of Münster, see Keen 1971, 152–53.

6. For a recent survey, see Randles 1994.

7. Perhaps this crisis of cosmography can be extended to the medical world. A similar emphasis on the need to travel, on the need to take popular lore and practices into account as well as the works of the learned, and on the value of drawing on experience characterizes the medical "primitivism" of the Italian surgeon and popular healer Leonardo Fioravanti (1518–88). The publication date of 1570 for his *Tesoro della vita humana*, an autobiographical record of his travels, discoveries, and travails, makes his vociferous criticisms of the physicians exactly contemporary with the "crisis of cosmography." On Fioravanti, see Eamon 1994, 168–93; and Ginzburg and Ferrari 1991.

8. Thevet's earliest published work, *Cosmographie de Levant*, was issued in 1554; the last of his works to be published, *Les vrais pourtraits et vies des hommes illustres Grecz,*

Latins, et Payens . . ., appeared in 1584. For obvious reasons, his unpublished works are not included in the present discussion.

9. How widespread this crisis of cosmography was outside France at this time is a matter for debate; see Rubiés 1993, 181 n.72.

10. They match the feathered cloak, skirt, and knee and ankle ornaments of the female figure labeled "Nobilis foemina in America" in A. de Bruijn's *Omnium pene Europae, Asiae, Aphricae atque Americae gentium habitus* (1581, 58).

11. In calling this correspondence into question we are not questioning the validity of Lestringant's analysis of the crisis itself.

12. For a similar polemical emphasis on eyewitness evidence as against literary sources in the work of Pierre Belon, whose account of his travels in the Near East appeared in the same decade as Thevet's *Cosmographie de Levant*, see Bertrand 1993.

13. For the combination of archaic woodcuts and more naturalistic representations in a fifteenth-century *tractatus de herbis*, see Tongiorgi Tomasi 1984.

14. For further discussion of the question of proximity in Heidegger, see Derrida 1972, 147–64; and 1978.

15. On the role of organic metaphors in Benjamin's essay, see esp. Derrida 1987, 203–35.

16. On this double bind see Derrida 1986, 147. Benjamin's theses are related to *visual*, rather than *textual*, translation in Mason 1996a.

17. This distinction obviously is based on the work of Wittgenstein and Austin in particular. For readings of the texts of these philosophers in terms of what they themselves say about texts, see Silverman and Torode 1980.

18. "Deus cornes de demi pié sur la teste, une petite au front."

19. "Ce que je préfère, dans la carte postale, c'est qu'on ne sait pas ce qui est devant ou ce qui est derrière, ici ou là, près ou loin. . . . Ni ce qui importe le plus, l'image ou le texte, et dans le texte, le message ou la légende." Walter Benjamin, who collected postcards in his childhood, also draws attention to the ambiguity of the postcard, saying that it is "like a page by an old master that has different but equally precious drawings on both sides" (1985, 92).

20. In some versions of the story of Saint Brendan, the Irish monk threw into the fire a book in which he had read of wonders he could not believe. His disbelief motivated a voyage of atonement, in the course of which he was confronted with marvelous places and people to convince him of God's power in creating wonders.

21. "Et m'étonne que Munster aye pris tant de peine à faire paindre en son oeuvre touts ces monstres comme si c'estoyent choses veritables."

22. Wittkower appositely comments on the woodcuts of monstrous peoples in Münster, "The visual appearance favors belief in what is left open to doubt in the text" (1977, 62).

23. On the monstrous human races in the Near East, see Samarrai 1993; in the Americas, Magaña 1982; in the North, Spies 1994; worldwide, Wittkower 1977.

24. Flint 1992; Friedman 1981; Mason 1990a, 1990b, 1994a. Perhaps the reader should be reminded that the terminology employed here is conventional, following the usage introduced by Friedman 1981. The "Plinian" figures in question are older than Pliny; their degree of monstrosity or humanity is precisely what is at issue; and the term *race*, of course, does not imply that they were conceived in terms of the categories of racist culture.

25. On the monstrous human races in the Greco-Roman world, see especially Pfister 1976; Romm 1992; and Wittkower 1977.

26. For example, the annotated edition by W. Guglinger (Krakow, 1526) or the *Som-*

maire des singularitez de Pline by Pierre de Changy (Paris, 1542) (see Céard 1977, 12).

27. Friedman 1981, 149f., gives a date in the eighth century and sees in it both a reflection of Celtic Irish learning, notions, and attitudes and familiarity with the Alexander cycle. For an annotated edition, see Bologna 1977.

28. Münster must have been familiar with this work from his time as a student in Tübingen, where his teacher, Konrad Pellikan, lectured on the *Margarita philosophica* (Grafton 1992, 102). The same iconographical pattern is found in a Sienese illustrated manuscript of Pliny's *Historia Naturalis* dating from ca. 1460, now in the Victoria and Albert Museum, London (MS. L. 1504–1896), reproduced in Whalley 1982.

29. For example, on the way in which "Strabo's attempt at revisionist Indography . . . turns out to be only marginally more restrictive than the efforts of earlier writers," see Romm 1992, 103.

30. Some editors, unable to accept such a level of credulousness on the part of the Ionian historian, emend the text at this point (see ibid., 92 n. 23).

31. "Cetera iam fabulosa: Hellusios et Oxionas ora hominum vultusque, corpora atque artus ferarum gerere: quod ego ut incompertum in medium relinquam." Tacitus here appears as a more critical ethnographer than many of his predecessors and successors. For an annotated bibliography of twentieth-century interpretations of this passage see Lund 1990a, 2187f.

32. George and Yapp (1991, 51–52) suggest an identification with the cheetah. For a recent discussion of the identification of the fabulous creatures in the Nile Mosaic of Palestrina, see Meyboom 1994.

33. The Boeotian poet Hesiod spoke of a half-dog people, and the Athenian dramatist Aeschylus also mentioned a dog-headed people (Strabo 1.2.35).

34. In the introduction to his annotated edition of Ralegh's *Discovery of the Large, Rich, and Beautiful Empire of Guiana* (1596), Ralegh's nineteenth-century admirer Robert Schomburgk lists further references to Amazons by Hernando de Ribeira, D'Acuña, Cyprian Baraza, de Condamine, Gilij, and others in order to show that if Ralegh had a preconceived opinion about them before he left England, "the belief was entertained by thousands at that period" (Ralegh [1596] 1970, lvii–lviii). Schomburgk also discusses Ralegh's credibility regarding headless men.

35. Drake Manuscript, f. 111r (black-and-white illustration in Lestringant 1990, 11; color reproduction of "this acephalous silhouette" in Lestringant 1994, fig. 7). The Drake Manuscript is located in the Pierpont Morgan Library, New York, N.Y. See also the facsimile edition (Histoire Naturelle des Indes 1996).

36. For a selection of twentieth-century explanations of the monstrous human races resulting from misperceptions of actual practices, see Mason 1991b, 9–12. The universality of the Plinian races rules out such an explanation.

37. Monstrous images played a particularly important part in the struggles between the pro- and anti-Lutheran factions (see Scribner [1981] 1994, 126ff.; and Warburg 1932, 2:487–558, 647–56).

38. Céard 1977, 43–59; Friedman 1981, 123–30; Mason 1991b, 6–8; Wittkower 1977, 56–57.

39. On the satirical use of *topoi* connected with the birth of a monstrous individual, see the remarks on Seneca's portrayal of the emperor Claudius as "quasi homo" in Lund 1994, 23–24 and 80.

40. Traditions related to the birth of individual monsters as portents go back at least to ancient Babylonia (see Wittkower 1977, 50 n. 58).

41. For instance, the discussion of individual hermaphrodites in Paré ([1585] 1971, 25) is based on Saint Augustine's treatment of hermaphrodites (*City of God* 16.8), but Augustine's hermaphrodites, following Pliny (*HN* 7.2), are a people.

42. Belleforest wrote a *Discours des presages et miracles advenuz en la personne du Roy, et parmy la France, dès le commencement de son Regne,* which was published in 1569 (Simonin 1992, 98).

43. The full title is *Anthropometamorphosis: Man Transform'd; or The Artificial Changeling Historically presented, In the mad and cruel Gallantry, foolish Bravery, ridiculous Beauty, filthy Finesse, and loathsome Loveliness of most Nations, fashioning and altering their Bodies from the mould intended by Nature; with Figures of those Transfigurations. To which artificial and affected Deformations are added, all the Native and Nationall Monstrosities that have appeared to disfigure the Humane Fabrick. With a Vindication of the Regular Beauty and Honesty of Nature. And an Appendix of the Pedigree of the English Gallant* (1653).

44. For some South American examples in the writings of Prudhomme, de la Condamine, and Gilij, see Magaña 1989, 135 n. 1.

45. The hypothesis that physical deformation resulting from a manual operation may eventually become hereditary was already advanced (in relation to the long-headed Makrokephaloi) in the pseudo-Hippocratic treatise *On Air, Places, and Waters.*

46. See the illustrations in Wilson 1993, 125; and Wittkower 1977, 69.

47. Friedman (1993, 52) mistakenly situates the event in the Midlands county of Leicestershire instead of in the north.

48. There is a precedent for the coincidence of a spate of publications on monstrous births with a period of political and religious turbulence in the 1560s; understandably, the powers that be were intent on controlling or neutralizing anything that augured a change in the status quo. See the remarks in connection with a woman who gave birth to a cat in 1569 in Cressy 1993, 1323–25.

49. It should be remembered that many of the sixteenth-century inquirers were collectors as well. Cf. Céard 1977, xxiii; and Mason 1994c.

50. On the tradition of exhibiting live "ethnographic specimens," see Kirshenblatt-Gimblett 1991, 402–7.

51. Pieter Pauw (1564–1617) was appointed to the chair of anatomy at the University of Leiden in 1592. He was responsible for the establishment of a museum of natural history in the anatomy theater there that was open to the public. He was succeeded by Ottho van Heurne (on whom see above).

52. On this belief see Huet 1993; and McGrath 1992.

53. "Non enim excursus hic eius, sed opus ipsum est" (Pliny, *Letters* 5.6).

CHAPTER 6: THE *LONGUE DURÉE* OF RITUAL PUNISHMENT

1. Illustrations of the punishment of "simple" drowning can be found in various works on judicial iconography, but these do not offer any pictures of the *poena cullei* (see Fehr 1923; Heinemann 1900; Schild 1980; and Von Amira 1922, 236–415. Cf. Edgerton 1985). Jan Willem Tellegen drew our attention to what may be its only illustration: appropriately, this picture can be found on a Dutch eighteenth-century tile that belongs to a series of dozens of tiles illustrating sections of the *Digesta.* For a discussion of this curious series, its designer, and its producer, see Tellegen-Couperus and Tellegen 1993.

2. For an excellent survey of the history of this punishment, see Bukowska Gorgoni

1979. The use of animals in the punishment of human beings should be clearly distinguished from the criminal trial and punishment of the animals themselves. On the latter, see, e.g., Von Amira 1891; Cohen 1986, 1993; Evans [1906] 1987; and Mason 1988, 1990c.

3. See esp. Briquel 1984; Bukowska Gorgoni 1979; and Magdelain 1984. Cf. Schild 1980.

4. See Foucault 1975; Elias [1939] 1969; and, e.g., Spierenburg 1984. Cf. Sharpe 1990.

5. For exceptions, see esp. Blok 1989; Evans 1984; Schild 1980; and Van Dülmen 1985.

6. The majority of the few postwar publications that refer to these older debates are in German. The relevant ones are Bukowska Gorgoni 1979; the volume *Du châtiment dans la cité: Supplices corporels et peine de mort dans le monde antique* (1984), on classical Roman and Greek punishment and criminal justice; Feucht 1967, which criticizes early German "sacrifice theories"; and Sturm 1961, which adds a Jungian interpretation. Leder 1980 merely presents a motley collection of punishments from many different regions and periods, combined with a simplified version of nineteenth-century "human sacrifice" theories.

7. For perceptive observations on links between the German discussions and the work of Durkheim, Mauss, and Gernet, see Thomas 1984. This is not the place to go into the causes for the turn away from the German tradition. Apart from the obvious political and ideological reasons, the separation of legal history, general history, and folklore studies (or *Volkskunde*) in many Continental countries may have been important too.

8. Momigliano was far too optimistic when he stated that "it is now clear to almost everyone that we can no longer maintain a distinction between historians' history and jurists' history" (1966, 239). Judging from Girard 1972, Van Dülmen 1985, Bartlett 1986, Blok 1989, and Cohen 1989 and 1993, interest in legal ritual and punishment may be increasing again among both historians and anthropologists.

9. For a useful survey of rapprochements between anthropology and history, see Ohnuki-Tierney 1990. In many respects modern anthropological literature hardly seems to improve on the work of Hubert and Mauss, who in their "Essai sur la nature et la fonction du sacrifice" stress both the complexity and the great variety of concurrent functions and the plurality of meaning of sacrifice while pointing to the importance of formal likenesses for the discovery of global patterns ([1898] 1964, esp. 1–8 and 89–103).

10. But see Hubert and Mauss [1898] 1964, 97. For anthropological studies of ritual in history or historical ritual, see Asad 1993, 55–79; and Bloch 1986. Cf. Kelly and Kaplan 1990. Bloch's useful introductory survey of theories of ritual and his pertinent criticism of both "functionalist" and "symbolic" approaches does not prevent him from an odd and unwarranted reductionism. To him there seems to be no ritual but religious ritual, and history, to which he turns as a last resort when all theoretical means to reach a conclusion have failed, is simplified as no more than the way in which rituals are affected over time by events.

11. See Van Gennep [1909] 1977 on rites of passage; cf. Blok 1989. See Girard 1972 on the scapegoat; Turner 1977 on ritual and community; and Cohen 1985 on ritual and social boundaries.

12. For a comprehensive formal analysis of the *poena cullei*, synchronic surveys of capital punishment during at least three phases of its existence should, of course, be added to this diachronic one.

13. The specific relation between type of offense and form of punishment played a key role in this controversy. Thus, some maintained that the *talio* principle was purely

Roman, whereas Germanic law was characterized by the so-called *Spiegelstrafen*. See, e.g., Briquel 1984, 225–28; Brunnenmeister 1887, 173–84; Friese 1898, 146–49; Kisch 1939; and Maes 1979, 214–15. Cf. Kelley 1990a, 93–96.

14. Or as Kelley puts it, "Associated with the 'barbarian' legal tradition is a view of Germanic national character which, especially since the Renaissance, has acquired the status of a grand cultural myth" (1990a, 95). For further information about the debates in German legal history and philosophy, see 209–57. To ignore the ideological overtones of both the "indigenous origins" and the "sacrifice or punishment" debates and to use the works of these German scholars without more ado would be extremely naive. On the other hand, to treat all their works as suspect and to regard all these scholars as forerunners of Nazi ideology simply because they lived during the century before the Second World War would be just as simplistic.

15. It should be emphasized that in German and Dutch the concepts public (*öffentlich* or *openbaar*) and state (*staatlich* or *staats-*) are far more closely connected than in English. Public punishment thus automatically means punishment by the state, or as Von Amira put it, "In so far as the society is a state, we therefore speak of 'staatlicher' or 'öffentlicher' punishments" (1922, 1).

16. For a summary of the strongly divergent opinions of almost twenty scholars involved in this German debate see Von Amira 1922, 1–7. For stringent criticism of theories of sacrifice, see Rehfeldt 1942 (which we have not been able to consult); and cf. Feucht 1967 and Ström 1942, neither of which rejects the evolutionary model itself, however. Ström, who prefers the term *irrational* to *prerational*, links up with anthropological debates through references to Lévy-Bruhl. For early-twentieth-century English and French branches of the study of sacrifice—in which connections with punishment play a relatively minor role and sacrifice is studied primarily in the context of the history of religious thought—see especially Hubert and Mauss [1898] 1964; cf. Hertz 1922.

17. See, e.g., Gorecki 1983; Leder 1980; and Sturm 1961. Gorecki does not hesitate to speak of postbarbaric societies and argues that punishment decreases in severity with the development of societies. In a more sophisticated form, comparable evolutionist assumptions can be found in many studies of criminal justice in early modern European states. The well-documented increasing severity of public punishment in many European countries during the fifteenth and sixteenth centuries should be enough to counter such theories of linear development. For a forceful critique of evolutionist approaches with respect to the judicial ritual of the ordeal, see Bartlett 1986, 153–66.

18. "Du privé au public, de la famille à la cité, tel est pour l'essentiel l'axe d'une recherche où les juristes, surtout, mais pas seulement eux, opèrent à l'aide de catégories qui, parce qu'elles sont absolues, ne peuvent s'articuler que dans un ordre successif. Depuis le commencement de ce siècle, ce modèle est resté remarquablement stable dans l'historiographie de la peine. . . . Dans le domaine romain et à quelques exceptions près, l'histoire de la peine tend soit à reconstituer—fût-ce à travers les modalités mêmes du supplice—l'ascendance de la fonction pénale, soit à exposer les divers offices que le châtiment, isolat déplacé dans l'histoire, aurait successivement assumés" (Thomas 1984, 5–6).

19. Bukowska Gorgoni (1979, 150–51) mentions Rogerius, Placentinus, and Bernardus Papiensis for the twelfth century and Hostiensis, Azo, Odofredus, and Bartolus, among others, for the thirteenth and fourteenth centuries.

20. Bukowska Gorgoni 1979, 150–52 and passim; cf. Grimm [1828] 1899, 2:278–82.

21. For this gloss, see esp. Bukowska Gorgoni 1979, 154; Friese 1898, 138 and 154; and

Steffenhagen 1920 (which we have not been able to consult); cf. Sturm 1961, 159. There are several modern editions of the *Sachsenspiegel;* see, e.g., the illustrated edition by Schott and Schmidt-Wiegand (1984), with bibliography.

22. For a parallel development in Spain during the fifteenth and sixteenth centuries see Bukowska Gorgoni 1979, 152–53.

23. See Bukowska Gorgoni 1979, 153–55; Caspar 1892, 25; Fischer 1936, 22; Grimm [1828] 1899, 2:279–80; His 1920, 500–501, and 1928, pt. 1, 86–87, and pt. 3, 124, 152; Sturm 1961; and Von Hentig [1932] 1954–55, 1:304–5. Cf. Von Amira 1922, 141–43.

24. A similar text can be found in Philips Wielant's *Practijcke criminele,* written during the late fifteenth or early sixteenth century, which was extensively used by Damhouder (see Wielant 1872, 118–20).

25. In Augsburg, for instance, the local ordinances prescribed breaking on the wheel for men who had murdered a close relative; women might be buried alive for this crime (Caspar 1892, 71).

26. For punishment in effigy, its relation to insult by libelous pictures, and the relation of a material representation to what or whom it was supposed to represent, see esp. Brückner 1966; Edgerton 1985; and Reinle 1984, 201–3. Cf. Blum 1983; Burke 1987, 95–107; Fehr 1923; Ginzburg 1991; and Kisch 1931.

27. Carpzovius [1625] 1652, 1.8.20, 21, 26, 27, 33, and 40.

28. We have not been able to consult Wild 1934 or Zinck 1933. In spite of references to *Säcken* in Damhouder and Wielant, we have not come across any actual examples in the Netherlands in the sixteenth or seventeenth century. See, e.g., Boomgaard 1992; and Maes 1979. Cf. Noordewier 1853, which specialize in legal curiosities; and Van Wijn 1801.

29. A perusal of recent studies of judicial practice in the Netherlands, parts of Germany, France, and England has not yielded any more examples. Systematic archival research in the Dutch criminal records for the period 1620–1800 (Egmond 1993b) turned up a dozen or so cases of parricide, which included the murder of parents, step-parents, parents-in-law, brothers and sisters, brothers- and sisters-in-law, uncles, aunts, cousins, and nephews. Men were sentenced to either hanging or breaking on the wheel, whereas women were strangled.

30. The history of the *poena cullei* in Spain forms a striking parallel: there too its inclusion in legal ordinances followed upon its discussion by jurists. Bukowska Gorgoni (1979, 153) mentions several sources stating that it was actually applied by several Spanish and Neapolitan courts during the sixteenth century. Sometimes the convict was killed before being put into the sack with the animals.

31. On the next page he declares that he does not want to make any definite statement about its "un-Germanness."

32. For various interpretations of the intensification of punishment in early modern Europe, see Cohen 1993, 159–61; Dean and Lowe 1994; Foucault 1975; Ginzburg [1989] 1990a; Sharpe 1990, 27–36; Van Dülmen 1985; and Weisser 1979. Cf. Langbein 1974 and 1977 on criminal procedure; and Moore 1987.

33. The tendency to claim direct connections with the past may have been especially strong in the circles of jurists. Their training and professional practice must have made nearly every one of them familiar with the success in court of legal argumentation based on "ancient" privileges and "traditional" customs and rights. See also Kelley 1990b.

34. The point is by no means a new one, but it still needs to be made because its considerable implications for the methodology, concepts, and questions of early modern legal history have only begun to make themselves felt (see Kelley 1990a, 229–34; and

Cohen 1993, 159–61). For excellent discussions of other traditions of scholarship and the transmission of culture, see Grafton 1991; Grafton and Blair 1990; and Pumfrey, Rossi, and Slawinski 1991.

35. See Briquel 1984, with further references to a previous discussion with Thomas in 1980; Brunnenmeister 1887; Düll 1935; Magdelain 1984; and Mommsen 1899, 537–38, 612–15, 643–46, 921–23.

36. See Brunnenmeister 1887, 198–238; and Düll 1935. Cf. Magdelain 1984, which combines an etymological discussion with an interest in the legal interpretations of *par(r)icidas;* and Briquel 1984, 229. Whatever their interpretations, all these scholars agree that there is no connection between *parricidas* and *patricidas.*

37. On Roman criminal procedure, see Kunkel 1962, 1980, and 1984, 11–31. On capital punishment, see Briquel 1984; Callu 1984; David 1984; Levy 1963; and Mommsen 1899.

38. "Alia deinde lex asperrimum crimen nova poena persequitur, quae Pompeia de parricidiis vocatur. qua cavetur, ut si quis parentis aut filii, aut omnino adfectionis eius, quae nuncupatione parricidii continetur, fata properaverit . . . poena parricidii puniatur et neque gladio neque ignibus neque ulla alia sollemni poena subicietur, sed insutus culleo cum cane et gallo gallinaceo et vipera et simia et inter eas ferales angustias comprehensus, secundum quod regionis qualitas tulerit, vel in vicinum mare, vel in amnem proiciatur, ut omni elementorum usu vivus carere incipiat et ei coelum superstiti, terra mortuo auferatur."

39. "Marcianus libro quarto decimo institutionem. Lege Pompeia de parricidiis cavetur, ut si quis patrem, matrem, . . . occiderit . . . ut poena ea teneatur, quae est lege Cornelis de sicariis." Mommsen includes a list of the various degrees of kinship subsumed under the notion of parricide according to the *Lex Pompeia* (1899, 645).

40. Mommsen supposes that the *poena cullei* only became the special punishment for parricide when "ordinary" murder was no longer punished by death in late Republican times. He declares that even for parricide the *poena* was eventually abolished during the last phase of the Republic (1899, 643–45). Düll (1935, 366 and 368) agrees with Mommsen that the *Lex Pompeia* abolished the punishment of *Säcken.*

41. For extensive and still unsurpassed comments, see the edition by Landgraf, which first appeared in 1882–84; we have used the second, revised edition of 1914. See also Bukowska Gorgoni 1979, 147; and Grimm [1828] 1899, 2:280.

42. This presupposes, of course, that it had first been abolished by the *Lex Pompeia* (see Düll 1935; and Mommsen 1899, 645–46).

43. Bukowska Gorgoni 1979, 147–48; Düll 1935, 366. On the considerable discretionary powers of Roman magistrates, who were responsible for the execution of capital punishment, see Levy 1963, 343; and Mommsen 1899, 912–13, 939–44.

44. Bukowska Gorgoni 1979, 149; Düll 1935, 366; Mommsen 1899, 646.

45. One Gaius Villius was drowned together with one or more serpents during the Gracchian period. The monkey, in the company of the snake or even by itself, is first mentioned by Juvenal (8.214). See Düll 1935, 367–68.

46. Dositheus (3.16 = Corp. Gloss. ed. Goetz. 3:38, 14ff.), an author from an outer area of the Roman Empire in the Near East, mentions them together with the snake and monkey. See Düll 1935, 368.

47. Modestin in *Digesta* 48.9.9; *Constitutio Constantini* in *Codex Justiniani* 9.17.1 and *Institutiones* I.4.18.6. See also Düll 1935, 367–70.

48. Besides the essays in Hobsbawm and Ranger 1983, see Kelley 1990b. Cf. Grafton and Blair 1990; and Pumfrey, Rossi, and Slawinski 1991. In a comment on an earlier ver-

sion of this chapter Esther Cohen suggested that the *poena cullei* might belong to a species of legal rituals that exist mainly on paper, in lawbooks, and seem to serve principally to create a self-perception of the group ordaining them (see also Cohen 1993, 92 n. 23). Although it is hard to imagine what sort of self-perception might be created in this instance, one would certainly expect there to be several more "phantom" legal rituals.

49. The word *monster* may perhaps be used to render the meaning of these terms, which are by no means easy to translate; according to Céard (1977), their various meanings continued to overlap until at least the sixteenth century. According to Brunnenmeister, the term *prodigium* should here be read as a bad omen for the whole nation. He also points out that the term *prodigium* was used in ancient Rome for many types of physical deformity, in particular for hermaphrodites (who were drowned) and "monstrous" births (1887, 193–96); for remarks in the same vein see Briquel 1984, 226. The term *prodigium* was also used in connection with vestal virgins who had committed the religious crime of *incestum* (Fraschetti 1984; cf. Bloch 1963. See also the discussion of terminology in Schrage, in press).

50. As pointed out above, Cicero mentions only the drowning in a sack and not the animals. Cf. Grimm [1828] 1899, 2:280; and Bukowska Gorgoni 1979, 158, for further quotations from Roman sources. As Schrage (in press) points out, certain monstrous births were likewise regarded as extremely polluting phenomena, denied any further contact with earth and sky, and drowned. Cf. Bloch 1963, 112ff.

51. "Vel in vicinum mare vel in amnem proiciatur ut omni elementorum usu vivus carere incipiat et ei caelum superstiti, terra mortuo auferatur."

52. On continuity and change in the relations between the living and the dead and on the legal position of the latter, see Cohen 1993, 134–45; Geary 1994; and Oexle 1983.

53. Coelius Rhodiginus's *Lectiones antiquae* figures most prominently among Thevet's sources. He also refers to Cicero (Lestringant 1991b, 59–77). The passage cited below draws on Cicero, *Rosc. Am.* 26/71–72.

54. Cf. Cicero, *Rosc. Am.* 26/71–72. Agents of purification, such as water, fire, and gold, must themselves be kept pure (cf. Parker 1983, 207–34).

55. The examples discussed here do not constitute the whole body of evidence regarding the "interpretation" of the *poena cullei*, but Cicero's *Pro Sexto Roscio Amerino*, the various texts in the *Corpus Juris*, and the interpretations by Doeplerus and Carpzovius certainly are the most influential texts. For a fairly exhaustive but still fragmentary survey see Bukowska Gorgoni 1979; cf. Mommsen 1899, 921–25.

56. These legal collections display certain similarities with collections of curiosities. On Renaissance collecting and the concepts of *museum* and *theatrum*, see Findlen 1989; cf. Findlen 1994. On antiquarians and the law, see Momigliano 1966, 1–39. Cf. Cohen 1993, 159–61.

57. Bearing in mind anthropological debates about totemism, identification with animals, and "magical" thinking, a further investigation of animal symbolism in the context of punishment in antiquity and early modern Europe might be worthwhile. On the "animalization" of convicts see Cohen 1993, 85–133, 170–80; and Mason 1988. On the role of animals in sacrifice see, among others, Girard 1972; and Hubert and Mauss [1898] 1964.

58. Cf. Van Dülmen 1985, 121–27, which describes the punishments of drowning, burning, and burying alive as rituals of purification, which were gradually replaced by deterrent punishments (175–79).

59. The monkey was perhaps a substitute for the slave, who was originally buried along with his master. Berkenhoff does not believe that the wolf's skin was meant to protect the public from the evil eye since the leather sack would already serve this purpose (Berkenhoff 1937, 114–15).

60. Berkenhoff, however, does not believe that the type of consciousness required by such an inversion could have existed in early Roman criminal law, which, according to him, was dominated by the thought of sacrifice (Berkenhoff 1937, 115). Von Hentig was the supervisor of both Fischer's and Berkenhoff's dissertations.

61. Some of the offshoots of these debates continued far into the postwar era. In his *Symbolische Todesstrafen* (1961) Sturm presents an unfortunate combination of Jungian archetypes, chthonic forces, "Schuldsubstanz," and purifying rituals. In Bukowska Gorgoni's survey of the *poena cullei*'s history, in contrast, only faint traces are left of a shift from the symbolic to the functional role of the animals (1979, 160–61).

62. It will be obvious that by *development* we do not mean simply change over time.

63. Of course this need not have made any difference to their actual appreciation of the punishment, though they might have minded discovering that they were not doing as the Romans did.

64. Bloch 1986. Cf. Asad 1993, 55–79; and Kelly and Kaplan 1990.

65. In the southern and northern Netherlands, in several parts of Germany and France, and in Switzerland drowning (in open water or in a tub) was fairly regularly imposed as a punishment from the fifteenth to the late eighteenth century. Generally speaking, it was imposed on women for various crimes for which men would have been hanged and on both men and women in cases of certain crimes against religion (see, e.g., Schild 1980, 204–6; and Van Dülmen 1985, 122–25. For drowning as an ordeal, see Bartlett 1986).

66. Grimm, for instance, declares that "the drowning in a sack was definitely a medieval punishment," which did not involve any animals, however, and was imposed for various crimes ([1818] 1899, 2:281–82). Caspar (1892, 25) maintains that the punishment of *Säcken* was based on an old Germanic idea. Berkenhoff believes that the drowning of a parricide in a sack originated independently in Roman and Germanic law, whereas the four animals constituted a "foreign," Roman element (1937, 113). To make matters even more complicated, this claim to fairly specific, Germanic origins for the *poena cullei* should be distinguished from a more abstract argument like that developed by Briquel 1984. Starting from the hypothesis that the connections between form of punishment and type of offense in Germanic, Celtic, and Roman society derive from a common Indo-European past and referring to the work of Georges Dumézil, Briquel distinguishes three domains, or *fonctions,* that serve to classify the offenses and are linked with various complementary pairs of capital punishment (such as hanging and drowning, or burning and burial). Cf. Cohen 1993, 191–93.

CHAPTER 7: IMAGES OF THE BARBARIAN

1. The drawings that Sir Hans Sloane acquired from John White's descendants around 1706 were not originals, as he supposed, but copies of White's original drawings (Rowlands 1994, 249).

2. White's dependence on an old English chronicle for his pictorial source indicates that despite his firsthand observations in Virginia, White was not adverse to using other iconographical sources. In view of the existence of a number of collections of books on

the costumes of the various peoples of the world at this time, one can understand Defert's interest in the extent to which such *Trachtenbücher* may be said to have guided the hand of the painter (1987, 541).

3. Similar Picts appear in a manuscript by Lucas de Heere, *Theatre de tous les peuples et nations de la terre avec leurs habits* (1568).

4. For the concept of "reading off," see Mason (1990a, 57); other examples taken from the Virginia expedition are discussed by Martinet (1987, 297).

5. The originality of Baumstark's essays on the *Germania* dating from the 1860s has been highlighted by Lund (1988, 11). For a complete survey of the literature on the *Germania*, see Lund 1990a.

6. It is because of the importance attached to this aspect of the interpretation of the *Germania* that we draw heavily in what follows on the recent works of Lund (1990a, 1990b, 1990c, 1993), including his full-length commentary on the *Germania* itself (1988). The history of scholarship on the *Germania* and full references to the recent literature can be found in those works. Since the text of the *Germania* is by no means uncontroversial, we have tried to avoid basing the main points of the argument on the reconstructions of the philologists.

7. We use the term *Germani* because Wells has argued that "probably the original Germans, 'Germani' in Latin, were a group of Celtic or Celticized tribes, originally settled east of the Rhine, some of whom had crossed to the west bank, others who in Caesar's time were trying to do so, as they were pushed westwards by pressure of the non-Celtic migratory tribes, such as the Suebi, to whom Caesar . . . transfers their name, and who subsequently come to monopolize it, as if *they* were the real Germans" (1974, 270, emphasis in the original) In this article Wells briefly indicates a number of interesting parallels between the classical ethnography of the Celts and the French ethnography of the Algonquian-Iroquoian tribes in Canada in the sixteenth and seventeenth centuries.

8. For this restrictive use of *ut,* see Tacitus's phrase "ut inter Germanos" (30.2), discussed below.

9. For Tacitus the moralist the argument is the same in both cases: the charms of a people that has not yet become perverted are the same as those of Rome in a less decadent era than Tacitus's own time. In this respect Tacitus operates like an Usbek in reverse: whereas the Persian traveler of Montesquieu's *Lettres persanes* denounces the conventions of the society that is strange to him, Tacitus accentuates the virtues of the strange society to indicate how far Rome has degenerated (see Volpilhac-Auger 1985, 116).

10. For the alignment of philosophical sects with barbarian cultures in the work of Sextus Empiricus, see Mason in press.

11. On the significance of this (absence of) color, see Vidal-Naquet 1981, 151–74.

12. For the wider significance of this practice and its relation to initiatory rites, see Gernet 1968, 161ff.; and Ginzburg [1989] 1990a, 192.

13. On the *Cronycke,* see Tilmans 1988. For surveys that take the discussions relating to the Batavi up to the modern period, see Morineau 1982 and Van der Woud 1990.

14. Van de Waal (1952, 1:199ff.) identifies these artists as Simon Frisius, Nicolaas van Geilenkercken, and Hendrick Hondius.

15. All page references to Clüver are to volume 1 of the 1616 edition. The identical illustrations were used for the 1631 edition, though they were inserted at a different point in the text in the later edition.

16. The etching is reproduced as fig. 60 in Van de Waal 1952, vol. 2.

17. In this respect Clüver's volumes are far removed from the discrepancies between text and woodcut that can be found in the *Cronycke* (see Van de Waal 1952, 1:128 and 290; and Tilmans 1988, 63–66).

18. For a detailed case study of the ways both social rank and cultural differences can be "read off" from clothing, see Adorno's semiotic studies (1981, 1986) of the dress of the Spaniards and the Peruvian Indians in the illustrations to a work written at about the same time as that of Clüver: Guaman Poma de Ayala's *El primer nueva corónica y buen gobierno*. Cf. Zuidema 1991.

19. On expressions such as *exterae* or *externae gentes,* see Lund (1990b, 17).

20. Animal skins had already made their appearance in the title print for Noviomagus's *Historia Batavica* of 1530, which Kampinga (1917, 75) took to be a reference to Batavians.

21. Lipsius (1588, 153) compared it with the *Pantrock* of his own day.

22. On the ease with which an author could be classified as "ancient" in the sixteenth century, see Paré's reference to Lycosthenes as an "ancient philosopher" even though this pseudonym belonged to a *sixteenth*-century author, Conrad Wolffhart (Paré [1585] 1971, 151 n. 6).

23. For religion, compare not only the print of the animal sacrifice (fig. 17) but also that of a funeral scene (fig. 30).

24. Van den Boogaart expresses a similar verdict in stating that Schöffer "unjustly minimizes the primitive features of the Teutons in these illustrations" (1979, 534 n. 57).

25. None other than Edward Gibbon had looked back on an ancestor who spent a year in Virginia, where his passion for heraldry found a singular gratification at a war dance of the native Indians, whose bark shields and naked bodies were adorned with what he took to be "the colors and symbols of his favorite science" (quoted in Kiernan 1989, 89).

26. For a series of illustrations of the cremation of widows taken from the Orient, see figs. 65–67 (from Varthema, Lodewijcksz, and Linschoten) in Knefelkamp and König 1988.

27. The homology between Europe's inner and outer others is discussed in Mason 1987.

28. This section is based on the fuller discussion of the Eckhout paintings in Mason 1989, where the gender-related aspects of the paintings and their alleged ethnographic realism are treated in more detail. There is now a facsimile edition of the first two volumes of crayon drawings in Theatrum Rerum Naturalium Brasiliae 1993.

29. The paintings have been frequently reproduced. See, e.g., Dam-Mikkelsen and Lundbaek 1980; Mason 1989; Whitehead 1985; and Whitehead and Boeseman 1989.

30. The dance was a popular subject in depictions of the early contact between Europe and the non-European world. At a feast organized to celebrate Johan Maurits's return to the Netherlands in 1644 the *pièce de résistance* was a dance executed by naked Indians, to the horror of some preachers and their wives who were among the guests (Worp 1911–18, 4:107).

31. Brazilian Indians also appear on some of the paintings made by Frans Post in Brazil, but since Post appears to have painted exclusively colonized Tupinamba (Van den Boogaart 1990, 396), his work can be ignored in the present discussion.

32. We deliberately write *"Tapuya"* because the term itself means simply "non-Tupi." The profile of the "Tapuya" is little more than a negative image of the Tupi: they are what the Tupi are not (see Mason 1989).

33. A miniature painting dated to around 1585–88 of a young woman adorned with exotic flowers that had recently been introduced to Europe, including a South American variety, has been attributed to Jacques Le Moyne de Morgues; this "Flora" corresponds to an engraving entitled *A young daughter of the Picts* (Hulton 1985, 25–26). Like John White, Le Moyne seems to have viewed Old World inhabitants through New World eyes.

34. The other four paintings not considered here (namely, the painting of a light-skinned male, corresponding to the Mameluca woman; the painting of an African man; the painting of an African woman and child; and the horizontal painting of a "Tapuya" dance) fall into line with this pattern (Mason 1989).

35. For the reception of Tacitus in Germany during this period, and particularly the cult of Arminius, see Ridé 1976.

36. The inclusion of prints illustrating the most gruesome episodes related by Las Casas, first in a Latin edition of the work published by De Bry, was a Dutch innovation (Swart 1975, 53).

37. Grotius dissociated himself from his earlier interpretation of Dutch history in the 1640s, but his work on the Batavian republic continued to have considerable influence (Schöffer 1975, 93 n.33).

38. Though Grotius was primarily interested in basing his parallels on the Indians of North America, the distinction between North and South would have been too precise for many European observers. Icons of America tended to have a *pars pro toto* character; hence, it was above all the early iconography of Brazil that delineated the contours of allegories of America as a whole (see Poeschel 1985; and Wendt 1989).

39. The Dutch artists whose works were commissioned were Abraham Bloemaert, Jan van Bijlert, Gerrit van Honthorst, Nicolaus Knüpfer, Palamedes Palamedesz, Crispijn de Pas the Elder and his son, Simon Peter Tilemann, and Adam Willaerts (Schepelern and Houkjær 1988, 10).

40. For accounts of the French in Florida, see Fishman 1995; and Sauer 1971, 192–212.

41. De Bry seems to have committed some errors of confusion or substitution in the utilization of the Floridan and Virginian material (Hulton 1984, 9 and 17).

42. Joppien (1978) has argued that Thevet's artist drew on the Aztec *Codex Mendoza* for some of the portraits in *Les vrais pourtraits et vies des hommes illustres*, including that of "Paraousti Satouriona, Roy de la Floride." However, although Joppien's argument is persuasive in the case of the Thevetian portraits of Motecuhzoma II and Atahualpa, any influence from this native American source on Thevet's king of Florida would appear to have been overshadowed by the influence of the "Germanic" iconography. For a detailed discussion of possible borrowings by European artists from Mexican screenfolds, see Mason 1997.

43. It should not be forgotten that the availability of Harriot's *Briefe and true Report of the new found Land of Virginia*, with White's illustrations, in volume 1 of De Bry's *Great Voyages* ensured that the work achieved a maximum European impact (Hulton 1984, 17).

REFERENCES

Abry, C., and A. Joisten, eds. 1992. *Etres fantastiques dans les Alpes. Le monde alpin et rhodanien*, nos. 1–4. Grenoble.

Achter, V. 1951. *Geburt der Strafe*. Frankfurt am Main.

Ackerman, J. 1985. The Involvement of Artists in Renaissance Science. In *Science and the Arts in the Renaissance*, edited by J. W. Shirley and F. D. Hoeniger, 94–129. New Jersey.

Adorno, R. 1981. On Pictorial Language and the Typology of Culture in a New World Chronicle. *Semiotica* 36, nos. 1–2: 51–106.

——. 1986. *Guaman Poma: Writing and Resistance in Colonial Peru*. Austin.

Agulhon, M. 1988. *Histoire vagabonde*. Paris.

Alpers, S. 1991. The Museum As a Way of Seeing. In *Exhibiting Cultures: The Poetics and Politics of Museum Display*, edited by I. Karp and S. D. Lavine, 25–32. Washington, D.C.

Altick, R. 1978. *The Shows of London: A Panoramic History of Exhibitions, 1600–1862*. Cambridge, Mass.

Von Amira, K. 1891. Tierstrafen und Tierprozesse. *Mitteilungen des Instituts für Oesterreichische Geschichtsforschung* 12:545–601.

——. 1922. *Die germanischen Todesstrafen: Untersuchungen zur Rechts- und Religionsgeschichte*. Munich.

Ampzing, S. 1628. *Beschrijvinge ende lof der stad Haerlem*. Haarlem.

Asad, T. 1993. *Genealogies of Religion: Discipline and Reasons of Power in Christianity and Islam*. Baltimore.

Austin, J. L. 1955. *How to Do Things with Words*. Oxford.

Barthelmess, K., and J. Münzing. 1991. *Monstrum Horrendum: Wale und Waldarstellungen in der Druckgraphik des 16. Jahrhunderts und ihr motivkundlicher Einfluss*. 3 vols. Hamburg.

Bartholinus, T. 1654. *Historiarum anatomicarum rariorum, Centuria I et II*. Amsterdam.

Bartlett, R. 1986. *Trial by Fire and Water: The Medieval Judicial Ordeal*. Oxford.

Becker, B. [1804] 1972. *Aktenmässige Geschichte der Räuberbanden an den beyden Ufern des Rheins*. 2 vols. Leipzig.

Beem, H. 1969. Joodse namen en namen van Joden. *Studia Rosenthaliana* 3:82–94.

Belleforest, F. 1575. *La cosmographie universelle de tout le monde*. 2 vols. Paris.

Benjamin, W. 1968. *Illuminations: Essays and Reflections*. Edited with an introduction by H. Arendt and translated by H. Zohn. New York.

——. 1985. *One-Way Street and Other Writings*. Translated by E. Jephcott and K. Shorter. London.

Benveniste, E. 1966. *Problèmes de linguistique générale*. Paris.

Berkenhoff, H. A. 1937. *Tierstrafe, Tierbannung und rechtsrituelle Tiertötung im Mittelalter*. Bühl-Baden.

Bertolotti, M. [1979] 1991. The Ox's Bones and the Ox's Hide: A Popular Myth, Part Hagiography and Part Witchcraft. In *Microhistory and the Lost Peoples of Europe: Selec-*

tions from Quaderni Storici, edited by E. Muir and G. Ruggiero and translated by E. Branch, 42–70. Baltimore.

Bertrand, D. 1993. Les stratégies de Belon pour une représentation exotique. *Nouvelle Revue du Seizième Siècle* 11:5–17.

Bhabha, H. K. 1994. *The Location of Culture.* London.

Biagioli, M. 1993. *Galileo Courtier: The Practice of Science in the Culture of Absolutism.* Chicago.

Blake, W. 1966. *Complete Writings.* Edited by G. Keynes. Oxford.

Bloch, M. [1949] 1953. *The Historian's Craft.* New York.

———. 1986. *From Blessing to Violence: History and Ideology in the Circumcision Ritual of the Merina of Madagascar.* Cambridge.

———. 1989. *Ritual, History, and Power: Selected Papers in Anthropology.* London.

Bloch, R. 1963. *Les prodiges dans l'antiquité classique.* Paris.

Blok, A. 1974. *The Mafia of a Sicilian Village, 1860–1960: A Study of Violent Peasant Entrepreneurs.* Oxford.

———. 1981. Rams and Billy-goats: A Key to the Mediterranean Code of Honor. *Man* 16:427–40.

———. 1989. The Symbolic Vocabulary of Public Executions. In *History and Power in the Study of Law: New Directions in Legal Anthropology,* edited by J. F. Collier and J. Starr, 31–55. Ithaca.

Bloom, H. I. 1937. *The Economic Activities of the Jews of Amsterdam in the Seventeenth and Eighteenth Centuries.* Williamsport, Pa.

Blum, C. 1983. La folie et la mort dans l'imaginaire collectif du Moyen Age et du début de la Renaissance (XIIe–XVIe siècles). In *Death in the Middle Ages,* edited by H. Braet and W. Verbeke, 258–85. Louvain.

Bolens-Duvernay, J. 1988. Les Géants Patagons ou l'espace retrouvé: Les débuts de la cartographie américaniste. *L'Homme* 28, nos. 2–3: 156–73.

Bologna, C., ed. 1977. *Liber monstrorum de diversis generibus.* Milan.

Van den Boogaart, E. 1979. Infernal Allies: The Dutch West India Company and the Tarairiu, 1631–1654. In *Johan Maurits van Nassau-Siegen, 1604–1679: A Humanist Prince in Europe and Brazil,* edited by E. van den Boogaart, 519–38. The Hague.

———. 1990. The Slow Progress of Colonial Civility: Indians in the Pictorial Record of Dutch Brazil, 1637–1644. In *La Imagen del Indio en la Europa Moderna,* Consejo Superior de Investigaciones Científicas, 389–403. Seville.

Boomgaard, J. E. A. 1992. *Misdaad en straf in Amsterdam: Een onderzoek naar de strafrechtspleging van de Amsterdamse schepenbank 1490–1552.* Zwolle.

Braekman, W. L. 1990. Marktlied op de walvis gestrand te Oostende (1827). *Volkskunde* 91:80–83.

Briquel, D. 1984. Formes de mise à mort dans la Rome primitive: quelques remarques sur une approche comparative du problème. In *Du châtiment dans la cité: Supplices corporels et peine de mort dans le monde antique,* 225–40. Rome.

Brückner, W. 1966. *Bildnis und Brauch: Studien zur Bildfunktion der Effigies.* Berlin.

Bruijn, A. de. 1581. *Omnium pene Europae, Asiae, Aphricae atque Americae gentium habitus.* Antwerp.

Brunnenmeister, E. 1887. *Das Tötungsverbrechen im altrömischen Recht.* Leipzig.

Bucher, B. [1977] 1981. *Icon and Conquest: A Structural Analysis of the Illustrations of de Bry's Great Voyages.* Translated by Basia Miller Gulati. Chicago.

Bukowska Gorgoni, C. 1979. Die Strafe des Säckens—Wahrheit und Legende. *Forschungen zur Rechtsarchäologie und rechtlichen Volkskunde* 2:145–62.

Burke, P. 1987. *The Historical Anthropology of Early Modern Italy: Essays on Perception and Communication.* Cambridge.

———. 1992. *History and Social Theory.* Cambridge.

———. 1995. America and the Rewriting of World History. In *America in European Consciousness, 1493–1750,* edited by K. Ordahl Kupperman, 33–51. Chapel Hill.

Burkert, W. 1987. Oriental and Greek Mythology: The Meeting of Parallels. In *Interpretations of Greek Mythology,* edited by J. Bremmer, 10–40. London.

Burkitt, I. 1991. *Social Selves: Theories of the Social Formation of Personality.* London.

Burmeister, K. H. 1964. *Sebastian Münster: Eine Bibliographie.* Wiesbaden.

Van Buuren, A. M. J. 1988. Eer en schande in enkele laat-Middelnederlandse literaire teksten. In *Soete minne en helsche boosheit. Seksuele voorstellingen in Nederland, 1300–1850,* edited by G. Hekma and H. Roodenburg, 23–41. Nijmegen.

Caisson, M. 1995. L'Indien, le détective, et l'ethnologue. *Terrain* 25:113–24.

Callu, J.-P. 1984. Le jardin des supplices au bas-empire. In *Du châtiment dans la cité: Supplices corporels et peine de mort dans le monde antique,* 313–59. Rome.

Campbell, J. K. 1964. *Honor, Family, and Patronage: A Study of Institutions and Moral Values in a Greek Mountain Community.* Oxford.

Campbell, M. B. 1988. *The Witness and the Other World: Exotic European Travel Writing, 400–1600.* Ithaca.

Canfora, L. 1979. Tacito e la "riscoperta degli antichi Germani": Dal II al III Reich. *Studi Urbinati di Storia, Filosofia e Letteratura* 53, nos. 1–2: 219–54.

Carozzi, C. 1983. La Géographie de l'au-delà et sa signification pendant le haut Moyen Age. In *Popoli e paesi nella cultura altomedievale.* Settimane di studio del Centro italiano di studi sull'alto medievo XXIX, 2:423–81. Spoleto.

Carpzovius (Carpzov), B. [1625] 1652. *Practica nova imperialis saxonica rerum criminalium.* 3rd rev. ed. Frankfurt.

Cary, G. 1956. *The Medieval Alexander.* Cambridge.

Caspar, C. J. 1892. *Darstellung des strafrechtlichen Inhaltes des Schwabenspiegels und des Augsburger Stadt Rechts.* Berlin.

Céard, J. 1977. *La nature et les prodiges: L'insolite au XVIe siècle, en France.* Geneva.

Certeau, M. de. 1975. *L'écriture de l'histoire.* Paris.

Chapman, W. R. 1985. Arranging Ethnology: A.H.L.F. Pitt Rivers and the Typological Tradition. In *Objects and Others: Essays on Museums and Material Culture,* edited by G. W. Stocking Jr., 15–48. Madison.

Cioffi, F. 1981. Wittgenstein and the Fire-Festivals. In *Perspectives on the Philosophy of Wittgenstein,* edited by I. Block, 212–37. Oxford.

Cipoletti, M. S. 1983. *Jenseitsvorstellungen bei den Indianern Südamerikas.* Berlin.

Van Cleeff-Hiegentlich, F. 1987. "Eerlyke smousen—Hoe zien die er uyt Myn Heer?" Of hoe er in de achttiende eeuw in de Republiek der Zeven Verenigde Nederlanden over joden werd gedacht—een verkenning. In *Vreemd Gespuis,* edited by Anne Frank Stichting, 56–65. Amsterdam.

Clericl, N. 1987. Native Americans in Columbus's Home Land: A Show within the Show. In *Indians and Europe,* edited by C. F. Feest, 415–26. Göttingen.

Clifford, J. 1988. *The Predicament of Culture: Twentieth-Century Ethnography, Literature, and Art.* Cambridge, Mass.

Clüver, P. 1616. *De Germania Antiqua*. Leiden.

Cohen, A. P. 1985. *The Symbolic Construction of Community*. London.

Cohen, C. 1994. *Le destin du mammouth*. Paris.

Cohen, E. 1986. Law, Folklore, and Animal Lore. *Past and Present* 110:8–37.

———. 1989. Symbols of Culpability and the Universal Language of Justice: The Ritual of Public Executions in Late Medieval Europe. *History of European Ideas* 11:407–16.

———. 1993. *The Crossroads of Justice: Law and Culture in Late Medieval France*. Leiden.

Colin, S. 1987. The Wild Man and the Indian in Early Sixteenth Century Book Illustration. In *Indians and Europe*, edited by C. F. Feest, 5–36. Göttingen.

Coombes, A. E. 1994. *Reinventing Africa: Museums, Material Culture, and Popular Imagination*. New Haven.

Copenhaver, B. P. 1991. A Tale of Two Fishes: Magical Objects in Natural History from Antiquity through the Scientific Revolution. *Journal of the History of Ideas* 52, no. 3: 373–98.

Cressy, D. 1993. De la fiction dans les archives? ou le Monstre de 1569. *Annales ESC* 48, no. 5: 1309–29.

Crosland, M. 1994. Anglo-Continental Scientific Relations, c. 1780–c. 1820, with Special Reference to the Correspondence of Sir Joseph Banks. In *Sir Joseph Banks: A Global Perspective*, edited by R. E. R. Banks et al., 13–22. Kew.

Dam-Mikkelsen, B., and T. Lundbaek. 1980. *Etnografiske genstande i Det kongelige danske Kunstkammer 1650–1800*. Copenhagen.

Damhouder, J. de. [1555] 1616. *Practijcke ende hant-boeck in criminele saacken*. Amsterdam.

Darwin, C. [1859] 1985. *The Origin of Species by Means of Natural Selection*. Edited by J. W. Burrow. Harmondsworth.

David, J.-M. 1984. Du *Comitium* à la roche Tarpéienne: Sur certains rituels d'exécution capitale sous la République, les règnes d'Auguste et de Tibere. In *Du châtiment dans la cité: Supplices corporels et peine de mort dans le monde antique*, 131–76. Rome.

Davis, N. Z. 1975. *Society and Culture in Early Modern France*. Stanford.

———. 1988. *Fiction in the Archives: Pardon Tales and Their Tellers in Sixteenth Century France*. Cambridge.

Day, M. 1994. Humana: Anatomical, Pathological, and Curious Human Specimens in Sloane's Museum. In *Sir Hans Sloane, Collector, Scientist, Antiquary, Founding Father of the British Museum*, edited by A. MacGregor, 69–76. London.

Dean, T., and K. J. P. Lowe, eds. 1994. *Crime, Society, and the Law in Renaissance Italy*. Cambridge.

Defert, D. 1987. Les collections iconographiques du XVIe siècle. In *Voyager à la Renaissance*, edited by J. Céard and J.-C. Margolin, 531–43. Paris.

Derrida, J. 1972. *Marges*. Paris.

———. 1978. *Éperons: Les styles de Nietzsche*. Paris.

———. 1980. *La Carte postale, de Socrate à Freud et au-delà*. Paris.

———. 1986. *Parages*. Paris.

———. 1987. *Psyché, inventions de l'autre*. Paris.

———. 1995. *Points . . . Interviews, 1974–1994*. Edited by E. Weber. Stanford.

Detienne, M. 1981. *L'invention de la mythologie*. Paris.

Doeplerus (Doepler), J. 1693–97. *Theatrum poenarum, suppliciorum et executionum criminalium oder Schauplatzes derer Leibes- und Lebensstrafen*. 2 vols. Leipzig.

Droixhe, D. 1978. *La linguistique et l'appel de l'histoire (1600–1800): Rationalisme et révolutions positivistes.* Geneva.

Du châtiment dans la cité: Supplices corporels et peine de mort dans le monde antique. 1984. Round table organized by the École française de Rome and the Centre national de la recherche scientifique, Rome, November 1982. Rome.

Duerr, H. P. [1978] 1985. *Dreamtime: Concerning the Boundary between Wilderness and Civilization.* Translated by F. Goodman. Oxford.

Düll, R. 1935. Zur Bedeutung der poena cullei im römischen Strafrecht. In *Atti del congresso internazionale di diritto romano: Bologna e Roma II,* 363–408. Pavia.

Van Dülmen, R. 1984. Das Schauspiel des Todes: Hinrichtungsrituale in der frühen Neuzeit. In *Volkskultur: Zur Wiederentdeckung des vergessenen Alltags (16.–20. Jahrhundert),* edited by R. van Dülmen and N. Schindler, 205–45. Frankfurt am Main.

———. 1985. *Theater des Schreckens: Gerichtspraxis und Strafrituale in der frühen Neuzeit.* Munich.

Duviols, J.-P. 1982. La colonie de Florida (1562–1565) et la découverte de nouveaux "sauvages." In *Etudes sur L'Impact Culturel du Nouveau Monde,* 2:31–43. Paris.

Eamon, W. 1994. *Science and the Secrets of Nature: Books of Secrets in Medieval and Early Modern Culture.* Princeton.

Edgerton, S. Y., Jr. 1985. *Pictures of Punishment: Art and Criminal Prosecution during the Florentine Renaissance.* Ithaca.

Egmond, F. 1986. *Banditisme in de Franse Tijd: Profiel van de Grote Nederlandse Bende, 1790–1799.* Amsterdam.

———. 1990. Crime in Context: Jewish Involvement in Organized Crime in the Dutch Republic. *Jewish History* 4:75–100.

———. 1993a. Children in Court: Children and Criminal Justice in the Dutch Republic. *Social and Legal Studies* 2:73–90.

———. 1993b. *Underworlds: Organized Crime in the Netherlands, 1650–1800.* Cambridge.

Egmond, F., and P. Mason. 1994. Armadillos in Unlikely Places: Some Unpublished Sixteenth-Century Sources for New World *Rezeptionsgeschichte* in Northern Europe. *Ibero-Amerikanisches Archiv* 20, nos. 1–2: 3–52.

———. 1995a. Een portret van Coenraet van Schilperoort (1577–1636). *Bulletin van het Rijksmuseum* 43, no. 1: 36–58; English summary on 81–83.

———. 1995b. Report on a Wild Goose Chase. *Journal of the History of Collections* 7, no. 1: 25–43.

Eisenman, S. F. 1992. *The Temptation of Saint Redon: Biography, Ideology, and Style in the Noirs of Odilon Redon.* Chicago.

Elias, N. [1939] 1969. *Über den Prozess der Zivilisation.* 2 vols. Bern.

Endelman, T. M. 1979. *The Jews of Georgian England, 1714–1830: Tradition and Change in a Liberal Society.* Philadelphia.

Erdman, D. V. 1954. *Blake: Prophet against Empire.* Princeton.

Evans, E. P. [1906] 1987. *The Criminal Prosecution and Capital Punishment of Animals.* London.

Evans, R. 1984. Öffentlichkeit und Autorität: Zur Geschichte der Hinrichtungen in Deutschland vom allgemeinen Landrecht bis zum Dritten Reich. In *Räuber, Volk und Obrigkeit: Studien zur Geschichte der Kriminalität in Deutschland seit dem 18. Jahrhundert,* edited by H. Reif, 185–258. Frankfurt am Main.

Fabre, D. 1996. Rêver. Le mot, la chose, l'histoire. *Terrain* 26:69–82.

Faris, J. C. 1992. A Political Primer on Anthropology/Photography. In *Anthropology and Photography, 1860–1920*, edited by E. Edwards, 253–63. New Haven.

Fehr, H. 1923. *Das Recht im Bilde*. Erlenbach.

Ferrari, M. 1987. Public Anatomy Lessons and the Carnival: The Anatomy Theatre of Bologna. *Past and Present* 117:50–106.

Feucht, D. 1967. *Grube und Pfahl: Ein Beitrag zur Geschichte der deutschen Hinrichtungsbräuche*. Tübingen.

Findlen, P. 1989. The Museum: Its Classical Etymology and Renaissance Genealogy. *Journal of the History of Collections* 1:59–78.

———. 1994. *Possessing Nature: Museums, Collecting, and Scientific Culture in Early Modern Italy*. Berkeley.

Fischer, J.-L. 1985. Lafitau et l'acéphale: Une preuve "teratologique" du monogénisme. In *Naissance de l'ethnologie? Anthropologie et missions en Amérique, XVIe–XVIIIe siècle*, edited by C. Blanckaert, 91–101. Paris.

Fischer, P. 1936. *Strafen und sichernde Massnahmen gegen Tote im germanischen und deutschen Recht*. Bonn.

Fishman, L. 1995. Old World Images Encounter New World Reality: René Laudonnière and the Timucuans of Florida. *Sixteenth Century Journal* 26, no. 3: 547–59.

Flint, V. I. J. 1991. *The Rise of Magic in Early Medieval Europe*. Princeton.

———. 1992. *The Imaginative Landscape of Christopher Columbus*. Princeton.

Foucault, M. 1975. *Surveiller et punir: Naissance de la prison*. Paris.

———. 1980. *Power/Knowledge: Selected Interviews and Other Writings, 1972–1977*. Edited by C. Gordon. New York.

Fraschetti, A. 1984. La sepoltura delle Vestali e la Città. In *Du châtiment dans la cité: Supplices corporels et peine de mort dans le monde antique*, 97–129. Rome.

Freud, S. [1900] 1976. *The Interpretation of Dreams*. Pelican Freud Library, vol. 4. Harmondsworth.

Frevert, U. 1995. *Men of Honor: A Social and Cultural History of the Duel*. Cambridge.

Friedman, J. 1993. *Miracles and the Pulp Press during the English Revolution: The Battle of the Frogs and Fairford's Flies*. London.

Friedman, J. B. 1981. *The Monstrous Races in Medieval Art and Thought*. Cambridge, Mass.

Friese, V. 1898. *Das Strafrecht des Sachsenspiegels*. Breslau.

Geary, P. 1994. *Living with the Dead in the Middle Ages*. Ithaca.

Van Gennep, A. [1909] 1977. *The Rites of Passage*. London.

George, W., and B. Yapp. 1991. *The Naming of the Beasts: Natural History in the Medieval Bestiary*. London.

Gerbi, A. 1973. *The Dispute of the New World: The History of a Polemic, 1750–1900*. Translated by J. Moyle. Rev. and enl. ed. Pittsburgh.

Gernet, L. 1937. Paricidas. *Revue de Philologie* 63:13–29.

———. 1955. *Droit et société dans la Grèce ancienne*. Paris.

———. 1968. *Anthropologie de la grèce antique*. Paris.

Gilmore, D. D., ed. 1987. *Honor and Shame and the Unity of the Mediterranean*. Washington, D.C.

Ginzburg, C. [1976] 1980. *The Cheese and the Worms: The Cosmos of a Sixteenth-Century Miller*. Translated by J. Tedeschi and A. Tedeschi. London.

———. 1981. Charivari, associations juvéniles, chasse sauvage. In *Le Charivari*, edited by J. Le Goff and J.-C. Schmitt, 131–40. Paris.

————. 1982. Datazione assoluta e datazione relativa: Sul metodo di Longhi. *Paragone* 33, no. 386: 9–17.

————. [1966] 1983. *The Night Battles.* Translated by J. Tedeschi and A. Tedeschi. London.

————. 1984. The Witches' Sabbat: Popular Cult or Inquisitorial Stereotype? In *Understanding Popular Culture: Europe from the Middle Ages to the Nineteenth Century,* edited by S. L. Kaplan, 39–51. Berlin, Amsterdam, and New York.

————. [1981] 1985. *The Enigma of Piero.* Translated by M. Ryle and K. Soper. London.

————. [1989] 1990a. *Ecstasies: Deciphering the Witches' Sabbath.* Translated by Raymond Rosenthal. London.

————. [1986] 1990b. *Myths, Emblems, Clues.* Translated by J. Tedeschi and A. Tedeschi. London.

————. 1991. Représentation: Le mot, l'idée, la chose. *Annales ESC* 45, no. 6: 1219–34.

————. 1992. Fiction As Historical Evidence: A Dialogue in Paris, 1646. *Yale Journal of Criticism* 5, no. 2: 165–78.

————. 1993. Microhistory: Two or Three Things I Know about It. *Critical Inquiry* 20:10–34.

————. 1995. Vetoes and Compatibilities. *Art Bulletin* 77, no. 4: 534–36.

Ginzburg, C., and M. Ferrari. 1991. The Dovecote Has Opened Its Eyes. In *Microhistory and the Lost Peoples of Europe: Selections from Quaderni Storici,* edited by E. Muir and G. Ruggiero and translated by E. Branch, 11–19. Baltimore.

Ginzburg, C., and C. Poni. 1991. The Name and the Game: Unequal Exchange and the Historiographic Marketplace. In *Microhistory and the Lost Peoples of Europe: Selections from Quaderni Storici,* edited by E. Muir and G. Ruggiero and translated by E. Branch, 1–10. Baltimore.

Girard, R. 1972. *La violence et le sacré.* Paris.

Glanz, R. 1968. *Geschichte des niederen jüdischen Volkes in Deutschland: Ein Studie über historisches Gaunertum, Bettelwesen und Vagantentum.* New York.

Goethe, J. W. von. [1809] 1971. *Elective Affinities.* Translated by R. J. Hollingdale. London.

Golubtsova, N. 1969. Le problème de la culture dans quelques oeuvres de la philosophie des lumières au 18e siècle. *Journal of World History* 11:657–74.

Gombrich, E. 1959. *Art and Illusion.* London.

Gorecki, J. 1983. *Capital Punishment: Criminal Law and Social Evolution.* New York.

Grafton, A. 1991. *Defenders of the Text: The Traditions of Scholarship in an Age of Science, 1450–1800.* Cambridge, Mass.

————. 1992. *New Worlds, Ancient Texts: The Power of Tradition and the Shock of Discovery.* Cambridge, Mass.

Grafton, A., and A. Blair, eds. 1990. *The Transmission of Culture in Early Modern Europe.* Philadelphia.

Green, D. 1985. Veins of Resemblance: Photography and Eugenics. *Oxford Art Journal* 7, no. 2: 3–16.

Greenberg, K. S. 1990. The Nose, the Lie, and the Duel in the Antebellum South. *American Historical Review* 95:57–74.

Greenblatt, S. J. 1980. *Renaissance Self-Fashioning.* Chicago.

————. 1990. *Learning to Curse: Essays in Early Modern Culture.* London.

————. 1991. *Marvelous Possessions: The Wonder of the New World.* Oxford.

Greene, J. P. 1993. *The Intellectual Construction of America: Exceptionalism and Identity from 1492 to 1800.* Chapel Hill.

Grendi, E. 1994. Ripensare la microstoria? *Quaderni Storici*, n.s., 86:539–49.

Grimm, J. [1828] 1899. *Deutsche Rechtsaltertümer*. Edited by A. Heusler and R. Hübner. 2 vols. 4th ed. Leipzig.

Groebner, V. 1995a. Der verletzte Körper und die Stadt: Gewalttätigkeit und Gewalt in Nürnberg am Ende des 15. Jahrhunderts. In *Physische Gewalt: Studien zur Geschichte der Neuzeit*, edited by Thomas Lindenberger and Alf Lüdtke, 162–89. Frankfurt am Main.

———. 1995b. Losing Face, Saving Face: Noses and Honour in the Late Medieval Town. *History Workshop Journal* 40:1–16.

Grottanelli, C. 1991. Discussione su "Storia Notturna" di Carlo Ginzburg. *Quaderni di storia* 17, no. 34: 103–16.

Guilleminot, G. 1987. Heurs et malheurs des jeunes voyageurs en France au XVIe siècle. In *Voyager à la Renaissance*, edited by J. Céard and J.-C. Margolin, 179–91. Paris.

Gundestrup, B. 1985. From the Royal Kunstkammer to the Modern Museums of Copenhagen. In *The Origins of Museums*, edited by O. Impey and A. MacGregor, 128–35. Oxford.

Gurevich, A. 1988. *Medieval Popular Culture: Problems of Belief and Perception*. Translated by J. M. Bak and P. A. Hollingsworth. Cambridge.

———. 1992. *Historical Anthropology of the Middle Ages*. Edited by J. Howlett. Cambridge.

Hanson, E. 1991. Torture and Truth in Renaissance England. *Representations* 34:53–84.

Hardy, T. 1979. *The Distracted Preacher and Other Tales*. London.

Heidegger, M. 1957. *Sein und Zeit*. 8th ed. Tübingen.

Heikkinen, A., and T. Kervinen. 1990. Finland: The Male Domination. In *Early Modern European Witchcraft: Centres and Peripheries*, edited by B. Ankarloo and G. Henningsen, 319–38. Oxford.

Heinemann, F. 1900. *Der Richter und die Rechtspflege in der deutschen Vergangenheit*. Leipzig.

Henningsen, G. 1990. "The Ladies from Outside": An Archaic Pattern of the Witches' Sabbath. In *Early Modern European Witchcraft: Centres and Peripheries*, edited by B. Ankarloo and G. Henningsen, 191–215. Oxford.

Von Hentig, H. [1932] 1954–55. *Die Strafe*. 2 vols. Berlin.

Héritier-Augé, F. 1992. Moitiés d'hommes, pieds déchaussés et sauteurs à cloche-pied. *Terrain* 18:5–14.

Hertz, R. 1922. La péché et l'expiation dans les sociétés primitives. *Revue de l'histoire des religions* 86:5–53.

His, R. 1920. *Das Strafrecht des deutschen Mittelalters*. Vol. 1. Leipzig.

———. 1928. *Geschichte des deutschen Strafrechts bis zur Karolina*. Munich.

Histoire Naturelle des Indes: The Drake Manuscript in the Pierpont Morgan Library. 1996. Preface by Charles E. Pierce Jr. Foreword by Patrick O'Brian. Introduction by Verlyn Klinkenborg. Translations by Ruth S. Kraemer. New York.

Hobsbawm, E. 1983. Introduction to *The Invention of Tradition*, edited by E. Hobsbawm and T. Ranger, 1–14. Cambridge.

Hobsbawm, E., and T. Ranger, eds. 1983. *The Invention of Tradition*. Cambridge.

Honour, H. 1975. *The New Golden Land: European Images of America from the Discoveries to the Present Time*. London.

———. 1979. Science and Exoticism: The European Artist and the Non-European World before Johan Maurits. In *Johan Maurits van Nassau-Siegen, 1604–1679: A Humanist Prince in Europe and Brazil*, edited by E. van den Boogaart, 269–96. The Hague.

———, ed. 1976. *L'Amérique vue par l'Europe*. Exhibition catalog, Grand Palais. Paris.

Hsia, R. Po-Chia. 1992. *Trent 1475: Stories of a Ritual Murder Trial*. New Haven.

Hubert, H., and M. Mauss. [1898] 1964. *Sacrifice: Its Nature and Function*. London.

Huet, M.-H. 1993. *Monstrous Imagination*. Cambridge, Mass.

Hulton, P. 1978. Images of the New World: Jacques Le Moyne de Morgues and John White. In *The Westward Enterprise: English Activities in Ireland, the Atlantic, and America, 1480–1650*, edited by K. R. Andrews, N. P. Canny, and P. E. H. Hair, 195–214. Liverpool.

———. 1984. *America 1585: The Complete Drawings of John White*. Chapel Hill.

———. 1985. Realism and Tradition in Ethnological and Natural History Imagery of the Sixteenth Century. In *The Natural Sciences and the Arts*, edited by A. Ellenius, 18–31. Uppsala.

Hunger, F.W.T. 1927. *Charles de l'Escluse*. The Hague.

Huussen, A. H. 1989. De Joden in Nederland en het probleem van de tolerantie. In *Een schijn van verdraagzaamheid: Afwijking en tolerantie in Nederland van de zestiende eeuw tot heden*, edited by M. Gijswijt-Hofstra, 107–29. Hilversum.

Israel, J. I. 1985. *European Jewry in the Age of Mercantilism, 1550–1750*. Oxford.

———. 1995. *The Dutch Republic: Its Rise, Greatness, and Fall, 1477–1806*. Oxford.

Janni, P. 1984. *La Mappa e il Periplo: Cartografia antica e spazio odologico*. Rome.

De Jongh, E. 1995. *Kwesties van betekenis: Thema en motief in de Nederlandse schilderkunst van de zeventiende eeuw*. Leiden.

Joppien, R. 1978. Etude de quelques portraits ethnologiques dans l'oeuvre d'André Thevet. *Gazette des Beaux-Arts*, 125–36.

———. 1979. The Dutch Vision of Brazil: Johan Maurits and His Artists. In *Johan Maurits van Nassau-Siegen, 1604–1679: A Humanist Prince in Europe and Brazil*, edited by E. van den Boogaart, 297–376. The Hague.

Kadir, D. 1992. *Columbus and the Ends of the Earth: Europe's Prophetic Rhetoric As Conquering Ideology*. Berkeley and Los Angeles.

Kampinga, H. 1917. *De Opvattingen over onze Oudere Vaderlandsche Geschiedenis bij de Hollandsche Historici der XVIe en XVIIe Eeuw*. The Hague.

Kaplan, Y. 1989a. Amsterdam and Ashkenazic Migration in the Seventeenth Century. *Studia Rosenthaliana* 23:22–44.

———. 1989b. The Portuguese Community in Seventeenth-Century Amsterdam and the Ashkenazi World. *Dutch Jewish History* 2:23–45.

Karp, I., and S. D. Lavine, eds. 1991. *Exhibiting Cultures: The Poetics and Politics of Museum Display*. Washington, D.C.

Katz, J. 1973. *Out of the Getto: The Social Background of Jewish Emancipation, 1770–1870*. Cambridge, Mass.

Keen, B. 1971. *The Aztec Image in Western Thought*. New Brunswick.

Kelley, D. R. 1990a. *The Human Measure: Social Thought in the Western Legal Tradition*. Cambridge, Mass.

———. 1990b. "Second Nature": The Idea of Custom in European Law, Society, and Culture. In *The Transmission of Culture in Early Modern Europe*, edited by A. Grafton and A. Blair, 131–72. Philadelphia.

Kelly, J. D., and M. Kaplan. 1990. History, Structure, and Ritual. *Annual Review of Anthropology* 19:119–51.

Kerber, L. 1970. *Federalists in Dissent: Imagery and Ideology in Jeffersonian America*. Ithaca.

Kiernan, V. G. 1989. Noble and Ignoble Savages. In *Exoticism in the Enlightenment*, edited by G. S. Rousseau and R. Porter, 86–116. Manchester.

Kirshenblatt-Gimblett, B. 1991. Objects of Ethnography. In *Exhibiting Cultures: The Poetics and Politics of Museum Display*, edited by I. Karp and S. D. Lavine, 386–443. Washington, D.C.

Kisch, G. 1931. Ehrenschelte und Schandgemälde. *Zeitschrift der Savigny-Stiftung für Rechtsgeschichte*, Germ. Abt. 51:514–20.

———— 1939. Die talionsartige Strafe für Rechtsverweigerung im Sachsenspiegel. *Tijdschrift voor Rechtsgeschiedenis* 16:457–67.

————. 1979. *Forschungen zur Rechts- und Sozialgeschichte der Juden in Deutschland während des Mittelalters*. 2 vols. Sigmaringen.

Klaniczay, G. 1984. Shamanistic Elements in Central European Witchcraft. In *Shamanism in Eurasia*, edited by M. Hoppál, 404–22. Göttingen.

————. 1990. Hungary: The Accusations and the Universe of Popular Magic. In *Early Modern European Witchcraft: Centres and Peripheries*, edited by B. Ankarloo and G. Henningsen, 219–55. Oxford.

Knefelkamp, U., and H.-J. König, eds. 1988. *Die Neuen Welten in alten Büchern: Entdeckung und Eroberung in frühen deutschen Schrift- und Bildzeugnissen*. Bamberg.

Koorn, F. 1986. Women without Vows: The Case of the Beguines and the Sisters of the Common Life in the Northern Netherlands. In *Women and Men in Spiritual Culture, XIV–XVII Centuries*, edited by E. Schulte van Kessel, 135–49. The Hague.

Kunkel, W. 1962. *Untersuchungen zur Entwicklung des römischen Kriminalverfahrens in vorsullanischer Zeit*. Munich.

————. 1980. *Römische Rechtsgeschichte: Eine Einführung*. 9th ed. Cologne.

————. 1984. *Kleine Schriften: Zum römischen Strafverfahren und zur römischen Verfassungsgeschichte*. Edited by H. Niederländer. Weimar.

Künzel, R. 1983. Over schuld en schaamte in enige verhalende bronnen uit de tiende en elfde eeuw. *Bijdragen en Mededelingen betreffende de Geschiedenis der Nederlanden* 98:358–72.

Laclos, C. [1782] 1972. *Les liaisons dangereuses*. Paris.

Lafitau, J.-F. 1724. *Moeurs des sauvages amériquains comparées aux moeurs des premiers temps*. 2 vols. Paris.

Landgraf, G., ed. [1882–84] 1914. *Ciceros Rede für Sex: Roscius aus Ameria*. 2 vols. Leipzig.

Langbein, J. H. 1974. *Prosecuting Crime in the Renaissance: England, Germany, France*. Cambridge, Mass.

————. 1977. *Torture and the Law of Proof: Europe and England in the Ancien Regime*. Chicago.

Lazzerini, L. 1994. Le radici folkloriche dell'anatomia: Scienza e rituale all'inizio dell'età moderna. *Quaderni Storici* 85, no. 1: 193–233.

Leder, K. B. 1980. *Todesstrafen. Ursprung, Geschichte, Opfer*. Munich.

Le Goff, J. 1977. *Pour un autre Moyen Age: Temps, travail et culture en occident: 18 essais*. Paris.

————. 1981. *La naissance du purgatoire*. Paris.

————. 1985. *L'imaginaire médiéval*. Paris.

Le Goff, J., and J.-C. Schmitt, eds. 1981. *Le Charivari*. Paris.

Le Roy Ladurie, E. 1979. *Le carnaval de Romans: De la chandeleur au mercredi des cendres 1579–1580*. Paris.

Léry, J. de. 1990. *History of a Voyage to the Land of Brazil, Otherwise Called America.* Translated with an introduction by J. Whatley. Berkeley and Los Angeles.

Lestringant, F. 1987. The Myth of the Indian Monarchy: An Aspect of the Controversy between Thevet and Léry (1575–1585). In *Indians and Europe,* edited by C. F. Feest, 37–60. Göttingen.

———. 1990. *Le Huguenot et le Sauvage: L'Amérique et la controverse coloniale, en France, au temps des Guerres de Religion (1555–1589).* Paris.

———. 1991a. *André Thevet: Cosmographe des derniers Valois.* Geneva.

———. 1991b. *L'atelier du cosmographe ou l'image du monde à la Renaissance.* Paris.

———. 1993. *Écrire le monde á la Renaissance: Quinze études sur Rabelais, Postel, Bodin et la littérature géographique.* Caen.

———. 1994. Le *Drake Manuscript* de la P. Morgan Library: Un document exceptionnel en marge des "nouveaux horizons" français. *L'Homme* 130, no. 2: 93–104.

Levenson, J. A., ed. 1991. *Circa 1492: Art in the Age of Exploration.* New Haven.

Lévi-Strauss, C. 1955. *Tristes tropiques.* Paris.

———. 1958. *Anthropologie structurale.* Paris.

———. [1962] 1969. *Totemism.* Translated by R. Needham. Harmondsworth.

———. 1973. *Anthropologie structurale deux.* Paris.

———. 1982. Eine Idylle bei den Indianern: Über Jean de Léry. In *Mythen der Neuen Welt: Zur Entdeckungsgeschichte Lateinamerikas,* edited by K.-H. Kohl, 68–70. Berlin.

———. 1985. *La potière jalouse.* Paris.

Levy, E. 1963. Die Römische Kapitalstrafe. In *Ernst Levy: Gesammelte Schriften zu seinem achtzigsten Geburtstag,* edited by W. Kunkel and M. Kaser, 2:325–78. Cologne.

Leys, R. 1991. Types of One: Adolf Meyer's Life Chart and the Representation of Individuality. *Representations* 34:1–28.

Lipsius, J. 1588. *Ad C. Cornelium Tacitum curae secundae.* Antwerp.

Lockhart, J. 1994. Sightings: Initial Nahua Reactions to Spanish Culture. In *Implicit Understandings,* edited by S. B. Schwartz, 218–48. Cambridge.

Löwenstein, S. M. 1985. Suggestions for Study of the Mediene Based on German, French, and English Models. *Studia Rosenthaliana* 19:342–54.

Lugli, A. 1983. *Naturalia et Mirabilia: Il collezionismo enciclopedico nelle Wunderkamern d'Europe.* Milan.

Luijten, G., et al., eds. 1993. *Dawn of the Golden Age: Northern Netherlandish Art, 1580–1620.* Exhibition catalog, Rijksmuseum. Amsterdam.

Lund, A. A., ed. and trans. 1988. *P. Cornelius Tacitus: Germania.* Heidelberg.

———. 1990a. Kritischer Forschungsbericht zur "Germania" des Tacitus. *Aufstieg und Niedergang der Römischen Welt,* pt. 2, 33, no. 3: 1989–2222.

———. 1990b. *Zum Germanenbild der Römer: Eine Einführung in die antike Ethnographie.* Heidelberg.

———. 1990c. Zur Gesamtinterpretation der "Germania" des Tacitus nebst einem Anhang zur Entstehung des Namens und Begriffes "Germani." *Aufstieg und Niedergang der Römischen Welt,* pt. 2, 33, no. 3: 1858–1988.

———. 1993. *De Etnografiske Kilder til Nordens Tidlige Historie.* Aarhus.

———, ed. and trans. 1994. *L. Annaeus Seneca: Apocolocyntosis Divi Claudii.* Heidelberg.

———. 1995. *Germanenideologie im Nationalsozialismus: Zur Rezeption der "Germania" des Tacitus im "Dritten Reich."* Heidelberg.

Lunsingh Scheurleer, Th. H. 1975. Un amphithéâtre d'anatomie moralisé. In *Leiden University in the Seventeenth Century: An Exchange of Learning,* edited by Th. H. Lunsingh Scheurleer and G. Posthumus Meyjes, 217–77. Leiden.

MacCormack, S. 1993. Demons, Imagination, and the Incas. In *New World Encounters,* edited by S. J. Greenblatt, 101–26. Berkeley and Los Angeles.

MacGaffey, W. 1994. Dialogues of the Deaf: Europeans on the Atlantic Coast of Africa. In *Implicit Understandings,* edited by S. B. Schwartz, 249–67. Cambridge.

MacGregor, A. 1989. The King's Disport: Sports, Games, and Pastimes of the Early Stuarts. In *The Late King's Goods: Collections, Possessions, and Patronage of Charles I in the Light of the Commonwealth Sale Inventories,* edited by A. MacGregor, 403–21. Oxford.

Maes, L. T. 1979. La peine de mort dans le droit criminel de Malines. In *Recht heeft vele significatie. Rechtshistorische opstellen van prof. dr. L. Th. Maes,* 213–43. Brussels.

Magaña, E. 1982. Note on Ethnoanthropological Notions of the Guiana Indians. *Anthropologica* 24:215–33.

———. 1989. Gilij: Ideología y mitología guayanesa. *Revista Montalbán* 21:125–51.

———. 1992. *Literaturas de los pueblos del Amazonas: Una introducción wayana.* Madrid.

Magaña, E., and P. Mason. 1986. Tales of Otherness: Myths, Stars and Plinian Men in South America. In *Myth and the Imaginary in the New World,* edited by E. Magaña and P. Mason, 7–40. Amsterdam.

Magdelain, A. 1984. Paricidas. In *Du châtiment dans la cité: Supplices corporels et peine de mort dans le monde antique,* 549–71. Rome.

Martinet, M.-M. 1987. Voyages de découverte et histoire des civilisations dans l'Angleterre de la Renaissance: De la monarchie maritime de Dee à la quête de l'Eldorado par Ralegh. In *Voyager à la Renaissance,* edited by J. Céard and J.-C. Margolin, 281–301. Paris.

Mason, P. 1986. Imaginary Worlds, Counterfact and Artefact. In *Myth and the Imaginary in the New World,* edited by E. Magaña and P. Mason, 43–73. Amsterdam.

———. 1987. Seduction from Afar: Europe's Inner Indians. *Anthropos* 82:581–601.

———. 1988. The Excommunication of Caterpillars: Ethno-anthropological Remarks on the Trial and Punishment of Animals. *Social Science Information* 27, no. 2: 265–73.

———. 1989. Portrayal and Betrayal: The Colonial Gaze in Seventeenth Century Brazil. *Culture and History* 6:37–62.

———. 1990a. *Deconstructing America: Representations of the Other.* London.

———. 1990b. De l'articulation. *L'Homme* 114, no. 2: 27–49.

———. 1990c. Una disputa entre frailes y hormigas. *Scripta Ethnologica Supplementa* 10:75–92.

———. 1991a. Continental Incontinence, *Horror vacui,* and the Colonial Supplement. In *Alterity, Identity, Image,* edited by R. Corbey and J. Leerssen, 151–90. Amsterdam.

———. 1991b. Half a Cow. *Semiotica* 85, nos. 1–2: 1–39.

———. 1993. Escritura fragmentaria: aproximaciones al otro. In *La formación del otro: De palabra y obra en el Nuevo Mundo,* vol. 3, edited by G. H. Gossen, J. J. Klor de Alva, M. Gutiérrez Estévez, and M. León-Portilla, 395–430. Madrid.

———. 1994a. Before and After Columbus. *New West Indian Guide* 68, nos. 3–4: 309–16.

———. 1994b. Classical Ethnology and Its Influence on the European Perception of the Peoples of the New World. In *The Classical Tradition and the Americas,* edited by W. Haase and M. Reinhold, 1, pt. 1:135–72. Berlin and New York.

———. 1994c. From Presentation to Representation: *Americana* in Europe. *Journal of the History of Collections* 6, no. 1: 1–20.

———. 1995. Colonial Culture and Its Limits. *Anthropos* 90, nos. 4–6: 576–81.

————. 1996a. Nicht wie ein Jagdgewehr oder ein Hut / Not Like a Rifle or a Hat. In *John Blake Kunstbunkertumulka München,* Exhibition catalog, Kunstsammlung Tumulka, Munich, 2–8 (German) and 21–27 (English). Munich.

————. 1996b. On Producing the (American) Exotic. *Anthropos* 91, nos. 1–3: 139–51.

————. 1997. The Purloined Codex. *Journal of the History of Collections* 9, no. 1.

————. In press. Ethnography, Ethnology, and Para-Anthropology: Sextus Empiricus and Hellenistic Comparative Method. *Aufstieg und Niedergang der Römischen Welt,* pt. 2, 37, no. 4.

Maus, K. E. 1991. Proof and Consequences: Inwardness and Its Exposure in the English Renaissance. *Representations* 34:29–51.

McGrath, E. 1992. The Black Andromeda. *Journal of the Warburg and Courtauld Institute* 55:1–18.

McGuire, B. P. 1989. Purgatory, the Communion of Saints, and Medieval Change. *Viator* 20:61–84.

McPhail, B. 1994. Through a Glass, Darkly: Scots and Indians Converge at Darien. *Eighteenth-Century Life* 18, no. 3: 129–47.

Menzhausen, J. 1985. Elector Augustus's *Kunstkammer:* An Analysis of the Inventory of 1587. In *The Origins of Museums,* edited by O. Impey and A. MacGregor, 69–75. Oxford.

Meyboom, P. G. P. 1994. *The Nile Mosaic of Palestrina: Early Evidence of Egyptian Religion in Italy.* Leiden.

Michman, J. 1989. The Jewish Essence of Dutch Jewry. *Dutch Jewish History* 2:1–22.

Miller, L. B. 1966. *Patrons and Patriotism: The Encouragement of the Fine Arts in the United States, 1790–1860.* Chicago.

Moens, J. 1977. Een "Koninklijke" walvis te Antwerpen in 1829. *Antwerpen* 23:155–68.

Moes, E. W. 1897. De blijde inkomst van Prins Willem van Oranje binnen Amsterdam in 1580. *Amsterdamsch Jaarboekje,* 1–8.

Momigliano, A. 1966. *Studies in Historiography.* London.

Mommsen, T. 1899. *Römisches Strafrecht.* Leipzig.

Moore, R. I. 1987. *The Formation of a Persecuting Society.* Oxford.

Morineau, M. 1982. Les Bataves: Des Gaulois réussis? In *Nos Ancêtres les Gaulois,* edited by P. Viallaneix and J. Ehrard, 59–68. Clermont-Ferrand.

Muir, E. 1981. *Civic Ritual in Renaissance Venice.* Princeton.

————. 1991. Introduction: Observing Trifles. In *Microhistory and the Lost Peoples of Europe: Selections from Quaderni Storici,* edited by E. Muir and G. Ruggiero and translated by E. Branch, vii–xxviii. Baltimore and London.

————. 1993. *Mad Blood Stirring: Vendetta and Factions in Friuli during the Renaissance.* Baltimore.

Muir, E., and G. Ruggiero, eds. 1994. *History from Crime.* Baltimore.

Müller, K. 1972. *Geschichte der Antiken Ethnographie und ethnologischen Theoriebildung.* Vol. 1. Wiesbaden.

Münster, S. 1550. *Cosmographei.* Basel.

Needham, R. 1971. Remarks on the Analysis of Kinship and Marriage. In *Rethinking Kinship and Marriage,* edited by R. Needham, 1–29. London.

————. 1978. *Primordial Characters.* Charlottesville.

————. 1980. *Reconnaissances.* Toronto.

————. 1985. *Exemplars.* Berkeley.

Neverov, O. 1985. "His Majesty's Cabinet" and Peter I's Kunstkammer. In *The Origins of*

Museums, edited by O. Impey and A. MacGregor, 54–61. Oxford.

Van Nierop, H. F. K. 1991. A Beggars' Banquet: The Compromise of the Nobility and the Politics of Inversion. *European History Quarterly* 21:419–43.

―――. 1993. *The Nobility of Holland: From Knights to Regents, 1500–1650.* Cambridge.

Nippel, W. 1990. *Griechen, Barbaren und "Wilde": Alte Geschichte und Sozialanthropologie.* Frankfurt am Main.

Noordewier, M. J. 1853. *Nederduitsche regtsoudheden.* Utrecht.

Nye, R. 1993. *Masculinity and Male Codes of Honor in Modern France.* New York.

Oexle, O. G. 1983. Die Gegenwart der Toten. In *Death in the Middle Ages,* edited by H. Braet and W. Verbeke, 19–77. Louvain.

Ohnuki-Tierney, E., ed. 1990. *Culture through Time.* Stanford.

Olivier de Sardan, J.-P. 1992. Occultism and the Ethnographic "I": The Exoticizing of Magic from Durkheim to "Postmodern" Anthropology. *Critique of Anthropology* 12, no. 1: 5–25.

Olmi, G. 1992. *L'inventario del mondo: Catalogazione della natura e luoghi del sapere nella prima età moderna.* Bologna.

Van Oostrom, F. 1987. *Het woord van eer: Literatuur aan het Hollandse hof omstreeks 1400.* Amsterdam.

Osborne, P. 1992. Modernity Is a Qualitative, Not a Chronological, Category: Notes on the Dialectics of Differential Historical Time. In *Postmodernism and the Re-reading of Modernity,* edited by F. Barker, P. Hulme, and M. Iversen, 23–45. Manchester.

Overing, J. 1985. There Is No End of Evil: The Guilty Innocents and Their Fallible God. In *The Anthropology of Evil,* edited by D. Parkin, 244–78. Oxford.

―――. 1987. Translation As a Creative Process: The Power of the Name. In *Comparative Anthropology,* edited by L. Holy, 70–87. Oxford.

Pagden, A. R. 1982. *The Fall of Natural Man: The American Indian and the Origins of Comparative Ethnology.* Cambridge.

Paré, J. [1585] 1971. *Des monstres et prodiges.* Edited by J. Céard. Geneva.

Park, K., and L. J. Daston, 1981. Unnatural Conceptions: The Study of Monsters in Sixteenth- and Seventeenth-Century France and England. *Past and Present* 92:20–54.

Parker, G. 1977. *The Dutch Revolt.* Harmondsworth.

Parker, R. 1983. *Miasma: Pollution and Purification in Early Greek Religion.* Oxford.

Peale, C. W. 1983. *The Selected Papers of Charles Willson Peale and His Family. Vol I. Charles Willson Peale: Artist in Revolutionary America, 1735–1791.* New Haven.

―――. 1988. *The Selected Papers of Charles Willson Peale and His Family. Vol II. Charles Willson Peale: The Artist As Museum Keeper, 1791–1810.* New Haven.

―――. 1991. *The Selected Papers of Charles Willson Peale and His Family. Vol III. The Belfield Farm Years, 1810–1820.* New Haven.

Peiresc, N, F. de. 1989. *Lettres à Cassiano dal Pozzo (1626–1637).* Edited with a commentary by J. F. Lhote and D. Joyal. Clermont-Ferrand.

Pellegrin, N. 1987. Vêtements de peau(x) et de plumes: La nudité des indiens et la diversité du monde au XVIe siècle. In *Voyager à la Renaissance,* edited by J. Céard and J. C. Margolin, 509–30. Paris.

Peristiany, J. G., ed. 1965. *Honor and Shame: The Values of Mediterranean Society.* Worcester.

Perrin, M. 1987. Creaciones míticas y representación del mundo: El ganado en el pensamiento símbolico Guajiro. *Antropológica* 67:3–31.

―――. 1992. *Les praticiens du rêve: Un exemple de chamanisme.* Paris.

Pfister, F. 1976. *Kleine Schriften zur Alexanderroman*. Meisenheim am Glan.

Picardt, J. 1660. *Korte beschryving van eenige Vergeetene en Verborgene Antiquiteiten der Provintien en Landen gelegen tusschen de Noord-Zee, de Yssel, Emse en Lippe.* . . . Amsterdam.

Piggott, S. 1976. *Ruins in a Landscape*. Edinburgh.

Poeschel, S. 1985. *Studien zur Ikonographie der Erdteile in der Kunst des 16.–18. Jahrhunderts*. Munich.

Poignant, R. 1992. Surveying the Field of View: The Making of the RAI Photographic Collection. In *Anthropology and Photography 1860–1920*, edited by E. Edwards, 42–73. New Haven.

Van de Pol, L. 1992. Prostitutie en de Amsterdamse burgerij: Eerbegrippen in een vroegmoderne stedelijke samenleving. In *Cultuur en maatschappij in Nederland, 1500–1850*, edited by P. te Boekhorst, P. Burke and W. Frijhoff, 179–218. Amsterdam.

Pregardien, D. 1985. L'iconographie des *Ceremonies et coutumes* de B. Picart. In *L'homme des Lumières et la découverte de l'autre*, edited by D. Droixhe and P. Gossiaux, 183–90. Brussels.

Pumfrey, S., P. Rossi, and M. Slawinski, eds. 1991. *Science, Culture, and Popular Belief in Renaissance Europe*. Manchester.

Ralegh, W. [1596] 1970. *The Discovery of the Large, Rich, and Beautiful Empire of Guiana*. Introduction and notes by R. H. Schomburgk. New York.

Randles, W. G. L. 1994. Classical Models of World Geography and Their Transformation following the Discovery of America. In *The Classical Tradition and the Americas*, edited by W. Haase and M. Reinhold, 1, pt. 1: 5–76. Berlin and New York.

Rehfeldt, B. 1942. *Todesstrafen und Bekehrungsgeschichte*. Berlin.

Reichler, C. 1989. La littérature comme interprétation symbolique. In *L'interprétation des textes*, edited by C. Reichler, 81–113. Paris.

Reijnders, C. 1969. *Van "Joodsche Natien" tot Joodse Nederlanders: Een onderzoek naar getto-en assimilatieverschijnselen tussen 1600 en 1942.* Amsterdam.

Reinle, A. 1984. *Das stellvertretende Bildnis: Plastiken und Gemälde von der Antiken bis ins 19. Jahrhundert*. Zürich.

Revel, J. 1994. Microanalisi e costruzione del sociale. *Quaderni Storici*, n.s., 86:549–75.

Rhees, R. 1982. Wittgenstein on Language and Ritual. In *Wittgenstein and His Times*, edited by B. McGuinness, 69–107. Oxford.

Ridé, J. 1976. *L'image du germain dans la pensée et la litterature allemandes de la redecouverte de Tacite à la fin du XVIème siècle (Contribution à l'étude de la genèse d'un mythe)*. Ph.D. diss., Université de Paris IV.

Rigal, L. 1993. Peale's Mammoth. In *American Iconology*, edited by D. C. Miller, 18–38. New Haven.

Rivière, P. G. 1971. Marriage, A Reassessment. In *Rethinking Kinship and Marriage*, edited by R. Needham, 57–74. London.

Romm, J. S. 1992. *The Edges of the Earth in Ancient Thought*. Princeton.

Rosaldo, R. 1986. From the Door of His Tent: The Fieldworker and the Inquisitor. In *Writing Culture: The Poetics and Politics of Ethnography*, edited by J. Clifford and G. E. Marcus, 77–97. Berkeley and Los Angeles.

Ross, D. J. A. 1963. *Alexander Historiatus: A Guide to Medieval Illustrated Alexander Literature*. London.

Rowlands, J. 1994. Prints and Drawings. In *Sir Hans Sloane. Collector, Scientist, Antiquary,*

Founding Father of the British Museum, edited by A. MacGregor, 245–62. London.

Rubiés, J.-P. 1993. New Worlds and Renaissance Ethnology. *History and Anthropology* 6, nos. 2–3: 157–97.

Rudwick, M. J. S. 1992. *Scenes from Deep Time: Early Pictorial Representations of the Prehistoric World.* Chicago.

Ruggiero, G. 1993. *Binding Passions: Tales of Magic, Marriage, and Power at the End of the Renaissance.* Oxford.

Salisbury, J. E. 1994. *The Beast Within: Animals in the Middle Ages.* London.

Samarrai, A. 1993. Beyond Belief and Reverence: Medieval Mythological Ethnography in the Near East and Europe. *Journal of Medieval and Renaissance Studies* 23, no. 1: 19–42.

Sauer, C. O. 1971. *Sixteenth Century North America.* Berkeley.

Sawday, J. 1995. *The Body Emblazoned.* London.

Schama, S. 1987. *The Embarrassment of Riches: An Interpretation of Dutch Culture in the Golden Age.* London.

———. 1995. *Landscape and Memory.* London.

Schepelern, H. D., and U. Houkjær. 1988. *The Kronborg Series: King Christian IV and His Pictures of Early Danish History.* Copenhagen.

Schild, W. 1980. *Alte Gerichtsbarkeit: Vom Gottesurteil bis zum Beginn der modernen Rechtsprechung.* Munich.

Von Schlosser, J. [1908] 1978. *Die Kunst- und Wunderkammern der Spätrenaissance.* 2nd ed., rev. and enl. Braunschweig.

Schmidt, B. 1994. *Innocence Abroad: The Dutch Imagination and the Representation of the New World, c. 1570–1670.* Ph.D. diss., Harvard University.

Schnapper, A. 1986. Persistance des géants. *Annales ESC* 41, no. 1: 177–200.

———. 1988. *Le Géant, La licorne, La tulipe: Collections françaises au XVIIe siècle.* Paris.

Schöffer, I. 1975. The Batavian Myth during the Sixteenth and Seventeenth Centuries. In *Britain and the Netherlands. Volume V. Some Political Mythologies,* papers delivered to the fifth Anglo-Dutch Historical Conference, edited by J. S. Bromley and E. H. Kossmann, 78–101. The Hague.

Schott, C., and R. Schmidt-Wiegand, eds. 1984. *Eike von Repgow: Der Sachsenspiegel.* Zürich.

Schrage, E. In press. Able to Contain a Reasonable Soul. In *Festschrift for Hans Ankum.*

Schwencken, C. P. T. 1820. *Notitzen über die berüchtigsten jüdischen Gauner und Spitzbuben, welche sich gegenwärtig in Deutschland und an dessen Gränzen umhertreiben nebst genauer Beschreibung ihrer Person: Nach Criminal-Akten und sonstigen zuverlässigen Quellen bearbeitet und in alphabetischer Ordnung zusammengestellt.* Marburg.

Scribner, R. W. [1981] 1994. *For the Sake of Simple Folk: Popular Propaganda for the German Reformation.* Oxford.

Severi, C. 1992. Le chamanisme et la dame du Bon Jeu. *L'Homme* 121, no. 1: 165–77.

Seznec, J. 1949. *Nouvelles études sur "La Tentation de Saint Antoine."* London.

Sharpe, J. A. 1990. *Judicial Punishment in England.* London.

Shulvass, M. A. 1971. *From East to West: The Westward Migration of Jews from Eastern Europe during the Seventeenth and Eighteenth Centuries.* Detroit.

Silverblatt, I. 1987. *Moon, Sun, and Witches: Gender Ideologies and Class in Inca and Colonial Peru.* Princeton.

Silverman, D., and B. Torode. 1980. *The Material Word: Some Theories of Language and Its Limits.* London.

Simonin, M. 1987. Les elites chorographes ou de la "Description de la France" dans la "Cosmographie universelle" de Belleforest. In *Voyager à la Renaissance*, edited by J. Céard and J.-C. Margolin, 433–51. Paris.

———. 1992. *Vivre de sa plume au XVIe siècle, ou la carrière de François de Belleforest.* Geneva.

Sliggers, B. C., and A. A. Wertheim, eds. 1993. *De tentoongestelde mens: Reuzen, dwergen en andere wonderen der natuur.* Exhibition catalog, Teylers Museum Haarlem. Haarlem.

Spaans, J. 1989. *Haarlem na de Reformatie: Stedelijke cultuur en kerkelijk leven, 1577–1620.* The Hague.

Sparrman, A. 1785. *A Voyage to the Cape of Good Hope.* London.

Spierenburg, P. 1984. *The Spectacle of Suffering. Executions and the Evolution of Repression: From a Preindustrial Metropolis to the European Experience.* Cambridge.

Spies, M. 1994. *Bij Noorden Om: Olivier Brunel en de doorvaart naar China en Cathay in de zestiende eeuw.* Amsterdam.

Stafford, B. M. 1991. *Body Criticism.* Cambridge, Mass.

———. 1994. *Artful Science: Enlightenment Entertainment and the Eclipse of Visual Education.* Cambridge, Mass.

Stallybrass, P., and A. White. 1986. *The Politics and Poetics of Transgression.* Ithaca.

Starobinski, J. 1989. *Le remède dans le mal.* Paris.

St. Cassia, P. 1991. Authors in Search of a Character: Personhood, Agency, and Identity in the Mediterranean. *Journal of Mediterranean Studies* 1:1–17.

Stedman, J. G. 1988. *Narrative of a Five Years Expedition against the Revolted Negroes of Surinam.* Edited with an introduction and notes by R. Price and S. Price. Baltimore.

Steffenhagen, E. 1920. Die Entwicklung der Landrechtsglosse des Sachsenspiegels: XI Johann von Buch und die Accursianische Glosse. *Sitzungsberichte der. phil.-hist. Klasse der Kaiserlichen Akademie der Wissenschaften* 194, no. 4.

Stewart, S. 1994. Death and Life, in That Order, in the Works of Charles Willson Peale. In *The Cultures of Collecting,* edited by J. Elsner and R. Cardinal, 204–23. London.

Stone, L. 1990. Honor, Morals, Religion, and the Law: The Action for Criminal Conversation in England, 1670–1857. In *The Transmission of Culture in Early Modern Europe,* edited by A. Grafton and A. Blair, 276–315. Philadelphia.

Storfer, A. J. 1911. Zur Sonderstellung des Vatermordes: Eine rechtsgeschichtliche und völkerpsychologische Studie. In *Schriften zur angewandten Seelenkunde, herausgegeben von prof. dr. Sigmund Freud,* Heft 12, 1–34. Leipzig and Vienna.

Ström, F. 1942. *On the Sacral Origin of the Germanic Death Penalties.* Lund.

Sturm, F. 1961. *Symbolische Todesstrafen.* N.p.

Sturtevant, W. C. 1976. First Visual Images of Native America. In *First Images of America,* edited by F. Chiapelli, 1:417–54. Berkeley.

———. 1988. La Tupinambisation des indiens d'Amérique du Nord. In *Les figures de l'indien,* edited by G. Thérien, 293–303. Montreal.

Sturtevant, W. C., and D. B. Quinn. 1987. This New Prey: Eskimos in Europe 1567, 1576, and 1577. In *Indians and Europe,* edited by C. F. Feest, 61–140. Göttingen.

Swart, K. W. 1975. The Black Legend during the Eighty Years War. In *Britain and the Netherlands. Volume V. Some Political Mythologies,* papers delivered to the fifth Anglo-Dutch Historical Conference, edited by J. S. Bromley and E. H. Kossmann, 36–57. The Hague.

Syme, R. M. 1979. *Tacitus.* 2 vols. Oxford.

Tambiah, S. J. 1990. *Magic, Science, Religion, and the Scope of Rationality.* Cambridge.

Taussig, M. 1984. History As Sorcery. *Representations* 7:87–109.

Tellegen-Couperus, O. E., and J. W. Tellegen. 1993. De Pandectentegels van Sybrand Feytema, *De Vrije Fries* 73:115–36.

Theatrum Rerum Naturalium Brasiliae. 1993. *Theatrum Rerum Naturalium Brasiliae. I. Icones Aquatilium, Icones Volatilium. II. Icones Animalium. Icones Vegetabilium.* Facs. ed. Compiled by C. Mentzel. Rio de Janeiro.

Thevet, A. 1584. *Les vrais pourtraits et vies des hommes illustres.* Paris.

———. [1554] 1985. *Cosmographie de Levant.* Critical Edition. Edited by Frank Lestringant. Geneva.

Thierry de Bye Dolleman, M. 1958. Het geslacht van Berckenrode. *Jaarboek van het Centraal Bureau voor Genealogie* 12:80–132.

Thom, M. 1990. Tribes within Nations: The Ancient Germans and the History of Modern France. In *Nation and Narration,* edited by H. K. Bhabha, 23–43. London.

Thomas, K. 1971. *Religion and the Decline of Magic.* Harmondsworth.

———. 1983. *Man and the Natural World: Changing Attitudes in England, 1500–1800.* Harmondsworth.

Thomas, N. 1991. *Entangled Objects: Exchange, Material Culture, and Colonialism in the Pacific.* Cambridge, Mass.

———. 1994. *Colonialism's Culture: Anthropology, Travel, and Government.* Cambridge.

Thomas, Y. 1984. Introduction to *Du châtiment dans la cité: Supplices corporels et peine de mort dans le monde antique,* 1–7. Rome.

Thompson, E. P. 1993. *Witness against the Beast: William Blake and the Moral Law.* Cambridge.

Tilmans, K. 1988. *Aurelius en de Divisiekroniek van 1517.* Hilversum.

Tongiorgi Tomasi, L. 1984. Dalla "medicina verde" al naturalismo: L'immagine botanica e zoologica nei manoscritti e nei primi testi a stampa sul finire del '400. In *Immagine e natura: L'immagine naturalistica nei codici e libri a stampa delle Biblioteche Estense e Universitaria, secoli XV–XVII,* edited by P. Tongiorgi, L. Tongiorgi Tomasi, and M. Goia Tavoni, 33–43. Modena.

Turner, V. 1977. *The Ritual Process: Structure and Anti-Structure.* Ithaca.

Vandenbroeck, P. 1987. *Beeld van de Andere: Vertoog over het Zelf.* Antwerp.

Vanderjagt, A. 1981. *Qui sa vertu anoblist: The Concepts of Noblesse and Chose publique in Burgundian Thought.* Groningen.

Veldman, I. 1974. Enkele aanvullende gegevens omtrent de biografie van Hadrianus Junius. *Bijdragen en Mededelingen betreffende de Geschiedenis der Nederlanden* 89:375–84.

Vernant, J.-P. 1980. Le mythe au réflechi. *Le Temps de la Réflexion* 1:21–25.

Verwer, W. J. 1973. *Memoriaelbouck: Dagboek van gebeurtenissen te Haarlem van 1572–1581.* Edited by J. J. Temminck. Haarlem.

Veyne, P 1983. *Les Grecs ont-ils cru à leurs mythes?* Paris.

Vidal-Naquet, P. 1981. *Le chasseur noir: Formes de pensée et formes de société dans le monde grec.* Paris.

Volpilhac-Auger, C. 1985. *Tacite et Montesquieu.* Oxford.

Van de Waal, H. 1952. *Drie Eeuwen Vaderlandsche Geschied-Uitbeelding 1500–1800: Een iconologische studie.* 2 vols. The Hague.

Warburg, A. 1932. *Gesammelte Schriften.* Leipzig.

Weijtens, M. J. 1971. *Nathan en Shylock in de Lage Landen.* Groningen.

Weisser, M. 1979. *Crime and Punishment in Early Modern Europe.* Bristol.

Wells, C. M. 1974. The Ethnography of the Celts and of the Algonkian-Iroquoian Tribes: A Comparison of Two Historical Traditions. In *Polis and Imperium: Studies in Honor of Edward Togo Salmon*, edited by J. A. S. Evans, 265–78. Toronto.

Wendt, A. 1989. *Kannibalismus in Brasilien: Eine Analyse europäischer Reiseberichte und Amerika-Darstellungen für die Zeit zwischen 1500 und 1654.* Frankfurt am Main.

Whalley, J. I. 1982. *Pliny the Elder: Historia Naturalis.* London.

Whatley, J. 1986. Savage Hierarchies: French Catholic Observers of the New World. *Sixteenth Century Journal* 17:319–30.

White, D. G. 1991. *Myths of the Dog-Man.* Chicago.

Whitehead, P. J. P. 1985. Faces of the New World. *FMR America* 9:125–40.

———. 1987. Earliest Extant Painting of Greenlanders. In *Indians and Europe,* edited by C. F. Feest, 141–59. Göttingen.

Whitehead, P. J. P., and M. Boeseman. 1989. *A Portrait of Dutch Seventeenth Century Brazil: Animals, Plants, and People by the Artists of Johan Maurits of Nassau.* Amsterdam.

Wielant, P. 1872. *Practijcke criminele.* Edited by A. Orts. Ghent.

Van Wijn, H. 1801. *Huiszittend leeven.* Vol. 1. Amsterdam.

Wild, F. 1934. Zur Säckung. *Mitteldeutsche Blätter für Volkskunde* 9:92ff.

Wilson, D. 1993. *Signs and Portents: Monstrous Births from the Middle Ages to the Enlightenment.* London.

Wischnitzer, M. 1965. *A History of Jewish Crafts and Guilds.* New York.

Wittgenstein, L. 1958. *Philosophical Investigations.* 2nd ed. Oxford.

———. 1993. *Philosophical Occasions, 1912–1951.* Edited by J. Klagge and A. Nordmann. Indianopolis.

Wittkower, R. 1977. *Allegory and the Migration of Symbols.* London.

Worp, J. A. 1915. *Briefwisseling van C. Huygens, 1608–1687.* Vol. 4. The Hague.

Van der Woud, A. 1990. *De Bataafse hut: Verschuivingen in het beeld van de geschiedenis (1750–1850).* Amsterdam.

Zinck, P. 1933. Zur Säckung. *Mitteldeutsche Blätter für Volkskunde* 8:61ff.

Ziolkowski, J. 1984. Folklore and Learned Lore in Letaldus' Whale Poem. *Viator* 15:107–18.

Zuidema, R. T. 1991. Guaman Poma and the Art of Empire: Toward an Iconography of Inca Royal Dress. In *Transatlantic Encounters: Europeans and Andeans in the Sixteenth Century,* edited by K. J. Andrien and R. Adorno, 151–202. Berkeley.

Library of Congress Cataloging-in-Publication Data

Egmond, Florike.
  The mammoth and the mouse : microhistory and morphology / Florike Egmond
and Peter Mason.
     p.   cm.
  Includes bibliographical references.
  ISBN 0-8018-5477-6. — ISBN 0-8018-5478-4 (pbk.)
    1. History—Methodology. 2. Historiography. I. Mason, Peter, 1952–   . II. Title.
D16.E32 1997
907.2—dc21   96-47416
                                                                  CIP